Praise for *Reimagining Equality*

"She eloquently recounts her family's journey 'from *being* property' in antebellum Arkansas 'to *owning* property' many years later in rural Oklahoma.... Her book is a complex and at times confounding portrait of the ways in which black men and women have struggled to surmount myriad forms of injustice to own homes.... This ambitious book provides just as dignified and well intentioned a performance as the one she gave at those hearings."

—MEGAN BUSKEY, *The New York Times Book Review*

"To begin with, Hill is a remarkably elegant and accessible writer. For those who wish to apprehend the gravitas of her intelligence and dignity, *Reimagining Equality* would be a good place to start ... a brilliantly lucid detailing of the apportionment of American real estate—and, along with it, the American dream—along the lines of race, gender and class.... From the 1800s to today, Hill meticulously tracks notions of communities split by the government's investment in racialized redlining of neighborhoods; of encompassing traditions of maternity riven by neonatalist notions about which mothers should be having more or fewer babies; and of 'ghetto lending practices' that have poisonously metastasized into today's bundled subprime mortgage crisis.... *Reimagining Equality* is an important achievement. Hill manages to humanize and reinvigorate the American promise of security in one's pride of home—even against the backdrop of harder-edged, more militaristically inflected calls to 'homeland security.' The kinder, gentler complications that Hill brings to bear in teasing out this contrast are an eloquent continuation of her giving voice to the invisible, the voiceless, the undocumented, the hopeless and, yes, the all too literally homeless."

—PATRICIA J. WILLIAMS, *The Nation*

"A cerebral kind of trip that delves into the intersection of equality and where you reside."

—JORIAN L. SEAY, *Ebony*

"With extraordinary grace and clarity, Anita Hill weaves the story of her family with that of other American families struggling to find and define homes for themselves. What emerges is a powerful story of our nation's ongoing quest for equality of opportunity, viewed through the eyes of the people who have been deeply engaged in that quest. Beautifully written, elegantly seen, compellingly argued."

—ROBERT B. REICH, author of *Aftershock*

"Combining the sincerity of memoir and the rigor of sociology, Anita Hill looks at home as a physical space, but also as a microcosm of American society. The women profiled in this engaging and moving book illustrate the challenges of living in America as a raced and gendered person while simultaneously demonstrating the beauty of resistance and the triumphs of family, community, and faith. Hill connects the dots between the home-making efforts of African Americans just after Reconstruction and the heartbreaking (and enraging) consequences of the subprime mortgage scandal. After reading this book, you will never see a house as just four walls and a roof. It is a dream and we, as Americans, are the dreamers."

—TAYARI JONES, author of *Silver Sparrow*

"Anita Hill's bravery, intellect, and commitment to justice galvanized a generation of women. If that weren't enough, it turns out she's also a wonderful storyteller. *Reimagining Equality* will change your ideas about home, race, and gender."

—PEGGY ORENSTEIN, author of *Cinderella Ate My Daughter*

"In a book that is rigorous and heartfelt, sharply analytical and deeply moving, Anita Hill examines the idea of what 'home' means to Americans. Bringing to bear her formidable skills as a scholar of American law, history, and culture, Hill has produced a personal narrative that reaches across color and class to explore how our family homes and our national home are inextricably linked to how we understand achievement, opportunity, and equality."

—HENRY LOUIS GATES JR., author of *Colored People*

To Chuck,
and to all the women and men
who have struggled to make
a home in our country.

"In her new book, *Reimagining Equality: Stories of Race, Gender, and Finding Home*, Professor Anita Hill has written a sobering and compelling book about the plight of woman historically and now. This book is a must-read for anyone who is committed to gender equality and will be invaluable to those who are trying to understand many of the burdens that women, black and white, face in their everyday lives.

"An easy read, this book has both tragic and triumphant stories and covers the lives of women through slavery to those who now live in the Obama era. They remind us that we still have to come to grips with issues of race and gender, and that we need to re-imagine the question of equality for all. I recommend it with great enthusiasm and excitement about its value to a large audience of readers."

—PROFESSOR CHARLES J. OGLETREE JR.,
author of *The Presumption of Guilt*

Featured in *Time, Newsweek, Vanity Fair*, the *New York Times Magazine*, the *Washington Post, People, Ms., Glamour, Ebony*, and many other publications.

Broadcast on ABC's *Good Morning America, CBS Sunday Morning, NBC Nightly News* with Brian Williams, *PBS NewsHour*, NPR's *Talk of the Nation*, MSNBC's *The Melissa Harris Perry Show*, PRI's *The Tavis Smiley Show, CNN Newsroom*, and MSNBC's *Andrea Mitchell Reports*.

REIMAGINING EQUALITY

REIMAGINING EQUALITY

Stories of Gender, Race, and Finding Home

Anita Hill

BEACON PRESS

BOSTON

Beacon Press
25 Beacon Street
Boston, Massachusetts 02108-2892
www.beacon.org

Beacon Press books
are published under the auspices of
the Unitarian Universalist Association of Congregations.

16   15   14   13   12   8   7   6   5   4   3   2   1

This book is printed on acid-free paper that meets the uncoated paper
ANSI/NISO specifications for permanence as revised in 1992.

Text design by Yvonne Tsang at Wilsted & Taylor Publishing Services

Names in chapter 5 have been changed to protect individuals' privacy.

Some epigraphs are adapted from the dictionary definitions.

Library of Congress Cataloging-in-Publication Data
Hill, Anita.
Reimagining equality : stories of gender, race, and finding home / Anita Hill.
p. cm.
Includes bibliographical references and index.
ISBN 978-0-8070-1443-1 (pbk. : alk. paper)
1. African Americans—Social conditions. 2. African American women—
Social conditions. 3. African Americans—Housing. 4. Home ownership—United States.
5. Equality—United States. 6. Nationalism—United States. I. Title.
E185.86.H655 2011
305.896′073—dc23   2011020232

CONTENTS

Introduction xi

CHAPTER ONE
Home: Survival and the Land 1

CHAPTER TWO
Belonging to the New Land 24

CHAPTER THREE
Gender and Race at Home in America 40

CHAPTER FOUR
Lorraine's Vision: A Better Place to Live 55

CHAPTER FIVE
Blame It on the Sun 78

CHAPTER SIX
Lessons from a Survivor:
Anjanette's Story 95

CHAPTER SEVEN
Home in Crisis: Americans on
the Outside of the Dream 116

CHAPTER EIGHT
Home at Last:
Toward an Inclusive Democracy 140

Acknowledgments 171
Notes 173
Index 187

INTRODUCTION

∗

Home: The place of one's dwelling or nurturing, with the conditions, circumstances, and feelings which naturally attach to it and are associated with it . . . not merely "place" but also "state."
The Oxford English Dictionary

This is a book about home.

As the first decade of the new millennium came to a close, the country was still reeling from a housing crisis that caused both physical and psychological distress. The centrality of home to individuals of all stripes was never more apparent. Millions of Americans, male and female, of all races, had been set adrift as a result of reckless personal and institutional financial behavior, the precipitous decline of manufacturing industries, and in the case of Hurricane Katrina, an unprecedented natural disaster. And whether as a place or as a state of being, the significance of home to neighborhood, city, and national well-being was becoming clear. Moreover, the crisis raised questions about whether our country is indeed a welcoming location of endless possibility to those seeking the American Dream. Our national identity was being challenged by the home ownership crisis.

Many have lost faith in homeownership, a bedrock of the American Dream. This loss is further complicated by the role of the home in defining equality and democracy—a role that is often overlooked, even though where one lives determines school assignments, voting opportunities, and often the availability of jobs, goods, and services. Yet little attention is paid to the complicated interrelationship between where one calls home, what happens inside the home, and equality outside the home.

I plan to examine home as a place and a state of being by interweaving discussions of law, literature, and culture with stories of individuals, focusing on women, and African Americans, in search of equality. These stories reflect each woman's experience in finding and shaping a home where she could achieve some measure of equality for herself and her family. Beginning with my own story, I invite readers to think about their experiences and yearning for home, even as they read of others whose experiences are different but who share a desire to be equal participants in our democracy. The women featured and I have learned over the course of our lives that home, as well as equality, need to be reconceived as our worlds change.

These stories of gender, race, and finding home guide us through a history of imagining and reimagining equality. They also address issues that have long been neglected in this country but must be grappled with in order to ensure that every American has the opportunity to achieve the sense of belonging that comes from being at home. As black women have come to head the majority of black households, they have become the primary "homebuilders." They have also become dominant forces as community builders in African American neighborhoods. Their determination to build their lives, their families, and their communities, despite harsh perceptions of them, is evidence of their belief in the promise of America, even in times when that promise may seem irreparably broken. Their struggle points to an important lesson: we may have reached the limits of current rights legislation's ability to assure liberty and equality for all. For these women and others who have yet to be perfectly at home in our nation, we need to find other strategies.

Black women know what it means physically, socially, and economically to possess a gender and a race.[1] They know that race and gender equality must both be realized if either is to be achieved. Like other women, they struggle to balance work and family obligations, and they suffer from violence in their homes and on the streets of their communities. Along with African American men in many racially isolated neighborhoods, they endure crime, inadequate schools, and a lack of public and private amenities. With all women and black men, they face limited employment and educational opportunities, as well as underrepresentation in political arenas. We have passed many laws to try to address these inequities, to level the playing field, and yet we have not finished the work. They struggle, as millions do, to find home in America.

•   •   •

How one conceives of home is deeply personal. As the poet T. S. Eliot wrote, "Home is where one starts from."[2] For me, home is inextricably linked to the story of how my family, in one generation, went from *being* property to *owning* property. In the first two chapters, I will explore the beginnings of the meaning I give to home by tracing the path that three generations of my family took to leave behind slavery and its vestiges. Their journeys kept them searching for an attachment to the land, their symbol of survival and belonging.

Mollie Elliott, one of my maternal great-grandmothers, was seventeen years old and a slave in 1864, when she gave birth to my maternal grandfather in Little River County, Arkansas. That son, Henry Elliott, went on to homestead eighty acres of land at the turn of the century, only to lose them. Nevertheless, he and his wife, Ida, summoned the courage to move, along with seven of their children, to Oklahoma. They settled very near the farm on which I and my twelve siblings were raised by Erma, their youngest daughter, and her husband, Albert Hill. From the bucolic vantage point of the small, rural community of Lone Tree, our family experienced sweeping social change—from Jim Crow to the civil rights era. My parents remained on the farm well into the 1990s, beyond the time when many Americans had left rural life for a more promising, urban existence. But being well into their sixties by the time the law's protections began to take hold, they saw the promises of equality not so much for change in their lives, but for the potential to transform the lives of their children. In particular, the advances ushered in by the civil rights and women's rights movements offered women born in the 1950s and '60s the kind of independence that Erma Hill could never fully imagine, much less realize. But this much she knew: neither the land, nor a house full of children, nor even a husband would define the place or the state of her daughter's home.

With the rights movements, my path to equality followed an entirely different trajectory from my mother's. Yet in 1973, Erma Hill approached my departure for college with optimism and with little thought of the challenges inherent in imagining a life not only outside rural confines, but also without the constraints of overt discrimination. And why not? The country was on the verge of a new day. A generation of children was making its way into the world to live out America's promise of equality, and she would enjoy a front-row seat knowing that she had prepared me to be a part of it.

As personal as the concept of home is, within its contours are principles with universal application. In chapter 3, I explore the history of how home became a preponderant symbol of race and gender advancement in the United States, simultaneously denoting belonging and independence. In 1776, likening the tyranny of husbands in the home to the tyranny of King George over the colonies, Abigail Adams implored her husband, John, to "Remember the Ladies" by including protections for them in the "new Code of Laws."[3] At the turn of the twentieth century, the African American leader Booker T. Washington urged fellow former slaves to abandon the "hovel" and establish respectable homes as evidence that they had earned the right to be recognized as citizens.[4] Washington's contemporary Nannie Helen Burroughs established a school for working-class African American girls, using the home as the foundation for their intellectual and economic enterprises. Renouncing both gender and race subservience, she encouraged her students to be wage earners and "professional" homemakers.[5]

To Adams, Washington, and Burroughs, home stood as a reference point from which equality and civic and economic participation sprang. Piercing the veil between the public and private spheres, Adams imagined women's equality as safety at home, which could be secured only by recognition in the Constitution. For Washington, African Americans' citizenship would emanate from their ability to establish homes that would affirm them as neighbors in the word's fullest and most meaningful sense. The keys to Washington's ideas for equality were community and interconnectedness. In Burroughs's vision, the economic recognition of work that women did in the home rightly established their social and political worth outside the home. In a society dominated by men, Burroughs saw and advocated the dignity and value in women's contributions and in women themselves. Home, a critical component of the American Dream, was at the heart of the quest for an inclusive democracy as pursued by women and people of color.

Through the stories of Adams, Washington, Burroughs, and others, I hope to show how home became a positive symbol of advancement. Advocates of equality took a concept that had represented gender and racial oppression and transformed it into a means of empowerment. Eighteenth- and nineteenth-century activists argued that liberation required society to reimagine the home, and that the freedom to choose where and how one lives was a vital component of a free society. Moreover, they laid the groundwork for aligning the interests of women and blacks with those of the entire society. Their ideas and their work would take root and develop into twentieth-century migration patterns and equal rights movements.

Nothing better represents the twisted path to racial and gender equality in America than the search for home as a place of refuge, financial security, and expression. At the end of the Civil War and well into the twentieth century, for African American families, the search for roots that had been lost to slavery became a search for land, a place where they could earn a living and escape the vestiges of bondage and the brutality of Jim Crow laws. Beginning in about 1915, during what is known in American history as the Great Migration, black men and women began to leave the rural South and make their way to northern industrial cities to find work and a new home. Despite racial restrictions in the North, the bright lines drawn by segregationists were starting to blur. Black women who were domestic workers started to form enclaves in rental housing in affluent neighborhoods. As the number of blacks in the North grew, the demand for housing began to exceed the supply of homes unencumbered by racially restrictive covenants. The idea of challenging those covenants by buying homes in white neighborhoods took hold; purchasing a home in a racially restricted neighborhood became a symbol of racial equality, a way for blacks to realize the desire of all Americans to find a place to belong. Litigation in the 1930s and forms of civil resistance to discrimination ultimately led Congress to pass equality-promising, antidiscrimination legislation in the 1960s.

But playwright Lorraine Hansberry complicated this view of the path to equality. Her real-life story of being a child caught in a landmark civil rights case, as well as her 1959 play *A Raisin in the Sun,* exposed the complexity of relying on the home as the fulfillment of racial justice. In chapter 4, I present Hansberry's experience as a story of race, gender, and commitment to a dream. Lorraine Hansberry was eight years old when her family moved into a white neighborhood in a Chicago suburb. Her father, Carl Hansberry, had won a 1940 Supreme Court case giving him the right to purchase the home in what had been a racially restricted community; but despite this victory, the family was harassed and their home vandalized. Lorraine Hansberry loosely based *A Raisin in the Sun* on her family's experience.[6] At the end of *Raisin,* the Younger family moves into a home over the protests of their new white neighbors. The conclusion is hopeful, but the complicated twists and turns the Younger family's story takes to reach that ending signal that their victory, like the Hansberrys', will be short-lived.

In 1960, within months of *Raisin*'s debut on Broadway, racial issues in America were being played out with sit-ins and marches in support of integration. Fatal violence in opposition to it soon followed. The battle for America as a welcoming place for African Americans erupted. In a span of just a few months in 1963, the civil rights leader Medgar Evers was shot to death in front of his home in Jackson, Mississippi, and four African American girls were killed when their church in Birmingham, Alabama, was bombed by Klansmen. Although civil rights legislation was enacted in 1964, the question remained whether people of all races could live together in the same neighborhoods.

I first saw the movie version of *Raisin* on television when I was a child coming of age in the 1960s. It was one of my first images of a black family on television, and it offered me an inside view of the civil rights struggle. Though often overlooked, Lorraine Hansberry's play also forecast the breakdown in black marriages, intraracial and interracial conflicts, and the impact of social change and materialism on all homes and communities. *Raisin* served as a contrast to the 1950s view of women and the home that was portrayed on television and in some popular women's magazines. As women's opportunities outside the home changed, so did their ideas about home and identity. As part of the women's movement, they challenged the notions that the home defined a man's masculinity and success, that women needed only to provide a "happy home" for their husbands and boys to be successful, and that children would reward them by being successes.

At each juncture, even as progress toward equality was made through the passing of civil rights laws, African American women, who found themselves outside the dream because of gender combined with race, had to develop a new image of equality. In a 1965 prescription to avert the decline of the Negro family, Daniel Patrick Moynihan, who was then the assistant secretary of labor, cited the "matriarchal structure" of black homes as a primary impediment to the achievements of black men and racial progress in American society. To Moynihan, racial equality outside the home could exist only when gender inequality existed in it, a proposition that ignored the fact that the average wages for black men, suppressed by racism, made it necessary for black women to work outside the home as well. Even more important, he ignored black women's growing educational achievements, which promised even greater opportunity for economic gains at a time when materialism was growing and encroaching on the home.[7] Black household income, even with two working adults, simply could not keep up with the image of the American Dream as an ever larger home with bigger and more technically advanced household products.

Though Moynihan's prescription for equality was flawed, his prognosis for urban blacks' existence was on target. Violence and decay in urban neighborhoods were indeed escalating, particularly by the late 1970s. Middle-class and wealthy whites increasingly left urban areas for the predominantly white suburbs, the development of which was subsidized by governments at the local, state, and even federal levels. More women began to work outside the home.

Women—whether married or single, homemakers or working outside the home—were still primarily responsible for the home and for protecting their children from harm, even as violence found its way into "good" neighborhoods. In chapter 5, I present Marla's story to show how those responsibilities came together in one home in Southern California. As she anguishes over the murder of her son Sam, killed just yards from her doorstep, Marla must confront the limitations of individual effort in combating the growing threats to the sanctity of home. After a lifetime of shaping her home to meet her family's needs, she must reassess the legacy she leaves to her two surviving children so that they may create the "happy home" she struggles to envision for herself.

Marla's story has several morals. First, as a sort of sequel to *A Raisin in the Sun,* it serves as a warning against making the fragile institution of home the focal point for civil rights advances. Second, as I explore the structural conditions that disadvantage Marla, her story cautions us to consider the limits that individuals face when attempting to withstand the pressures put on home life in modern America. Finally, it shows that when neighborhoods are vulnerable, entire cities are at risk. In 2009, as the housing crisis unfolded, the danger of relying too heavily on access to home ownership as a measurement of progress became even more obvious, especially to black women. But rather than "dry up like a raisin in the sun," the dream of home ownership for black women flourished.[8]

In 1998 I purchased a home for the fourth time, moving from Oklahoma to Massachusetts and buying an 1887 Victorian that I imagined as my dream home. In truth, I didn't move to New England for the real estate. I was looking for a new intellectual home. After years of hearing from individuals, mostly women, who had suffered various forms of discrimination, I felt I needed to be outside a law school environment to rethink the role of the law. The disconnect between the laws on the books and women's experiences persuaded me that laws alone were not enough. I was beginning to understand, in fact, that as important as rights are to identifying inequality, true equality for all Americans requires us to consider how it can be expressed in those things that are most familiar and compelling, such as home. I took a position at a public-policy school, hoping that collaboration with academics and practitioners in other disciplines would help me learn what needed to be done to fulfill the promises of equality that I had so strongly believed in when I left Oklahoma for the first time decades earlier.

Deeply invested in home ownership as a part of my personal dream, I bought my Victorian and became a participant in the buying boom that was happening across the country. Low interest rates and government policies promoting home ownership as essential to the American Dream fueled the home-buying movement, painting a picture of a vital economy. Behind the public scenes, however, something very harmful, even sinister, was taking place. From the 1990s to 2008, predatory and subprime lending were on the rise, feeding on policymakers' increasing promotion of home ownership as a way for individuals to establish themselves as respected citizens. At best, lending practices were a way to bridge the growing gap between the real estate haves and have-nots. At worst, they were a recipe for individual and community disaster. In time, the worst was realized.

Instead of accumulating wealth, as the policymakers had promised, black women became more likely to lose what they had. Half of the African Americans borrowing money to purchase a home were women, but they were more likely than men to be borrowers in the subprime lending market.[9] That means they were more likely to be charged higher rates and fees. Black neighborhoods suffered economically, and a sense of community—the place where people congregate to share their views of the world—was also lost. Some black women survived the financial minefield. Anjanette Booker, whose story is detailed in chapter 6, managed to keep her home in Baltimore as well as build a sense of community through her work as a hairdresser.

Yet the community problems persist. In 2009, the mayor and city council of Baltimore sued Wells Fargo for economic losses that they attributed to the bank's lending practices. The allegations included charges of behavior that legal experts had called a "subprime lending spree."[10] If the city's 2008 projection of nearly half a million home foreclosures was correct, then Baltimore is in dire straits. In January 2010, a federal court judge dismissed the claim, citing "other factors leading to the deterioration of the inner city."[11] The city, however, filed an amended complaint in April 2010, saying that Wells Fargo's targeting of the city's minority neighborhoods for subprime loans had "inflicted significant, direct, and continuing financial harm on Baltimore."[12]

Anjanette Booker's story illustrates that what is at stake in making sure that people can make a home in any neighborhood goes beyond the individual; it extends to the entire city and beyond. Moreover, the city's response and the civil rights laws of the 1960s may prove inadequate to address the problems that face Baltimore, the state, and the nation. As it sheds light on those issues, this story calls upon us to look beyond the rights we've come to count on as the insurers of our freedoms from race and gender bias and once again to reimagine equality.

The crisis is more than the collapse of the housing market, it is a crisis of home—a tragic turning point in the search for equality in America. In chapter 7, as I explain why the plights of women like Booker matter to us all, I raise the question of whether the idea of home as a repository of the American Dream and the signifier of equality can coexist with the concept of housing as a measure of national economic prosperity.

The mortgage meltdown was never simply a problem of individual borrowers who overextended themselves in a fickle market, nor did its consequences fall on only a few communities. The collapse reflected systemic failures and exacerbated a host of problems in cities throughout the country. Baltimore is not suffering alone; the city of Memphis and the state of Illinois also sued Wells Fargo, the country's fourth-largest bank and one of the beneficiaries of the federal bank bailout program. And Wells Fargo, which repaid the government in December 2009 and posted earnings of $3.06 billion for the second quarter of 2010, was not the only bank caught up in the subprime frenzy. The combination of accepted industry-wide practices and a variety of social conditions that predate the housing crisis created the current state of affairs in cities like Detroit, New Orleans, Baltimore, and Memphis. They, along with places like Las Vegas, Milwaukee, and Charlotte, will have to reinvent themselves over the next few decades. The challenge for these urban areas has become how to avoid repeating the past. The challenge for the nation is how to make these and all cities more egalitarian in terms of who is at home in them.

In the years leading up to the housing collapse, both liberals and conservatives tapped into a yearning to realize the American Dream, a deeply rooted desire that transcends political ideology. Neither camp, however, seemed to understand the vulnerability of those most likely to take out subprime or unconventional loans, particularly those living in economically stressed neighborhoods or in neighborhoods where housing prices were hyperinflated or where public services were lacking. American leaders did little to make sure that the dream went beyond simply holding a deed to heavily mortgaged property. Banks and politicians failed to understand that the fates of those borrowers in struggling neighborhoods and the nation's economy were linked. As a result, because both gambled on the housing market, millions were displaced—not simply from their houses, but from their belief in an America where they could establish themselves and their families for generations to come. The long-term consequences of this lapse in leadership have yet to be given serious consideration.

The universality of the damage done goes beyond the economic losses claimed in lawsuits. The actions of lenders and our leaders' failure to impede them are more appropriately viewed as an assault on the American

Dream of finding a place to be truly at home. As author Christopher Clausen puts it, "What is at stake is not only the stability of the larger economy but something psychologically even more important—a shared ideology of... mobility."[13] That ideology of mobility has forever been linked to the idea of equality. Throughout American history, the desire to escape racial and gender bias has motivated the search for a place of refuge, satisfaction, and expression.

In his 2010 book *The Making of African America: The Four Great Migrations,* historian Ira Berlin tells of a four-hundred-year search for home, a series of four migrations to escape repressive forces and embrace something more hopeful. Even today, migration on a smaller and more intimate scale continues; women and people of color, displaced by the housing crisis, grapple with whether to stay put or to venture into unfamiliar roles and communities. Moreover, recent census data tells the story of young, educated African Americans, many of them women, choosing to make their homes in the South, reversing the journey of their ancestors. Latinos are changing the demographic landscape of southern cities and suburbs in America as well. Americans, whatever their race or gender, do not move for the sake of moving. They move to find a place where they truly belong. Others opt to remain in familiar places where they can create the homes they desire, even if the locations are less promising ones. The choice is often between a place where expectations of equality were not realized and a place where they can be reimagined—where they can live the American Dream.

Home ownership alone is not the answer assuring that individuals enjoy even the "place" of home, let alone the state, of being at home in America. The full participation of all citizens is much too important to be left to the whims of the housing market. In 2011 migration, along with a sense of rootlessness, is taking place on a much larger scale among Americans caught in the crisis of home. In chapter 8, I explore the pivotal question for all of us: What can our leaders do to ensure that the home remains an integral and achievable part of the American Dream? Punishing a handful of lenders in isolated lawsuits throughout the country is not a national strategy for addressing the displacement of millions. Administrative programs that cover just a fraction of the households suffering from the collapse of the market address only the end result of a crisis of home, which is rooted in inequalities that have plagued the country throughout its existence. History shows us that more fundamental approaches, those that require us to rethink our ideological investment in home ownership and our equating of home ownership with "home," are necessary to address the predicament we confront today.

In 2008, two events spurred me to think anew about equality in the United States. One, the presidential election campaign, took place in full public view. The other occurred in the quiet of my home, as I sorted through the seventeen years of correspondence that I had received from people throughout the country since my testimony before the Senate Judiciary Committee in the Clarence Thomas hearing. I saw the richness of the content of those letters, which came to represent a community in which I had become a member. I culled them for what they taught me about belonging to that community. Between those letters and the real prospect of living in a country that, for the first time in history, might be headed by either a white woman or a black man, I began to feel more at home in America than I had since 1991, when the public rejected the testimony of my life experience.

In 2009, when the first African American family to call 1600 Pennsylvania Avenue home moved into the country's most symbolic house, the political dimensions of the concept of home could not be ignored. President Obama, the son of a white American from Kansas and a black African from Kenya, and First Lady Michelle Obama, a descendant of slaves, were perfectly positioned to bring us to a new understanding of what it means for every citizen to feel at home in this country. Their personal and family stories are emblematic of the struggle of America to become a more inclusive democracy. The calls for proof of President Obama's place of origin, Hawaiian birth certificate notwithstanding, indicate that a vocal minority of Americans are still not "at home" with Barack Obama as president. Nevertheless, even in this time of crisis, he has an opportunity to resurrect and expand the American Dream and to lead the country to see home as something more than individual ownership of a house. Chapter 8 will focus on that reimagining.

From Abraham Lincoln to Barack Obama, presidents have shaped who is at home in America and whom America is at home with. Lincoln's signatures on the Homestead Act of 1862 and the Emancipation Procla-

Home:
A place that provides access
to every opportunity
America has to offer.

—A. H.

mation redefined our thinking about who belonged. Together they gave blacks, and others who had been locked out of the American Dream because they lacked the resources to buy land, a chance to put down roots, to enjoy the benefits of citizenship, and to be represented by their government. The American family was greatly enlarged, but not complete, as Native Americans were left out and many others, including the newly freed slaves, remained vulnerable.

Other presidents have made similar contributions to the expansion of democracy. Franklin Delano Roosevelt's New Deal ideas promoting home ownership opportunities were so strong that they prompted African Americans to reinvest in the country's political system and defect from the party of Lincoln to the Democratic Party. Lyndon Johnson's unyielding support for the passage of civil rights legislation, enforcement of housing nondiscrimination laws, and efforts to provide better housing for the poor also come to mind. Lincoln, Roosevelt, and Johnson confronted inequality and moved the country toward a stronger democracy. Yet none saw America reach its capacity as an inclusive community. Each left work to be done by future generations.

Barack Obama's presidency became another milestone in the full citizenship of African Americans and others who had felt left out politically in the previous twenty years. But the first black president's achievements must mean more. Like Lincoln, Obama must seize the moment of crisis to enlarge our concept of home for all Americans, particularly those who have been displaced by the economic and housing crises. Just as previous presidents came to hold special places in the hearts of the disenfranchised, the enslaved, and those without property, President Obama could become a champion of the displaced. Having been raised mostly by a single mother and her parents, he helps us think more broadly about what a family is. So can Michelle Obama, the descendant of slaves and slaveholders. The Obamas' personal histories are living stories of dislocation and progress in the search for home in America.

To move the country forward, the president will have to confront lingering inequality by engaging us in a discussion about the meaning of home, by enforcing laws that protect against housing discrimination, and by establishing policies that encourage the building of communities of equals. True, for the first time in our country's history, the house "at the center of a nation's identity," as C-SPAN called the White House, is presided over by an African American family.[14] But the job of creating a more inclusive democracy is not the president's alone. One of my greatest privileges as a university professor is to work with a generation that sees race and gender differently than mine. Its members challenge conventional categories and long-held thinking. Indeed, today 2.9 million people, a majority of them under the age of thirty, identify themselves as multiracial. As much as they believe in equality, for them a discussion of rights is abstraction. If we are to engage young Americans in a struggle for progress, we must understand that some ways of excluding those viewed as different will not be addressed by a discussion of rights and find new ways to talk about what it means to belong and live the American Dream. Our schools—at every level, elementary to university—must rise to the challenge of giving young people new ways of understanding equality and how it works in their lives.

The more than twenty-five thousand letters I have received from the public over the course of nearly two decades extend beyond the specific issues of the day. Consequently, my letters offer long-view lessons about equality that remind me of our common desires to be truly at home in America. Among their many messages is that, at its best, the American Dream is an application of our shared values. The views of the letter writers, like those of my students, reflect a larger portrait of the American Family. However, most of those who wrote to me won't return to school to learn how to realize that vision. They must be able to look within their own homes, as well as to religious institutions, the media, local leaders, and even businesses, for programs and policies that include the experiences of the disenfranchised and that promote our connections.

While he is in the White House, President Obama can make "home" the symbol of equality that Americans have envisioned in the past and that many of us continue to pursue. But it will take all who believe in an inclusive democracy to ensure that the American Dream stays alive and remains real for generations to come.

CHAPTER ONE

Home

Survival and the Land

Home: 1. The country or place of origin. 2. The house and
grounds with their appurtenances habitually occupied by a
family. 3. The family environment to which one is attached.
Webster's Third New International Dictionary

THE LUGGAGE

In August 1973, three weeks past my seventeenth birthday, I packed my
clothes in three hand-me-down Samsonite suitcases and left the only
place I had ever called home. Even at that age, I wanted a "better place,"
just as my grandparents had more than a hundred years earlier. College
was my first stop on the road to that better place—wherever it was.

Situated in Stillwater, Oklahoma State University was only three
hours by car from the farming community of Lone Tree, where I'd grown
up, but it was a world away from what I was leaving. The university had
built its first high-rise dormitories only several years earlier, and as a
freshman on scholarship, I was assigned to live in one. The twelve-story
concrete-and-steel structure known as Willham Hall would be my home
for the next two years.

In just about every way, our family's house in Lone Tree stood in stark
contrast to my new dwelling. Like the other homes in our community,
ours was a one-story wooden structure. A front room led to a dining
room, followed by a kitchen and utility porch joining three bedrooms
and a single bath. As the youngest child, I was the last to leave my parents' house, but I could recall when my parents, six of my brothers and sisters, an elderly uncle, and I shared a home that was a beehive of intimate
activity—with sibling squabbles, parental admonitions, family meals,
music, homework, and chores. Willham Hall was bustling as well, but

the activity inside was, like its exterior, much more impersonal, even institutional. Its hundreds of residents and I were there for the purpose of learning. For the most part, we treated the building and each other like the temporary measures we were.

Lone Tree, a smattering of small family-owned farms, had no post office, no streetlights or signs, and little hint of any government presence. Our "town hall" was the two-room Lone Tree Missionary Baptist Church, which at one time doubled as an elementary school for black children. Lone Tree's African American citizens worshiped there on Sundays. During the week, they occasionally gathered there to discuss issues of concern to the community, matters like who would contact the county commissioner to make sure equipment was sent to grate the unpaved roads. The few whites who lived among us spent Sunday mornings elsewhere. Though my college town of Stillwater was no booming metropolis, it had paved roads, stoplights, a city hall, a mayor, a police force, and more than one post office. But the university campus was the hub of my experience; because I didn't own a car, I knew very little of what went on beyond the university's sprawling acreage.

On the day I left for Oklahoma State, my belongings—notebooks, paper and pens, a few sets of twin sheets, a popcorn popper, and a new hi-fi record player, all graduation gifts—fit into a few boxes that my brother Bill and I loaded onto the back of a pickup. My neatly pressed clothes were packed in the luggage that bore the initials of my benefactor, Iola B. Young, a retired schoolteacher who was the most educated black woman in Lone Tree. Her friends, my mother among them, knew her as I. B. To my generation, she was Miss Young.

In dividing her possessions among her friends, Miss Young decided that the luggage was something that I could use. It was worn, but I was happy to have it. It was, after all, a matching set, and I needed something to put my clothes in. Miss Young, unlike the other women in our community, had escaped the manual labor of farm work and earned her living with her mind; I was determined to do the same. The wear on the suitcases suggested that they were well traveled. Had I been looking for a sign of my own long journey ahead, I might have found it there, but much of the gift's import was lost on me then. Years later, I would begin to understand why my mother accepted it with mixed emotions.

In 1973, however, I was a seventeen-year-old about to embark on an adventure. Having grown up in an era that promised new opportunities for young black women like me, I was off to claim them. In time, I would also begin to understand that my passage was not just my own; it also signified the most recent steps in a journey that had begun more than a hundred years earlier, when my ancestors, like so many blacks, set out in pursuit of the home that America had promised them with the ratification of the Fourteenth Amendment.

A *New York Times* article published October 7, 2009, "In First Lady's Roots, a Complex Path from Slavery," detailed the ancestral origins of First Lady Michelle Obama. It confirmed that an extraordinary amount of detective work is required to unravel African American family history. It also provided a glimpse into how unaware many of us are about the details of our past; Mrs. Obama had no knowledge of some of the stories that were ultimately revealed. Long before the *Times* article appeared, Harvard professor Henry Louis Gates Jr. was receiving widespread acclaim for his project that traced the genetics and genealogy of prominent African Americans. Gates's work, heralded as inspiring, has spawned courses at universities throughout the globe. "The desire to know who you are and where you come from is universal," transcending geography, age, and race, said Professor Gates.[1] Using public information and genetic technology, Gates set out to map the passages of black Americans from location to location within the United States as well as from regions in Africa.

Informed and motivated by these stories and by a family legend, I began to retrace the path taken by my mother's family, beginning with my only known maternal great-grandmother, Mary Elliott, from southwest Arkansas to eastern Oklahoma, where I was born. I wanted to know not only where they lived, but also—and more important to me—who they were and *how* they lived.

MOLLIE (NÉE MARY) ELLIOTT TAYLOR: THE LAST GENERATION OF SLAVES

Mary Elliott was born a slave in 1847, in one of the Elliott households in Oauchita County, Arkansas. The white Elliott family, whose ancestors could be traced to the Revolutionary War, were among the state's political and economic elite planter class. Camden, the Oauchita County seat, was set on the Oauchita River and had become a busy trade center because of its steamship connections to New Orleans. As it did throughout the South, cotton drove much of the business that operated out of Camden. By the late 1850s whites in the county prospered, shipping as many as forty thousand bales of cotton annually from Camden and building fine homes to reflect the area's wealth. As cotton output and prices rose, so did the number of slaves bought by whites in the region. Camden was booming by 1860, nearly tripling its population from the previous decade; it had two newspapers, numerous churches, manufacturing enterprises, and a number of lawyers. At the outset of the Civil War, more than half of the county's twelve thousand inhabitants were slaves.

It was in Oauchita County that Mary married Sam Elliott, also a slave, in 1863. They were both teenagers; she was sixteen years old. Like all other slaves who lived as wife and husband, their marriage was not recognized legally. Sam's and Mary's lives on the Elliott family farm were unremarkable, at least according to written records. Sam and Mary worked the land outside of Camden and lived together in slave quarters: a log cabin that likely had one or two rooms and a dirt floor. When Captain F. Heinemann of the Union army came to occupy Camden in 1864, he found "a small place, [whose] homes indicate a fairly well situated and intelligent population."[2]

Life in bustling Camden and Oauchita County, however, was about to change. In April 1864, during what became known as the Camden Expedition, Union troops advanced from Little Rock to occupy Camden as part of a push toward Shreveport, Louisiana. Brigadier General Frederick Salomon of the Union army established his headquarters in the home of James T. Elliott, a major in the Confederate army. Elliott family members were allowed to live on the second floor of the home. Troops camped out on properties throughout the area, taking over mills and raiding trains and steamships to commandeer food for the advancing army. The area was in turmoil as soldiers prepared for the battle of Poison Springs. The white inhabitants of Oauchita County, mostly Confederate sympathizers, were under siege and living in an enemy-occupied territory.

Mary Elliott, pregnant with her first child, was put up for sale. A family in Sevier County, Arkansas, near the Texas and Oklahoma borders, purchased Mary just as slavery was about to end. A healthy woman in her late teens might have sold for as much as twelve hundred dollars, and Mary's pregnancy added to her value; the prospect of an additional slave made her an even more attractive buy.

Though not as wealthy as their Camden neighbors to the east, Sevier County's planters were thriving. Cotton production, continually on the rise throughout Arkansas, was moving westward to the state's far southwest corner. The high yields from Sevier's rich bottom soil meant that more field hands were needed to keep up with the output. But purchasing slaves during the Civil War became an act of faith. Planters held out hope that the Confederate army would prevail, that Arkansas would remain a slave state, and that their way of life would endure.

A battleground now stood between Mary and Sam. The war raged on, but nearly two years into it, in January 1863, Abraham Lincoln signed the Emancipation Proclamation. Yet Mary, like many who would not learn until much later of their liberation, continued to live as a slave. And when she gave birth to a son, William Henry, in May 1864, her husband was a hundred miles away, still enslaved on the Elliott farm in Oauchita County, just as she continued in bondage.

With Confederate general Robert E. Lee's surrender to the Union's Ulysses S. Grant in 1865, the war ended. With the adoption of the Thirteenth Amendment to the Constitution, the chance for lives as free people came to nineteen-year-old Mary and her twenty-month-old son Henry, as it did for millions of black Americans throughout the country. Marriage took on added importance for the newly freed slaves. At the end of the Civil War, a black corporal in the U.S. Colored Troops rallied his command, saying: "The Marriage Covenant is at the foundation of all our rights. In slavery, we could not have legalised [sic] marriage: Now we have it . . . and we shall be established as a people."[3]

Like the corporal, early black Americans attached their ability to marry to their ability to establish a residence, a community, and a national home. The first Africans who would be called Americans—the largest group of immigrants in the country's history—had to start from scratch, or worse, from bondage. So strong was slavery's pull that the ability to establish a family outside of its influence did not fully materialize for almost a generation after the end of the Civil War. Yes, at the end of the war blacks could marry. Thanks to the efforts of the Bureau of Refugees, Freedmen, and Abandoned Lands, better known as the Freedmen's Bureau, they did. But many of the marriages performed by government officials involved individuals brought together by their owners. Yet some attempts were made to mend families that slavery had fractured. Government officials reunited hundreds of black families in Arkansas; army officials even performed wedding ceremonies.

Mary and Sam's family, however, was never restored. Why they were not among those taking vows is unclear. As a free man, Sam could have joined Mary in Sevier County. Or Mary, who had no longstanding ties to her new home, might have returned to Oauchita County. But it probably would have been difficult. After the Civil War ended, the Freedmen's Bureau opened an office and refugee camp in Camden, most likely because of its proximity to river travel. Thousands of destitute, hungry, and ill-clothed freedmen and displaced whites flooded the area. By 1865 diseases like dysentery and rubella had spread through the overcrowded camp and surrounding areas.

The horrific health situation endured for three years. An 1866 news story in the *Ouachita and Union County Reports* noted that "old and diseased freedmen and freedwomen are constantly turned away by their employers and former owners." Those who were no longer able to work were unwelcome as tenants on plantation properties. One historian has noted that "Mississippi and Arkansas river steamboats often dumped ailing black passengers at [the] nearest port."[4] By 1867 the vessels that had once hauled cotton and healthy, valuable enslaved blacks were now loaded with aged, infirm free blacks. Oauchita County was no place for Mary to return with her young son. The *Arkansas Gazette Weekly* reported in 1867 that, owing in part to an epidemic of cholera, the black population was rapidly disappearing. Just how Sam Elliott survived is unknown. What is known is that neither Sam nor Mary ventured to cross the hundred miles of dense cypress and pine groves to reunite their family.

Mary Elliott remained in Sevier County, living in the shadow of her former slaveholder's farm and most likely in one of his slave cabins. In 1867 Sevier County was partitioned by an act of the Arkansas legislature. Mary lived in the newly established portion, Little River County, but her situation remained the same. She was free, but she continued to work the land to make a home for herself and her son, Henry, in what was still a relatively new community. Conditions in Little River County for newly freed slaves were far from idyllic. Former Confederate soldiers bent on continuing the war, bandits, and Ku Klux Klansmen terrorized, beat, robbed, and even killed former slaves.

Work in the fertile bottomland of the region was plentiful. Indeed, maintaining the agricultural economy in the wake of the Civil War was in the interest of both the North and the South. A Freedmen's Bureau agent, Second Lieutenant Hiram F. Willis, set up his office near where Mary and Henry lived. Willis made it one of his primary responsibilities to enforce employment contracts for freed slaves. If his competence in acting on behalf of blacks was measured by the number of threats on his life and challenges to his authority he received, then he did his job well. The white farming population in Arkansas was so invested in the slavery system that the idea of paying blacks for work offended their very notion of race and class order.

In the end, through violence, these "Lost Causers" prevailed. In October 1868, a group of six gunmen ambushed Lieutenant Willis while he was on his way to settle a dispute between a local farmer and black contract workers. Willis and two others were shot and killed. Shortly thereafter, as the political will for Reconstruction waned, the federal government closed the Arkansas Freedmen's Bureau offices in 1869, leaving Mary and other former slaves in the area to negotiate with whites on their own. Although some had obtained basic literacy skills, Mary had not. Henry was nearly six years old, but the area had no school for black children. It did, however, have plenty of farm work.

For the next five years, Mary raised her son alone on the subsistence wages she earned in the fields of Little River County. Henry worked at her side. In 1874, Mary married Charley Taylor, a widower alongside whom she had worked as a slave in Sevier County; they had been neighbors since their liberation. Marriage did little to change their housing situation. As if to say goodbye to her old life, Mary began to call herself Mollie and moved into Charley's home, the cabin next to hers. Mollie, my great-grandmother, and Charley had three daughters together: Anna, Maria, and Bettie, the first known generation of freeborn children in my mother's family. Over the years, Mollie's household would include two adult daughters, one widowed and one separated; their children; and Charley's mother. In time, her daughters moved to Missouri and Nebraska, but Mollie never lived far from Henry, my grandfather. Theirs was a bond forged by the cruelty of slavery that had separated Mollie from her husband and other family and left Mollie and Henry with only each other for the first ten years of his life. Their bond endured until his death, many years before hers. Mollie Taylor was 107 when she died in Oklahoma, where she had moved to be near Henry and his family.

IDA (CROOKS) AND WILLIAM HENRY ELLIOTT: AN UNEASY FREEDOM

Ida Crooks was born in 1874 in New Boston, Texas, just across Arkansas's western border. When Ida was twelve, her brother, Danny, was killed by a white man in a dispute over land. Ida, her widowed father, and her older sister left New Boston soon after to start a new life in Little River County, Arkansas. There, in 1887, Ida met Henry Elliott, Mollie's son.

Three years later, Ida and Henry formed an unlikely union. She was the fifteen-year-old mother of a toddler; he was a twenty-four-year-old widower and father of three. She was known to be free-spirited; he was quite serious, even pious. But perhaps Henry saw something familiar in Ida. Henry had grown up witnessing the difficulties women and their children faced without men in their homes. Ida and Henry Elliott had one thing in common: they were the children of the last generation of slaves. As part of the first generation of African Americans who could begin to form families outside slavery's sway, they represented the best chance to form "a people," as the black corporal had imagined when he spoke to his troops at the end of the Civil War.

The Emancipation Proclamation came of age through couples like Ida and Henry. Yet the freedom that Ida enjoyed, even decades after the Civil War, was fraught with uncertainty. Her ability to shape her own existence was premised on the institution of marriage and on a peaceful coexistence with the white population in Arkansas. Both factors were largely beyond her control.

When she married Henry in 1890, Ida, who had never been on her own, was about to have her first home. To Ida and Henry's generation, marriage may have been promoted as "the foundation of all our rights," but Ida may not have been thinking of race or rights when she married. She was more likely thinking of her own good name and that of her son, Arthur, born out of wedlock. Even though he kept his biological father's name (Newsome), Arthur became legitimate, in terms of the social norms, when Ida married. And by marrying Henry, an older widower, Ida regained whatever respectability she had lost. Socially, marriage helped establish Ida and Arthur as *people*—if not completely free, at least respectable. Yet her marriage to Henry was more than a formality. Over the years, they grew together as a couple and, with their children, as a family.

By all accounts, Ida Crooks Elliott was confident and determined. But as a teenager, she could not have known how marriage, motherhood, and racial violence would come to overpower her ability to manage the home she lived in and her security within it. Indeed, what marriage meant for Ida was different from what it meant to the young Civil War corporal and his troops, or even to Henry. Along with her first home came the daunting responsibility of caring for three stepchildren, the oldest of whom was nine, in addition to her two-year-old son. Ida's marriage legitimized her motherhood, and within that construct she proved to be incredibly prolific. After their marriage, every two years or so, Ida brought more Elliott babies into the world. By the turn of the century, five more children had joined the Elliott household. That meant more food to cook and clothes to wash and, invariably, sick children to care for. Two daughters and a son would die before the age of six.

THE PARADOX OF BLACK MOTHERHOOD

In 1903, President Theodore Roosevelt called on native-born women to prove their patriotism by bearing children; by then, Ida Elliott was giving birth to her seventh child. But at the turn of the twentieth century, black women, including Nannie Helen Burroughs, were also beginning to express a desire to free themselves from the limits on their lives. Angelina Weld Grimké's 1916 play *Rachel* even suggested that women reject marriage altogether.

Rachel is a coming-of-age play about a black woman in the early twentieth century whose experience is shaped by her emerging understanding of race and gender, and even class. Grimké, the great-niece of a noted abolitionist and suffragist, Angelina Emily Grimké, sought to show the brutality of lynching—not only the immediate horrors of the act, but also its repercussions for generations to come. Grimké chose a female protagonist as the play's subject, even though men were typically the ones hunted and killed by lynch mobs. Though Rachel is not herself lynched, she is not immune from lynching's harm. After she learns that her father and half brother had been lynched ten years earlier, Rachel is transformed from a woman who loves and longs for "brown and black babies" into a woman who believes that they are best left unborn. Rather than risk bringing children into a world filled with violence and racism, Rachel ultimately chooses to break off her engagement. Grimké makes clear that Rachel's decision costs her. By the play's end, she is no longer her bright, vibrant, and hopeful self. Vacillating between near-hysterical laughter and deep remorse, Rachel struggles to make peace with her decision.

Grimké's drama sparked harsh criticism. The NAACP had commissioned *Rachel,* but critics rejected it as overly propagandist. The NAACP's male leadership denounced Grimké's message, claiming that her rejection of motherhood was a recipe for racial genocide, which the organization could not support. The play and its message for women sat dormant for decades, until it was presented in 1991 by students at Spelman College, a historically black women's college in Atlanta.

Roosevelt's resistance to women's use of birth control was not unlike the NAACP's resistance to Grimké's suggestion that black women reject motherhood. But the president, intent on balancing the impact of fertile immigrant populations, was directing his message at white women of English and Dutch descent, not black American women. The country's population was changing to reflect the influx of immigrants from southern and eastern Europe, namely Italians, Greeks, Hungarians, and Poles who were flooding into the country. They rendered futile Roosevelt's efforts to shape the racial and ethnic image of the United States.

Ida Elliott lived Roosevelt's message, whether she meant to or not and whether he wanted her to or not. In 1915 Ida gave birth for the last time. She bore thirteen children in all, although the number of children born to African Americans in general was on the decline.

Local customs, culture, and a lack of available birth control probably had the greatest influence on Ida's decisions about marriage and children—more so than the president of the United States or intellectuals like Grimké. In southeast Arkansas's black and rural communities, big families were respected and children were valued for their labor. Women were expected to produce and care for large numbers of them. Ida's marriage to Henry and her many children may have enhanced her respectability, but each child made her more conscious of the racial violence around her. To establish the kind of home she wanted, she needed each member of the household to feel secure. Security was not the province of men alone; black women shared in that responsibility. And at the start of the twentieth century, the past and present brutality wrought by racial distinctions left Ida with grave feelings of uncertainty about how much control she would ever have over her own life or her children's lives.

PROMISED LANDS

For many black families in the area, the only response to the harshness of Arkansas was to leave it. According to historian Kenneth Barnes, in the 1880s and 1890s about 650 black Arkansans sought to find a home in Liberia, which was thought to be, as one settler wrote to relatives, "the colored man's home, the only place on earth where they have equal rights."[5] More blacks left for Liberia from Arkansas than from any other state. To reach their destination, they had to trek halfway across the country to New York before boarding a steamer headed for the "African Promised Land." Hundreds of cotton farmers and field hands were promised twenty-five acres of land and a chance to grow coffee. Full citizenship in the United States had proved so elusive that they sold their few possessions to scrape together the money they needed to reverse the Atlantic transit of their forebears.

So strong was the allure of an idealized nation to call "home" that black Arkansans were willing to abandon their houses, extended families, neighbors, and friends to "return" to a place they had never been, where they would be a majority race. But in that place—where "there are no white men to give orders, and when you go in your house, there is no one to stand out, and call you to the door and shoot you when you come out"[6]—these pilgrims also found dense jungle and wetlands that had to be cleared before any planting could be done. Virulent strains of malaria wiped out many. Others went bankrupt when coffee prices plummeted in the 1890s, after Brazil flooded the world market with its own product.

Some returned to the States, but some, having risked everything to get to Liberia, stayed.

Black Arkansans who chose not to make the long journey to Africa, but still longed for a home that promised a more certain freedom, opted to settle nearby in Oklahoma Territory. It was accessible and, in the minds of many, largely devoid of the overt racism common in the South. That notion about Oklahoma was accurate, in part. Slaves who had been held by Indian tribes suffered less abuse and had more independence than slaves on Southern plantations. The more humane nature of black-Indian relationships endured after slavery ended, just as the harsher tenor of black-white in the South endured.

Available transportation and the proximity of the region to Arkansas made Oklahoma Territory an attractive destination. The structure of farm ownership there was also appealing, because it differed so vastly from the plantation system that existed in Arkansas and other southern states. In Oklahoma, small individual plots were the norm. Southern plantation owners with huge acreages required many field hands to sustain their enterprises, but in Oklahoma blacks, whites, and Indians could own and sustain their own relatively small allotments.

In the late nineteenth century, the cultural and racial climates of Oklahoma also contrasted with those in the Deep South. In 1889 the federal government opened land to the general public that had been set aside for Indian tribes, and settlers from throughout the South found their way to Oklahoma Territory. The subsequent building boom that swept through Oklahoma in the 1890s drew even more speculators and settlers to the territory, a substantial number of them black. In one incident in 1891, hundreds of blacks fled racial violence in Arkansas, spending the night under wharves with whatever belongings they could carry before heading down the Arkansas River on steamers to Oklahoma Territory.[7] The home that had once been promised to the area tribes was now a mecca for blacks and whites seeking their own version of the American Dream, a dream granted to them at the expense of the Indian population.

For many blacks, Arkansas had become a place to leave. Ida and Henry not only stayed, but made a commitment to the state that eventually became a critical part of the family legacy. In 1895, after years of working the land of white farmers, William Henry Elliott applied to the federal government for eighty acres of uncultivated land close to his birthplace, near where his mother, Mollie, had been a slave. Ida and Henry began the process of finalizing their ownership of the allotment. In January 1896 they built their first home on the land, a two-room log cabin. It was just the beginning of their claim to the homestead.

Each year they cleared more of the pine and oak trees that were native to the property. The first year, they planted four acres of cotton and corn in the soil, which had been enriched by centuries of forest foliage. They added a smokehouse and planted an orchard. By 1902, when Henry applied for the final patent, or deed, they were farming twenty acres. By virtue of the Elliotts' hard work, the log cabin had become home to thirty-seven-year-old Henry, twenty-eight-year-old Ida, and their seven children. They were the first in the Elliott and Crooks families to own property. "Repatriating" to Africa or resettling in Oklahoma was not for them.

Ida and Henry were at home in Arkansas, but as they went about securing their place in Little River County, violence was escalating. Racial terrorism in Arkansas included both mass killings and individual lynchings, and Little River County escaped neither. The Supreme Court's infamous *Plessy v. Ferguson* decision in 1896 legalized separation along color lines and succeeded in legitimizing racial intimidation as an extra-curricular tool in the furtherance of segregation.

FEAR AND TERRORISM IN BLACK AND WHITE

In March 1899, a group of fifty white citizens of Little River County set out to kill a number of its black citizens who were rumored to be planning a race war. By one newspaper account, as many as twenty-three black men were hunted down and either shot or hanged, most for being "smart and troublesome niggers," as one observer put it.[8] Fear gripped blacks throughout the county. Some attempted to escape to New Boston, Texas, just across the Arkansas border. Ironically, Ida's family had left New Boston years earlier and settled in Little River County after her brother, Danny, was killed by a white man in a dispute over land. No one was ever tried in the incident. Similarly, law enforcement turned a blind eye to the 1899 murders of those "troublesome niggers."

Many modern-day analyses of the horrors of lynching attempt to expose the dubious reasoning that was often used to explain why so many

African Americans died at the hands of lawless mobs. These explanations debunk the myth that black men were lynched as punishment for sexual assault, pointing out that the victims were often seen as a threat to the economic order in the agrarian South. Unlike Angelina Grimké, most writers tend to look at the public impact of lynching. Even today, few focus on how such a lawless act reaches into the private sphere, with profound consequences as far-reaching as they are unpredictable. Such brutality is not simply directed at individuals; it alters the sense of security of the family members and neighbors left behind.

The story of one of my grandparents' neighbors, who was murdered at the hands of a mob, helps illustrate that. In 1910 Dock McClain, a black farmhand whose census record indicates that he could neither read nor write nor identify his parents' places of birth, was arrested by the Little River County sheriff for stabbing Ernest Hale, a prominent local white farmer. The gash McClain carved was so deep that those who found the wounded man claimed to have seen his heart beating inside his chest. For days after the stabbing, as Hale struggled for his life, McClain sat in the Ashdown County Jail awaiting a trial. On the night of May 14, as officials transported their prisoner to a nearby facility, seventy-five whites surrounded the sheriff and his deputies. At eleven o'clock the mob hanged the accused, Dock McClain.

Word of Dock McClain's death spread quickly among the blacks in the small community outside Ashdown, where he and his wife, Mary, shared a home. The next morning, on Sunday, May 15, 1910, Mary McClain awoke in her rural home to her new status of widow. According to a report in the *Arkansas Gazette,* the state's largest newspaper, her husband's demise was quiet and swift. The sheriff who was transporting Dock McClain from the Ashdown jail to a "safer" location across the Texas border was overcome by the mob without a single shot being fired. The mob took custody of McClain, and within minutes he was dead.

Depending on the account, lynching was the fate that befell as many as twenty-six black men in Little River County from 1893 to 1910. Some lynchings were conducted away from public scrutiny, like the killings in March 1899 in which virtual hunting parties scoured the woods and river bottomland to find their victims. Others were carried out quite publicly.

In some instances, Jim Crow trials and executions resembled lynchings. Newspaper accounts detailed gruesome hangings in front of large crowds of both black and white onlookers, as in the 1883 case of Joseph Young. Even before seventeen-year-old Young was tried and convicted for sexual assault, he had been savaged thoroughly by law enforcement officials as well as dehumanized by the press. In reporting the trial, the *Arkansas Gazette* described Young as inhuman. In implementing his execution, the county sheriff and a posse of seventy-five men armed with Winchester rifles escorted Young to his hanging as his father, a local mill worker, and scores of black citizens held a prayer vigil on Joseph's behalf. Yet even with the horde of deputized whites ready to shoot Joseph and onlookers, the sheriff found it necessary to shackle the prisoner's arms and legs and place an iron collar around his neck.

Trials were often dispensed with. When Dock McClain was hanged, "so quietly did the lynchers work," the *Gazette* reported, "that the sleeping town knew nothing of the crime,"[9] as if that somehow diminished the violence carried out against Dock, as well as Mary and her children, seventeen-year-old Lizzie and thirteen-year-old Ezekiel. At the time of the lynching, the family had been without Dock for weeks, but now the isolation took on a permanence. Mary's worst fears had been realized and her twenty-year marriage brought to a brutal end.

In the following years, a banner waved outside the NAACP headquarters in New York City, some fifteen hundred miles away, reading "A Man Was Lynched Yesterday." As part of a national campaign against the lynchings that were occurring throughout the South, the organization marked each newly reported incident with the banner. In Little River County in 1893, 1899, and 1910, that banner could have read, "A Neighbor Was Lynched Yesterday." In 1910, Mary McClain's banner would have been even more personal: "My Husband, My Children's Father, Was Lynched Yesterday." After the worst outcome imaginable of her husband's arrest, Mary had to confront what life would be like for her and her children after Dock's horrible, unjust death.

The lynching changed Mary's life forever. The death of a spouse, violent or otherwise, can be devastating, even with today's counseling and the availability of antidepressant drugs. In the aftermath of Dock's lynching, Mary might have experienced what would now be called post-traumatic stress disorder. In 1910, although the American Psychiatric Association did exist, the *Diagnostic and Statistical Manual of Mental Disorders* did not, and post-traumatic stress had yet to be identified. In the early twentieth century, an intense psychological reaction to a traumatic event likely meant admittance to an insane asylum. Even that treatment would have depended on whether such places existed for "colored" women in Arkansas. Today, survivors or victims of violence can find support groups and organizations that raise awareness. In 1910, the loved ones of lynching victims would not have joined together to draw attention to their plight. Out of fear, few dared speak of such matters in the light of day.

The biggest question facing Mary McClain was whether she should take her children and move from where her husband met his tragic end. She chose to remain in Little River County, where she might regularly encounter members of the Hale family and where living reminders of Dock's death would be unavoidable. She might have thought it unwise to move her children from a life that was familiar to a place where they would confront new and unknown demons. She and Dock had been farm laborers, born and raised in Arkansas. Even if she had wanted to, would she have had the means to make such a move? She could continue to pick cotton and work the fields she had known since childhood.

The lynching would have also affected how neighbors interacted with Mary and her children. Was there a stigma attached to being the family of a man whose death was a manifestation of the racism that cloaked the entire community? Would Mary and her children be shunned or ridiculed by their neighbors, black or white? Would neighbors feel sympathy for Mary? She must have heard the jokes that blacks made about racial violence as a way of calming their fears. But this form of gallows humor was no longer an abstraction, and Mary's experience was one that most of her neighbors undoubtedly dreaded.

Black people had learned to trust one another for survival, assured that at the very least they shared a collective interest in avoiding racial violence. In rural black Arkansas, trusting other blacks was second only to trusting God. But Dock McClain's lynching hit so close to home that it may have threatened that collective interest. Would Mary be able to trust anyone?

Mary's neighbors and friends would have expected her to be angry. The unfairness of her situation magnified the unfairness of the everyday racism they all experienced. Their collective history included generations of slaves who had learned, out of necessity, to hide their feelings. Did Mary take out the anger she masked from others on her children "for their own good"? Did the lessons she learned from her forebears serve her as she taught her children that their very survival might require them to swallow the hurt and the bitterness? At age thirteen, Ezekiel would have had a difficult time, and his anger at life's unfairness might have easily defied a mother's teaching. No evidence of Ezekiel remains in public records.

Historical records cannot tell us how the McClains and their community coped in the aftermath of Dock's lynching. What is known is that seven years after her father's murder, Lizzie McClain, at the ripe age of twenty-four, married Willie Brown in Little River County. Lizzie's wedding in 1917 made her part of the third generation of African Americans to marry in hopes of being established as "a people." But as the subsequent history of racial violence would show, marriage was not the panacea that the black Civil War corporal had hoped for in his speech to his troops.

Lizzie was four years older than the average marrying age for women at the turn of the century. She may have delayed marriage, but to forgo marriage and children, the way Grimké's title character did in *Rachel,* would not have been an easy choice. She may not have understood or even cared about the political implications of such a choice, but Lizzie was no doubt aware of the cultural implications. In the early 1900s, black women were striving for respectability, and one way to achieve it was through motherhood within marriage. Whether Lizzie had children is not clear from the public records, but her choice to marry in the same community where her father was so violently killed shows a commitment to home.

Mary McClain died in 1925 and was buried in Newsome Cemetery in Little River County, among the neighbors and friends she and Dock McClain had shared. The cemetery is seven miles east of Ashdown, Arkansas, just off State Highway 317 and not far from Yarborough Landing, a new lakeside housing development named after the slave-owning family who once owned the land. Turn right off the highway at a white house and follow the dirt road into a wooded area, and you will soon reach the cemetery entrance. Amid the rough stones that mark the graves of African American men and women, most of whom were born in the nineteenth century, is the grave of Mary McClain. The headstone gives her date of death and the fraternal organization that likely paid for the marker: 1/9/1925, Nelson Chamber 2134, Red Bluff, Arkansas. It does not tell us that she was a wife, a mother, and a woman who struggled to deal with the cruel circumstances life had dealt her fifteen years earlier, when a violent mob lynched her husband.

Mary lived long enough to see her children reach adulthood, which may have been her greatest triumph. That a local organization paid for her headstone suggests that she was a valued member of the community. No headstone exists for Dock McClain in Newsome Cemetery, or in any other cemetery in Little River County.

There are, however, numerous public records of the Hale family. Ernest Hale, whose encounter with Dock ultimately led to the lynching, had ventured out on his own at age fourteen. Rather than live in comfort with his physician father and be attended by black servants, he chose to live in a neighbor's smokehouse, doing farm work for room and board and token pay. Exactly what prompted him to leave home is not clear, but he could not have known that his future would be as bright as it was. He soon accumulated enough money to buy ten acres of land. In 1910, when Dock McClain stabbed him, Hale was on his way to becoming one of the county's most prominent farmers. He survived the attack and continued to live on a nearby farm; by 1914 he had accumulated thousands of acres of the rich land that surrounded his father's home.

Two years after the stabbing, unmarried and living alone at age thirty, Hale brought a twelve-year-old black child into his household. The boy, known as Goody, was being raised by a widow in the community, and Hale promised the mother of eight that he would provide Goody with a home and send him to school. Goody lived in Ernest's home until adulthood, then moved into a home of his own on the Hale property. Hale kept his promise, even after he married and had children of his own, staying in contact even after Goody left Arkansas.

We can only wonder why Ernest Hale chose to defy social custom and take a black child into his home. One theory is that it had to do with Lillian, a mulatto girl who grew up in Hale's boyhood home. Lillian was Ernest's half sister, the daughter of his father and the Hale family's cook. Ernest, twelve years older than Lillian, broke another taboo when he developed a friendly relationship with her that lasted long into adulthood, often visiting her openly in her home.

Ernest Hale's affection for Lillian and Goody may explain why he became known as a "friend to blacks in Little River County." Another possible explanation is that it was guilt or remorse over McClain's lynching. Within days of Dock McClain's arrest, Hale's brother Archie shot a black man; Archie, who was ten years younger than Ernest and living in their father's home, claimed the man had threatened him with a knife. From then on, Ernest's relationship with his younger brother was strained. The two feuded—occasionally with guns in hand, threatening to shoot each other—until Archie's death in 1957. Ernest died a year later. His son and grandchildren still live in Little River County on the land that Ernest amassed.

Hale's grandsons offered me a much more simplistic recollection of the McClain incident than Mary McClain's grandchildren might have. The Hales were told by family members over the years that Ernest was near death for days after the stabbing and that the person who assaulted him "was hanged." The McClain lynching is nonetheless part of their family legend and may have influenced Ernest Hale's decision to make a black child a member of his household. It also may have influenced the racial attitudes of his grandsons, who want people to "know the truth" about what happened in 1910. I am flattered that the Hales entrust me with telling the truth about their grandfather. I too want to know the truth. Their truth may be simply that he was stabbed and almost died and that the culprit was hanged. Neither I nor they believe that Ernest Hale conspired to have Dock McClain lynched.

Through my cousin Faye, I have an account of Hale's life that is not entirely different from the grandsons'. She expresses little doubt that McClain stabbed Hale. And she, like Hale's descendants, did not know of the lynching. "Our parents tried to keep those kind of things away from us," Faye said, referring to herself and her siblings.

My cousin's and the Hales' stories don't supply any information about what provoked Dock McClain. Frankly, I don't know how to define provocation in the context of the virulent racism in existence at the time. No matter the circumstances of the assault on Hale, McClain's lynching was an act of lawless barbarism.

But I want to know something different about Ernest Hale. I want to know how the pieces of Ernest Hale's life came together to lead to his apparent rejection of his brother's act of vengeance. I suspect that when Hale, as a boy, lived in an unheated barn rather than his father's comfortable home, he learned what life as an outcast was like. Through that experience, he might have had some idea of what life was like for Dock McClain and his family. I suspect that at the very least, when Ernest Hale saw Goody, he was reminded of himself as a boy. When Hale saw the child he would take into his home, he might have imagined Goody growing up ignorant and subject to the whims of racial hostility then so prevalent in the South and done what he could to prevent it.

The truth I want to know about Hale is whether his very real kinship with Lillian—his time in her home—allowed him to see himself in people of other races. Lillian is not a part of the story the grandsons know. Indeed, I learned of Lillian through Faye, and they learned of Lillian through me. With so many parts, from different sources, a whole truth is likely unknowable. But what we do know is that Ernest Hale defied convention and found a new way of living in community with his black neighbors in Little River County. And perhaps that is as much of Hale's truth as one need know. My grandparents' reality was different.

A BETTER PLACE

In 1914, four years after an angry mob killed Dock McClain, my grandfather, Henry Elliott, had his own brush with a near lynching. Following a dispute with one of his white neighbors, Henry was warned about a possible plot to kill him. Ida and Henry had reason to take the threat seriously, and certainly no reason to believe that local law enforcement would intercede on his behalf. Fearing for his life and for his family's sense of security, Henry temporarily left my grandmother Ida and their seven children in search of a better place to raise his family.

Ida lived with the memory of her brother Danny's murder after a fight with a white man. When Henry was threatened, Ida's oldest son, Arthur, was nineteen years old—close to the same age Danny was when he was killed. The fact that Arthur was entering manhood made him vulnerable enough; his quick temper put him at even greater risk. Yet he was not the only vulnerable member of the Elliott household. At fifty, Henry's age and status in the community were not enough to protect him. Henry was ambitious and industrious in his efforts to provide for his family. He was a founding member of the New Hope Baptist Church and did business with the whites in the community. Ida knew that despite his years of respectable living, Henry would have been as helpless as Joseph Young's father had been in trying to dissuade a mob intent on harming a member his family. At the time, Henry and Ida were also raising four other sons, all under the age of ten, and two daughters, ages sixteen and fourteen. Ida, who had seen two of her daughters die of tuberculosis, worried constantly about losing her husband or a son to lynching. Had Henry's fate been the same as Dock's, Ida would have had to face life as the provider for her family at the age of forty-one. She would have been left alone to protect her children from poverty and persecution.

After leaving Little River County for a few weeks to avoid a lynching, Henry returned and relocated the family to a new and, he hoped, safer home. Henry and Ida and seven of their children followed in the footsteps of earlier migrants and made their way west to Oklahoma. They left behind their house, Henry's and Ida's parents, and four of their children. Those who stayed witnessed the last recorded lynching in Little River County, in 1917.

Family members tell two different stories about Henry and Ida's decision to leave Little River County and about the 1914 threat of lynching. With some coaxing, my uncle George Elliott told me that the family left after a white neighbor tried to force Ida to cook and clean for his wife. On Ida's behalf, Henry declined this "offer" of employment. The white neighbor responded to the "racial insult" with intimidation, saying Henry and his family would be visited by the night riders, the lynch mobs. My cousin, Faye, who was raised in Little River County, recalled a more ominous scene involving hooded white men and a direct threat. Denying an accusation that he was harboring a black fugitive, Henry ordered the white vigilantes off his property. Henry had been tipped off to his neighbors' plot to kill him for "sassing white men." One of his friendlier white neighbors had issued a rather direct warning: "Leave or you will be lynched." Whatever the precise details, in an era when racism was continually escalating into violence, the Elliotts had been persuaded to uproot their family, seeking safety and a better life in Oklahoma.

Economics probably played a role in their decision as well. In order to acquire the seeds and supplies he needed each year for farming his land in Arkansas, Henry signed crude documents that gave his lenders control over what he could obtain and the value of items he received. An 1897 entry found in the Little River County Mortgage Record reads:

> I, W. H. Elliott . . . in consideration of the sum of fifty dollars, to me in hand paid by W. P. Goolsby . . . and for the consideration of such supplies of provision, merchandise, money, etc., as the said W. P. Goolsby supplies . . . hereby grant, bargain, and sell to said W. P. Goolsby the following described property . . . Six acres of cotton that I may raise in my farm . . . One Bay mare, five years old. . . . Conditioned that should I pay to him on or before 1st November 1897 (with 10% from date) such sums that I may be due to the aforesaid W. P. Goolsby.[10]

By the time the Elliotts left Little River County, they were no longer living on the land they had homesteaded. Henry and Ida were farming for others and living in a rented home. No family member has an explanation for how the Elliotts turned from homeowners into renters. By that time cotton prices had plunged, jeopardizing their ability to make a living from their farming, notwithstanding Ida and Henry's enterprising ways. They had tried to raise corn, but that did not provide the income they needed to prosper. The plantation system that had been the hallmark of the South still favored large landholdings and cheap or free labor. Small farms, whether owned by blacks or whites, were at a competitive disadvantage. For years the Elliotts' homestead had been mortgaged heavily, on terms that always favored the mortgage holders. Sometimes the terms even granted the lenders the right to charge whatever interest rate they saw fit and to determine the amount owed.

We do know that whatever motivated the Elliotts to pick up and leave must have been a powerful force. The combination of the violence, the threats, and the economy was probably enough to drive the family from Little River County, the only home Henry had known. My uncle George Elliott said that for the first time in his life, he saw his father, Henry, cry as they boarded the train headed for their new life in Wewoka, Oklahoma. Mixed with the memory of his father's sadness was the excitement George felt as he embarked on his first train ride. The family members were leaving their home, their community, their vegetable garden, and the crape myrtle and pear trees. The New Hope Baptist Church—the church Henry and Ida had helped found—would be traded for a church called Paradise. But part of the family was still in Arkansas: Zodia, the oldest daughter, who was married and had a baby boy; Bettie, Ida's step-daughter; Rosa; and Arthur, who was not yet married. In time, the Elliott homestead would fall into the hands of the Hale family. But what mattered more to Henry and Ida was a new start. They left behind the eighty acres they once owned, and in doing so, they dared to imagine a new home for themselves and their younger children.

CHAPTER TWO

Belonging to the New Land

Home: The place, region, or state to which one properly
belongs, in which one's affections properly centre,
or where one finds refuge, rest, or satisfaction.
The Oxford English Dictionary

In cultivating the rugged acreage in Arkansas, Henry and Ida Elliott had faced and conquered untamed land to make a home. In pulling up their roots to move the 250 miles to Seminole County, Oklahoma, they were cutting their ties to the land of their enslavement and starting over in a place where their family would be known only as free people. In 1914 Henry, now fifty years old, and Ida, forty-one, put whatever energy they had into making a new home in a new land. The terrain surrounding Wewoka, the county seat, was flatter and less forested than Little River County's, much better suited to farming. But the state's topography was not its biggest draw; Henry came to Oklahoma because he envisioned it as a home of promise for his children. The frontier setting, multiracial population, and uncharted social and legal environment all contributed to the popular idea that the Southern Plains location was a twentieth-century melting pot.

In 1943 Rodgers and Hammerstein honored the spirit of Oklahoma with a Broadway musical named for the state. The theatrical production—set at the turn of the century, just before the Elliotts made their journey—paints a picture of Oklahoma as a romantic locale with endless opportunities for all who venture within its borders. The diverse characters in *Oklahoma!*, all rugged individuals with various backgrounds, come together for the communal good in the territory's effort to achieve the holy grail of statehood. Assimilation is a theme throughout the production, and its ultimate message is one of unification, as the individuals become "we," singing, "We know we belong to the land." Everyone learns to get along. Aunt Eller, the show's matriarch, speculates that once statehood is granted, the farmers, ranchers, and merchants will "all behave theirsel's and act like brothers." Even the musical's staging conveys a message: men and women dance together in elaborately choreographed synchronism. In *Oklahoma!*, establishing a cohesive community is the key to establishing statehood.[1]

Interestingly—or perhaps tellingly—the musical has no specifically African American or Native American characters, and its utopian picture of assimilation and nation building hardly matches the reality of the black experience in Oklahoma before statehood. However, some read the dark-skinned Jud Fry as the racial outsider, interpreting him as either black or Native American. It is worthy of note that Jud is the play's sole holdout from conversion to solidarity. That is, he is the one who refuses to give up his personal freedom for the good of the whole and a "unitary American identity."[2] It is further worth noting that Richard Rodgers and Oscar Hammerstein II excluded racially offensive language contained in the play from which their work was adapted.[3]

Passed one month after Oklahoma achieved statehood, Senate Bill One mandated segregated transportation and called for violators, individual or corporate, to pay fines ranging from five to one thousand dollars. When the measure became law on December 18, 1907, it was Oklahoma's first legislation and the signal of even more destructive race relations in the state's future. As whites began to enter Oklahoma in greater numbers, they brought with them their sense of superiority in the racial hierarchy, as well as the violent enforcement of that hierarchy that blacks who had left Arkansas were hoping to escape.

In the early days of Oklahoma Territory, lynching was primarily a way of enforcing economic interests, and the main victims of such mob violence were white cattle rustlers. Over time, white transplants from Tennessee, Louisiana, Arkansas, and Mississippi congregated in the eastern and southern parts of the territory; the southeastern corner of the state became known as Little Dixie. Following statehood, as the population growth of whites outpaced that of blacks or Indians, lynchings took on a clear racial basis. Blacks became the most frequent victims of mob violence, although Native Americans were occasionally lynched; whites rarely found themselves on the wrong side of the vigilantes' noose. In 1904 Boynton, an eastern Oklahoma Territory town, was the site of a race riot that left at least one black resident dead. In nearby Henryetta in 1907, white residents lynched a black man accused of murder, then torched the black neighborhood.[4] Through law and lawlessness, the promise of Oklahoma as a utopian melting pot faded. The state emerged in racial custom and culture as a Dixie outpost.

Even with all its flaws, Oklahoma came to be seen as an appealing alternative to life in the South. Beginning in the 1890s, activists promoted the notion of colonizing the state for blacks; although the idea never materialized, a proposal to make Oklahoma a "black state" reportedly went as far as the president, first to Benjamin Harrison and later to Theodore Roosevelt.[5] In neighboring Kansas, William L. Eagleson, an African American newspaper editor, founded the Oklahoma Immigration Association to achieve the goal of resettling one hundred thousand blacks from southern states to Oklahoma. He teamed with Edward P. McCabe, Kansas's first black state auditor, to buy land to incorporate black towns. His plan also included enfranchisement; the politically savvy McCabe worked to establish blacks in various locations in numbers significant enough to constitute voting blocs.

Blacks responded. A group of delegates even went to Washington to protest the enactment of Senate Bill One, but President Roosevelt refused to interfere with the state's autonomy. Despite the open hostility directed toward blacks, or maybe because of it, black towns sprang up virtually overnight. Blacks then occupied settlements carved out of the territories that had belonged to the Creek, Seminole, and Choctaw nations. Black townships developed parallel to white towns, mixed towns, and Indian towns. Outside of organized municipalities, black enclaves provided a kind of community and security unattainable in multiracial settings.

After statehood, Oklahoma became well known for all-black towns like Boley and Langston, planned communities run by black governments that were often associated with economic opportunities and access to the railroads. These homogenous towns were a response to both the freedom Oklahoma promised and the racial animus blacks experienced there. The federal government sanctioned racial separation with the Supreme Court's 1896 decision in *Plessy v. Ferguson*, which upheld segregation on trains. For whites, the *Plessy* reasoning meant that blacks could be separated not just on trains, but in all political and economic capacities. Separate municipalities were a logical extension. Blacks also followed the *Plessy* logic, engaging in preemptive segregation by establishing towns as expressions of black independence and self-determination: by us, for us.

By 1914, when the Elliotts determined that Arkansas could no longer be their home and that Liberia was not a feasible option, they joined the ranks of blacks who chose to keep the United States as their nation-home. Even as they boarded a segregated train to Oklahoma, they attempted to redefine what that citizenship meant to them. Lone Tree, the community the Elliotts settled in not long after the move to Wewoka, bore similarities to the all-black townships.

Although Henry and Ida never again owned a home, that did not stop them from looking for security and a chance to belong. They found it in family and in the church. By 1930 Henry and Ida lived in a black enclave in rural Oklahoma surrounded by family members. Zodia, Ida and Henry's oldest, was estranged from her husband and lived nearby with her four children and a boarder she took in to help make ends meet. My mother, Erma, was Henry and Ida's youngest daughter; she and my father and their first child lived and farmed within walking distance of her parents. So did two of my uncles. Henry's stepmother, Alice, lived with Henry and Ida and their youngest son, Floyd. Henry's sister Ann joined him in Oklahoma before moving on to Missouri and Nebraska, where she made her home in Omaha.

Ida was no longer able to work the farm, but she could still cook her signature buttermilk cake, braid her granddaughters' hair, and, according to my sister Elreatha, regale her grandsons with stories of how she could once "pick cotton all day and square-dance all night." The Elliott family members still picked cotton. But Ida was no doubt oblivious to the likelihood that her grandsons were more interested in dancing to "Ma Rainey's Black Bottom" than in their grandmother's do-si-dos. Ida, Henry, and Alice looked after the children who were too young to join their parents in the fields. In time, Ida's daughters and daughter-in-law took care of their elders. Ida and Henry had moved from the church called Paradise to worshiping at Lone Tree Missionary Baptist Church, where Henry was also a founding deacon. After services, Ida and Henry, their children, and their grandchildren ate Sunday meals together. If not a prosperous life, theirs was a good life; but as the Depression hit with full force, that life became increasingly unsustainable.

Rural black enclaves and townships provided a sense of security and belonging for people like Henry and Ida, but ultimately, turning inward to avoid racism did not give them the freedom they desired. Too often, it succeeded only in increasing their distrust toward whites, which was what had led to the formation of the enclaves in the first place. The members of these communities were limited not only in their income, education, and social opportunities, but also in their political strength. The racism and sexism that marginalized blacks had legal and cultural manifestations. In the end, the idea that blacks and whites and Indians could live as separately as "fingers on the hand" proved untenable.[6]

In her 1998 novel *Paradise,* the Nobel laureate Toni Morrison explores the extremes that can result when segregation by a dominant group pushes the self-isolation of a subordinate group to its geographical limits. The black families in *Paradise* are driven to the remotest edge of the country's frontier, to Oklahoma, where they attempt to establish their own utopia. They call their town Ruby, and much like the plantations of the past, it soon develops a stifling structure because of its insularity. Ruby is its own community and nation, premised on both physical and intellectual isolation. In what they believe are efforts to cleanse Ruby of racism, the town leaders turn first on each other, then on a neighboring enclave of women who have taken refuge in a place they call the Convent.

Paradise begins and ends as the Ruby men slay the Convent women, who were about to begin a ritual to purge themselves of the burdens of sexism and racism that they had carried throughout their lives. Through their tragic demise, we glimpse how threatened the men of Ruby were by women's ownership and shaping of their own space. Though the Convent was a place to which Ruby's residents had no claim, the men of Ruby were willing to deny the Convent's residents the sense of owning and belonging that the men themselves coveted. That is no surprise. Conformity dominated the vision that the leaders of Ruby had for their paradise. But by their refusal to accept new ideas and vehement insistence on rigid submission to their ideals, they ensured their own demise. With or without their acquiescence, the world around them changed. From them we learn the impossibility of achieving equality though isolation and exclusion. By constructing their liberation through an ability to expel from their separatist compound the blacks who did not think like them, the leaders created their own prison in which they were both wardens and inmates. They replicated what they sought to escape—the order that had been imposed on them by whites—and, in time, imposed that same scheme's ultimate control mechanism, violence.

The real black towns of Oklahoma did not end with catastrophe, nor did they self-destruct as the fictional Ruby did. They wasted away and often disappeared. Cut off from the economies and social networks of the rest of the world, they could not sustain the people within them, and their inhabitants lost the will to hold on to them.

In time, that fate befell Lone Tree. Mercifully, Henry and Ida would not witness the demise of their community. When Henry died in 1936 and Ida followed in 1937, they were surrounded by two new generations of Mollie Elliott's descendants, poised to make good on the promise of Oklahoma, the promise of a new home.

ERMA ELLIOTT HILL AND ALBERT HILL:
HOME AT LAST

My mother was three years old when her parents, Henry and Ida, fled Arkansas. Aside from stories told by her parents and siblings and an occasional visit to Little River County, Oklahoma was the only home she ever really knew. Erma was the youngest daughter, the family darling, and her father's favorite. Despite her shyness, she was strong willed and somewhat accustomed to getting her way.

Shortly after the Elliotts moved to Lone Tree, Erma met Albert Hill, the boy that she would marry when she was sixteen, despite her parents' misgivings. Teen marriages were not unusual in 1927. Their marriage license lists their ages as sixteen, the legal age for marriage. In fact, Albert was only fifteen. As the youngest of three children, Albert—nicknamed "Be" by a Creole uncle, short for *bebe*, "baby"—was not ready to leave his mother's home. At seventeen, Erma gave birth to her first child in her mother-in-law's Miss Hill's kitchen. By nineteen, pregnant with their second child, she exerted her will and threatened to leave her husband if he didn't get them their own home by the time the baby was due.

With a dowry of a cow and a calf from Ida and Henry, and with money from Albert's grandfather, Erma and Albert began to cobble together the pieces to assemble a home. In time came the land and the house that she and Albert built themselves, just as Ida and Henry had done thirty years before. On their land, Erma and Albert raised thirteen children and grew much of their own food. By the time I, the thirteenth, was born in 1956, the rural community called Lone Tree—where they had lived most of their lives—felt like home to Erma. She and Albert had achieved what Ida and Henry had lost: ownership of their own farm. Lone Tree had survived—not as the family enclave that her parents envisioned, but as a community of loving neighbors nevertheless. Erma Hill knew its residents through the kind of familiarity that came from knowing the songs they sang, the prayers they prayed, the food they ate. She made sure her children did too. On Sundays, when Ralph Hutton—brother of the schoolteacher, Iola Young—sang about letting the light God gave him shine "all around my home," we knew what home he meant. We had been in it.

We shared social activities, assembling in the church or the school for birthdays and funerals. We did the same kind of work. Those who were not farming at the time had farmed in the past, had been raised by farmers, or were being raised by farmers. The community also helped shape and reinforce the religious, work, and family values I'd first learned from my parents. The people who lived down the road from our house were, in more modern lingo, my homies. We all felt rooted in the place and at home together, even though the houses were separated by expanses of fields and woods. So in 1973, when my mother and I knocked on Miss Young's door for the luggage that would carry my belongings to college, we felt a comforting familiarity in her home, which was set back from a dusty road.

My mother and Miss Young were perhaps as different as two women could be in such a small rural community. My mother never finished high school. She married at sixteen, was a mother by seventeen, and every two years or so for the next thirty years, she bore another child. I was her youngest, born two months shy of her forty-fifth birthday. My mother had spent more than half her life negotiating the restrictions of overt racial segregation. She sent ten children to segregated schools and attempted to protect them from the harshness of segregation's intended message of inferiority. Erma Hill watched her three youngest children graduate from integrated schools, shielding them from the vestiges of segregation and racism that hung in the air at previously all-white schools. She made it clear that homework, even when she didn't understand the lessons, was our priority. We were obligated to do it, just as we were to help feed the livestock, wash and iron our clothes, and mop the floors. She grilled us daily, laboring with us to make sure that we appreciated the difference between a living earned from backbreaking labor and a living earned sitting at a desk. My mother understood the end game and made it clear that I would need an education that exceeded hers if I expected to get anywhere in the world.

Miss Young was married but had no children. She worked outside the home and earned more money as a teacher than most others in the community, men or women, earned from working their farms. She even went by her initials, I. B., something typically done only by men. Being a teacher was a socially acceptable undertaking for African American women in a segregated society; being one helped Miss Young escape some of the class constraints of our community. Like many African American schoolteachers, she was one of the most respected and vital members of the community.

By 1959, five years after the Supreme Court's ruling in *Brown v. Board of Education* banned segregation in public schools—and when desegregation finally edged its way into the Oklahoma schools—the new, integrated system deemed Miss Young dispensable. She, along with many other experienced black teachers, found herself looking for a job after the black schools closed and black students were educated in what had once been all-white schools. During the first few years of the integrated system, she often used her Samsonite luggage as she traveled the dusty roads to teach at a high school hours away from our community. Each weekend she would return to her husband and their small, secluded farmhouse on one of the single-lane roads that connected Lone Tree's residents. But Miss Young grew weary from all the commuting, and her health began to fail. As soon as the English teacher was eligible for a pension, she retired and came home to Lone Tree for good.

When my mother and I went to collect the luggage, Miss Young greeted us at the door with a smile that couldn't cover the fact that she was in her final days. She was dressed in a loose-fitting housedress that in no way resembled the neat and proper clothing she had worn when she taught my brothers and sisters English. She looked tired, drawn, and defeated.

For all their differences, Erma Hill and Iola Young shared a faith in education. To them, education promised liberation, even if they had not experienced it. Miss Young often stressed the value of education and encouraged my parents to view me as gifted; my mother treated all her children as if they were gifted. If nothing else, my mother knew she had given us the gift of understanding how to work hard and how to survive. My mother raised me to believe that I must be responsible for supporting myself and any children I might have. "I don't want a daughter of mine to have to rely on a man for money," she asserted. I was eleven when she first declared that to me; at the time, I had no idea of the personal frustration behind her statement. As the mother of thirteen, she exhibited amazing organizational and management skills in the areas of human and fiscal resources—skills that far surpassed the settings in which she could display them: our home and farm. Her identity was tied to motherhood, and she grieved as she watched each of her children leave home, even as she reaffirmed, "I didn't raise you to stay here."

For forty years, children were the center of her life. Her empty-nest experience was palpable: I heard it in her voice when we spoke after I left home; I saw it in her face when she welcomed her grandchildren for long summer visits and when she said goodbye to them as they returned to their homes. Despite her desire for independence from the demands of marriage and parenting, she showed no signs of rebellion. She lived the freedom she craved through her six daughters. Gender and race constraints were inescapable elements of Erma Hill's life. The same was true for her neighbor Iola Young. They had made the best bargain with tradition that the times afforded them, and they lived to see a day when change was in the air.

My mother and Miss Young knew that their worlds and their lives would not be my world or my life. They knew that they wanted something different for me. Neither woman told me where I should go or what I should do, but each expected me to do better than she had done. To ensure that, they knew I would have to travel to where I could make decisions without regard to my race and gender and where others would respect those choices. Erma Hill, who had never spent much time outside of Lone Tree, had seen enough of the world to know that the change her parents sought in moving to Oklahoma was now happening at a much faster pace elsewhere.

My mother was largely detached from the legal developments that had drastically changed the country: the passage of the Civil Rights Act of 1964 and the Voting Rights Act of 1965. She watched the 1960s revolutions on a black-and-white television set and read stories in *Life* magazine about experiences that contrasted with her own. She had voted in every election, but never discussed politics at the dinner table. Erma's instincts told her that attitudes in Oklahoma had not kept pace with those in other parts of the country.

In 1977, four years after being given Miss Young's luggage, I began to understand my mother's ambivalence toward her friend's gift. By the time I graduated from Oklahoma State, my mother had saved enough money and S&H Green Stamps for a new set of Samsonite luggage—blue with silver hardware, bearing *my* initials. With it I headed to New Haven, Connecticut, and Yale Law School, taking along the work ethic she had instilled in me to face the challenges there and thereafter. My mother, who had modeled her life largely after her mother's, knew that she could not fully understand, much less prepare me for, the life I would have. It is a testament to her courage and to her confidence in me that she sent me anyway.

In 1992, when my uncle George reluctantly spoke about his family's departure from Arkansas, he seemed to revert to the frightened and excited five-year-old he had been at the time. His most searing recollection was the sight of his father crying, but my mother spoke of it in more guarded terms. She shrugged her shoulders when asked how she felt about leaving her childhood home. "That was just the way it had to be," she said. Yet in their voices and in their careful choice of words, I sensed a longing for what had been left behind.

When she died, at the start of a new millennium, Erma Hill was the last Elliott family member still living in Lone Tree. She had seen the family compound, built when she was a young bride in the 1930s, dissolve as her siblings, then her own children, left the land in Okmulgee County for work in Tulsa and beyond. She remained especially committed to two things: the land and the Lone Tree Missionary Baptist Church. She gardened each year as if she were still feeding a large family, and she attended church long after my father had given up on the Sunday ritual. I believe she held on to both fiercely because they reminded her of who she was and they made her feel at home in a fast-changing world.

ANITA HILL: A LONG JOURNEY HOME

When I began to explore my family history, I was in search of the perfect past. What I found were surprises and a messy, complicated reality that forced me to abandon the myths that filled my head about family, progress, and success. I was stunned to find that my grandmother had a child before marrying my grandfather and becoming mother to a total of fifteen children. I accepted that neither of my grandparents could read or write when they married in 1890, but I was disappointed that my grandmother never gained those skills, even though her husband managed to do so, perhaps by teaching himself or picking them up from his children.

I understood, in the abstract, the brutality of racism in the nineteenth and early twentieth centuries, but was somehow convinced that it didn't matter today. When my uncle George recalled how his parents left Arkansas in fear of racial violence, he warned me that if I told anyone, "they might use it against you." It took months of probing into the family history for me to appreciate how thoroughly he understood the power of racial memories.

Sociologists speak of the push and pull factors that prompt migration. Blacks migrated from the South to avoid the harsh realities of segregation and embrace better opportunities. I had wanted a family story about movement toward the positive. What I found was a family driven from its home, making the best of the situation. It pained me all the more to learn that my grandparents had come so close to their American Dream—owning, then losing, the eighty acres of land they had homesteaded. I would never be able to walk into one cemetery and see the headstones for three generations of my family. I understood why my mother rarely spoke of her childhood home and why we were not encouraged to visit it. To my surprise, learning why I had never set eyes on the place where my mother was born disrupted my present sense of rootedness. My grandparents' exile from their home in Arkansas resulted in a family diaspora that was, in its own way, as profound as my distant ancestors' wrenching displacement from the shores of Africa.

With slavery, a system was put in place to deny black people their liberty. In researching my family history, I was forced to come to terms with the reality that the system established to correct slavery's depravities had failed my mother and her siblings—people I loved—as well as their parents, people I learned to love by uncovering their stories.

Americans like to believe that their ancestors were fierce protectors of their homes, patriots of a sort. But in searching through the history of Little River County, I could not distinguish between the patriots and the refugees. Nor could I exclude strangers from my history. I was not related to the McClains or the Hales, but they were a part of my family story. None of them escaped the violence born of racism, and I ached for them all—relatives and nonrelatives, black and white, those I knew and those I had never met.

I wanted irrefutable evidence that Mary McClain and her children had triumphed over the demons that her husband's lynching might have unleashed. I wanted to know that Mary, Lizzie, and Ezekiel had found a loving community that firmly secured their roots in Little River County. I wanted to correct what I considered a gross sin of omission in the official report of Dock McClain's lynching: its failure to tell the tale of his survivors. I never found what I was looking for; the last record I could locate was Mary's tombstone.

I wanted to believe that even as his stab wounds healed, Ernest Hale became a beacon for racial healing among whites in his community. Hale fed and sheltered Goody and made sure he was educated, even beyond the eighth-grade level that Hale had attained. Hale went on to hire blacks as foremen, positions of authority that most white farmers reserved for other whites. Hale's example of racial magnanimity, however, did nothing to alter the community in a way that would have allowed my grandparents—his neighbors—to remain in the place they called home. Yet in talking with Hale's grandsons, who are still attached to the land that Ernest farmed, I got the sense that he had planted the seed of hope that we could live together as neighbors.

In April 2009, August Wilson's play *Joe Turner's Come and Gone* returned to Broadway. Set in 1911—the year my mother was born—it is, as the *New York Times* theater critic Ben Brantley observed, "about nothing less than the migration and dispersal of a race and culture, searching for an identity and home." Brantley noted that despite the seeming calm of the everyday experiences of the play's characters, "there's a storm whipping within and around the breezy talk, a gale-force wind that picks up and scatters people as if they were dandelion seeds. That wind is cold, uncaring history, propelling an entire population of men and women, only fifty years out of slavery, as they try to find footholds on a land that keeps shaking them loose."[7] As I learned my grandparents' story, I was nearly overwhelmed by how easily uprooted they were and how thorny their path from refugees to citizens had been. The deep roots that they had hoped to establish in Arkansas never took hold.

Henry and Ida Elliott, however, kept their faith—in God and the church, in each other, and in the belief that life would be better, if not for their children, then for their children's children—even if it meant moving to a different land. The feeling of being uprooted that I felt as I uncovered their story had a surprisingly positive side. Henry and Ida's struggle taught me that home need not feel like something that was forever lost. In moving to Oklahoma, they affirmed their belief that home can be found if one is willing to risk pursuing it. I realized how proud I was that my grandparents' brave commitment to the future pressed them to move to an unfamiliar place in search of a home for their family. Erma Hill then fulfilled and exceeded her parents' vision of equality by remaining on the land and raising her children to live a better life. My mother followed in their footsteps when she gave me luggage and sent me on my way. Each time they put down roots, Mollie, Ida, and Erma must have believed that they were making progress, and I am forever in their debt. If I could speak to them today, I would want more than anything to reassure them that none of their efforts were in vain. Their search for liberation was the prelude to my search for equality. Each of us travels the same path—a route to home. To my surprise, understanding their journey helped me understand my own.

For me and others in my generation, family stories force us to reconcile our desire to feel rooted with our need to seek our own place. When my mother and Miss Young each sent me off with a set of luggage, they encouraged me to leave behind a world in which household roles were dictated by gender and where community divisions were delineated by race. I had to define what home would become. Since then I've gone through several sets of luggage as I've packed my belongings to move from homes in New Haven; Washington, DC; Tulsa and Norman, Oklahoma; and finally Waltham, Massachusetts (with layovers in Northern and Southern California and Munich, Germany). I always knew that I was searching for more than a house. I was looking for the place where I belonged.

I am also privileged to have grown up during the 1960s, an era of seemingly endless possibilities. My appreciation for the exquisiteness of that time is influenced by my mother, whose life was shaped by the gender and race limitations she experienced and by what she learned from her mother's experience. Despite what she witnessed in her lifetime in Oklahoma, my mother instilled in me a will for optimism. Together we formed a vision of progress shared by many Americans, one that acknowledged the steepness of the road to equality but assumed that the trajectory was linear and continuous. Now, much of what I believed was possible in the 1960s has yet to be accomplished, and the progress of equality seems to have stalled. Rather than retreat, we must reassess and reimagine our goals and how to achieve them, understanding that the route to equality is a winding path that ends at a yet-to-be-determined place of refuge from prejudice and violence. The granting of rights will guide—but alone, will not assure—our arrival.

In April 2009, while researching this book, I visited the Sallie Bingham Center for Women's History and Culture, a Duke University library, to discuss donating my papers to the center's archives. Handing over my papers, at fifty-three years old, symbolized a finality to my work that I had trouble reconciling with my doubts that we are achieving gender equality. Moreover, I was amused by the idea that I had experienced enough for researchers to study. But I was attracted to Duke for one reason in particular: John Hope Franklin, the noted historian who wrote the seminal book *From Slavery to Freedom: A History of African Americans*, had trusted his papers to the university.

I'd had the opportunity to talk with Dr. Franklin on a few occasions, and we spoke about our shared native state, Oklahoma. His assessment of racial progress there was that even as more and more rights were gained, Oklahoma uniquely defied the dominant narrative of a continuous march to equality. In 2008 Dr. Franklin had traveled from Duke University, where he was a professor emeritus, to Tulsa for the groundbreaking of a park to be named in his honor. I had planned to visit the park and attend one of the programs honoring the historian whose work I'd followed throughout my career. Then I had hoped to have one more conversation with Dr. Franklin about our home state and to ask his advice about donating my personal papers. But that trip never happened; neither did the conversation I had hoped to have.

The last stop on my April visit to the Duke campus was the John Hope Franklin Research Center, a three-story office building with a gallery devoted to world peace art. The weather was unseasonably warm, and I was tired but determined to find the center, which is on the outskirts of Duke's sprawling campus. A month earlier, Dr. Franklin had died, and a memorial book and video of the historian's ninety-four years greeted visitors. Certainly the world had lost a great historian, and Duke had suffered a significant loss. But I pondered what his death meant to me and other Oklahomans. As the video ended and I added my name to the list of those who had paid tribute, it dawned on me that this man was my mother's contemporary. They shared the same race and the same "can't sit around and do nothing" mind-set. But their life stories were vastly different. My mother lived in rural Oklahoma most of her life. Dr. Franklin grew up in a similar environment, but in the end, he traveled the world. His was a story of movement; hers was of staying.

On that day in 2009, I thought about questions I would have asked John Hope Franklin, the man President Bill Clinton had called upon to be chairman of his President's Initiative on Race: Is the story of Oklahoma's progress more accurately a story of the country's progress? How did my mother's experience fit within Dr. Franklin's understanding of progress? What if the struggle for equality in America is bigger than simply a discussion of the evolution of rights as defined by law? Would it then need to include an account of how people live, in addition to what rights they enjoy?

Ira Berlin, a historian and ambitious raconteur, has attempted to capture the entire African American experience from the 1600s to the present as a series of migrations—"the story of a people uprooted and searching for home."[8] In his book *The Making of African America,* Berlin builds on the long-prevailing slavery-to-freedom narrative so brilliantly developed by his friend and colleague Dr. Franklin. Berlin is correct in his assessment that the story of African America is not one of linear progress. It is a "contrapuntal narrative" of "movement and place; fluidity and fixity."[9] What would equality look like if we imagined it from the perspective of those who seek it not by moving, but by staying and building? My mother's greatest gift to me was the freedom to leave. But over time I have come to realize that the most enduring lessons Erma Hill passed on to me were about how, once planted, to stay and make a home.

In the chapters that follow, I will focus on "place" and "fixity" in the lives of African American women. Their stories are about home: the place and the state of being, a pathway to equality. They all, in some ways, represent a measure of how far we've come, but also point to where we as a country need to move next. In order to understand those stories, one must understand how early in our country's history African Americans and women adopted home as a symbol of their belonging and independence.

CHAPTER THREE

Gender and Race
at Home in America

Home: 1. Any valued place, original habitation, or emotional attachment
regarded as a refuge or place of origin. 2. The place where one was
born or spent his early childhood, as a town, state, or country.
The American Heritage Dictionary of the English Language

Since before the United States was formed, the home has figured promi-
nently in the imaginations of individuals committed to gender and racial equality. At the urging of individuals devoted to equality and full
citizenship, home became a powerful symbol of race and gender advancement, the great signifier of our belonging and independence, in the public
imagination as well.

In March 1776, Abigail Adams was keenly aware of the domestic
abuse that women in the colonies suffered when she implored her husband, John, to "Remember the Ladies" in her memorable letter. She
sought protections for women, in particular married women, in the Declaration of Independence. Though women were largely ignored in the
language set out in that document—and later in the United States Constitution, completed just over a decade later—Abigail Adams introduced
two powerful ideas into the public discourse: that women needed legal
protections that differed from those conceived of by men and granted to
protect the power held by men, and that those safeguards must reach into
the core of married women's experiences—the home. Women of all races
and backgrounds knew that this hallowed space, often thought to be beyond the law's reach, was indeed a place where they could be tyrannized
and that any chance they had to live as independent members of society
must begin there.

Exactly what Adams had in mind when she wrote to John is unclear. She lived at a time when a married woman could not own property, not even the home in which she lived, in her own name. Perhaps Adams wanted her husband to allow wives control over property—at least inherited property—something that was denied to them under English law. She most likely thought that women could best protect themselves from physical harm in the home if they were specifically granted the same rights that the men of the revolution were presumed to have. Those rights certainly would have exceeded the rights women enjoyed in England, but Adams viewed the break from British control as the opportunity for a new way of looking at every citizen's participation. She relished women's aggressive resistance to British authority during the Revolutionary War. Most likely the plea in her letters was for a formulation of the law that would protect women from the "cruelty and indignity" of men who would treat women "only as the Vassals of [their] sex."[1]

Already Adams enjoyed an independence in her marriage that few women of any race knew. Gail Collins, author of *America's Women*, calls Adams "a widow to the Revolution."[2] With her husband away for long stretches of time, Abigail Adams raised their children, took care of the family's finances, and ran their farm. She renounced England as a "tyrant state" in her own voice.[3] Yet John Adams dismissed Abigail's plea for women's independence in the home with no more than a laugh.

FROM BABYLON TO ZION

As limited as Adams's political influence was, her home life was privileged well beyond what many women experienced. Many women, regardless of race or class, were subject to the cruelty Abigail described in her letter to John. For some, home may well have been a prison. Indeed, for most black women prior to the Civil War, home was a plantation or farm in the rural South from which there was no escape. Undoubtedly, despite romantic portrayals to the contrary, most aspired to leave the harshness of slavery for some kind of "promised land" where they could enjoy even a modicum of freedom. Harriet Tubman's engineering of the Underground Railroad is legendary. Yet even at the end of the war, my maternal great-grandmother Mollie Elliott and her son Henry lived within a stone's throw of her former owner. Liberation is not always freedom. In addition to remaining on the slaveholder's property, like so many other former slaves, they continued to work his land years after the war was over.

A few slave women managed to escape Southern bondage to reside in the North or West. One such fortunate soul was Sybela Owens, writer John Edgar Wideman's great-great-great-grandmother. Wideman credits Sybela, a runaway from a farm in Maryland in 1859, as a founder of a community named Homewood that continues even today, where Wideman spent much of his early life.[4]

No more compelling example of the important role that black women played in establishing the family home exists than that of Biddy Mason. In 1848 Miss Mason, a mother of three daughters—one of whom was nursing at her breast—accompanied her owner, Robert Smith, along with his family and ten other slaves, on a journey from the Smith farm in Mississippi to a brief stay in Utah before settling in San Bernardino, California. On each portion of the journey, which took the caravan through Tennessee, Kentucky, Missouri, Iowa, Nebraska, Wyoming, Utah, and Nevada, Miss Mason's job was to walk behind the wagons and herd the livestock. It's also likely that during the trip she assisted in the birth of Robert Smith's child, as well as that of a child born to fellow slave Hannah Owens. The caravan arrived in San Bernardino in 1851, a year after California entered the Union as a free state. According to state law, individuals who had been brought into the state as slaves became free people once they took up residence there.

For five years Smith's party remained intact, with Biddy Mason and her fellow, ostensibly, former slaves working for Smith in San Bernardino. In 1856 Robert Smith decided to move his family, along with Miss Mason and the other slaves, to Texas. Mason resisted and petitioned the court for a declaration of her freedom, as well as that of the others Smith had brought to live in California. Smith's argument—that Mason and the others were members of his household who had been duped into asking to be freed—fell on deaf ears. The judge ruled in Mason's favor, on her behalf and on behalf of the other former slaves.

Biddy Mason's story does not end there. She became known for her medical skills and earned a living as a midwife and healer for residents of all races in Los Angeles. Eventually, with $250, she purchased what she called "the Homestead," a lot on Spring Street in what is today downtown

Los Angeles. She continued to purchase land extending from Spring Street to what is now Broadway, between Third and Fourth Streets—but not for speculation, as many were doing during that period. Mason used her holdings to house her extended family and to stake family members who wanted to enter business, enabling them to make the successful transition from rural and frontier life to independent urban living.

According to historian Dolores Hayden, Mason's use of the property was "as an urban, economic base for her family's activities." In 1872 Mason gathered a group of black locals for a meeting in her home to organize the First African Methodist Episcopal Church. Her home became the location for her philanthropy, which she supported with income derived from other property. In 1884 she instructed a local grocer to open accounts for families made "homeless by season floods." In 1891, when Mason died at her home in Los Angeles, her grandsons had to turn away hundreds who, unaware of her passing, sought out her services as a midwife and healer. Biddy Mason's life story is a remarkable testament to her will to find her way out of slavery and create a home where she and her family would live as truly free people. After her death, Mason's family held the land until the beginning of the twentieth century.[5]

Biddy Mason was not alone among black female pioneers seeking refuge in the western United States. Religion drove some free black women to set up home in unlikely locations—like Boulder and Salt Lake City, and as far west as Hawaii—as missionaries. For example, in 1843, two years after hearing a sermon by a Mormon missionary, Jane James abandoned Presbyterianism. James, who had been born free in Connecticut, left the state of her birth and "followed the convert's departure from 'Babylon' to 'Zion'" to make her home as a live-in maid, first for Joseph Smith in Illinois and then for church leader Brigham Young in Utah. Later she married and set up her own home in Salt Lake City.[6]

Whether they came as servants or slaves, one common denominator in many of these women's experiences is the effort they made to overcome discrimination, establish their place in the communities where they settled, and thereby advance the race. Unlike Biddy Nelson, most of the women were not wealthy; some died impoverished. Yet many left a mark on the communities they helped establish. They were our founding mothers.

HOME, THE GRAND SIGNIFIER

Historians often view the "Great Migration" of blacks from the rural South to the urban North as a mass movement of black men and women made in anticipation of economic opportunity and freedom from racism. But such a description suggests a tidiness that is not altogether true. The movement was not simply from south to north or even west, nor from rural to urban. At the turn of the twentieth century, it was as if the "gale-force wind," to borrow Ben Brantley's image, that "picks up and scatters people as if they were dandelion seeds"[7] deposited blacks in places beyond and between destinations like Los Angeles, Chicago, Detroit, and New York.

My mother's family was like so many black families that struggled to find their footholds on the land. Yet my grandparents took a different course than that of those who headed for the nation's cities. Henry and Ida Elliott left the site of Henry's enslavement in Arkansas in 1914 and moved west, still holding on to a belief in the land and a way of life that was fading.

With all such migrations, there is a push and a pull. According to historian Ira Berlin, the migration of African Americans incorporated "dispossession" and "unspeakable brutality" even as it occasioned opportunity for transforming culture and reshaping politics.[8] At the turn of the twentieth century, southern blacks moved from their ancestral homes for a number of reasons. Some, like my grandfather, moved to escape violence. Nevertheless, he and others also moved in the direction of greater promise. It was during this time in particular, as our locations became more diverse, that where we called home became an indication of our race's advancement.

Educator and African American leader Booker T. Washington made the link between blacks' dwellings and their place in the nation. In Washington's imagination, a home that would come to be known as the "tasty little cottage" became a model American home and thus the symbol of African American equality.[9] Washington declared that the one-room cabins of the "great mass of negroes" were "the greatest embarrassment to the progress of the race."[10] He proposed to replace the "log hovel that had been [the freedmen's] abode for a quarter of a century" after slavery with a "comfortable, tasty, framed-cottage."[11] Integral to his formula for race improvement, this domestic ideal would be situated "in the middle of a garden, with fruit and flowers and vegetables growing all about."[12] According to Washington, such a cottage was the precursor to honorable participation in public life.

Washington wrote an article in which he described a black couple whose well-kept home, with its beautiful flower garden, so captivated a local white woman that in due course she ventured inside to examine the residents' books and papers. Soon, thanks to the endorsement of their white visitor, "there [were] few people in that community more highly respected than" Washington's couple—or so the legend went. Their model of domestic life was "more powerful than all the laws Congress can pass in the direction of bringing about right relations between blacks and whites," an object lesson in community building.[13] Washington's story may have been little more than a fable, but we should not dismiss the connection between the home and full citizenship he made in the minds of his followers and donors to his college.

Fable or not, Washington's instinct about the role the physical abode could play in engendering racial equality was not entirely misplaced. Washington knew that in twentieth-century America, blacks' status as citizens began with their ability to establish a home in, and belong to, an American residential neighborhood.

Yet Washington's insight was limited. To the public, including his donors, Washington refused to acknowledge how law, politics, and even popular literature worked together to define black uplift and negated his effort to define black citizenship via the home. He was undoubtedly wrong about the ease with which "right relations" could be achieved. (By way of illustration, in 1915, the year Washington died, D. W. Griffith's *Birth of a Nation*, glorifying Klan activity, became the country's top-grossing film following its screening in the White House.) As other race leaders in the early twentieth century pursued racial justice in the courts, Washington claimed that neither social integration nor civil rights were necessary for black uplift. The word "Tuskegee" means "warrior" in the Muskogee (Creek) language, but Washington's critics would assert that the head of the famed institution was more a social conformist than a fighter. Nonetheless, he led the Tuskegee Institute (now Tuskegee University) from its founding in 1881 to his death in 1915. Though historians have found evidence that he secretly supported civil rights initiatives, in his public pronouncements Washington advocated a formula for "negro" advancement based on individual effort and accommodation.

Washington proposed that, by building and maintaining the "tasty little cottage," blacks would demonstrate that they were capable of self-improvement and worthy of citizenship. He was so certain of his ideal and his method that he remained steadfast even when his critics were potential financial supporters. In 1895 Washington solicited funds to build his model home on the Tuskegee campus, a two-story cottage that would serve as a "permanent object lesson" for the students and presumably the race. A. W. Parker, a wealthy Long Island attorney and potential benefactor, warned that the cost of such a cottage ("four to five hundred dollars") was so out of the reach of Tuskegee graduates that it was "preposterous" to think it could serve as a model for social change. He estimated that less than 1 percent of the school's graduates could expect to afford more than a two-room cottage upon graduating from Tuskegee. Parker suggested that Washington either abandon the idea of a model or build three or four more modest one-story homes. Washington fired back that he meant to build something that would represent "an ideal toward which [blacks] could aspire" as they grew "in education." In the meantime, the cottage would be used as a laboratory for teaching the female students "the principles of housekeeping." Two days after he heard from Washington, Parker sent him a check for five hundred dollars, noting that he was funding the two-story home to teach black women how to keep house. Like many of the campus buildings, including a chapel and residence halls, the home was built with student labor.[14]

The reality of the black experience in Tuskegee, Alabama, might have given Washington second thoughts about the feasibility of his model cottage as a vehicle of African American advancement. Until the 1920s, blacks lived primarily in the South, in and around towns like Tuskegee. They either farmed on their own small plots of land or, more likely, worked on the larger plantations owned by white farmers. Parker was absolutely correct in his assessment that Washington's cottage was beyond the reach of a Tuskegee graduate, let alone most of the farm laborers who lived near enough to visit it. In truth, opportunities in the North were not entirely better.

But together Parker and Washington stumbled on the future. The building of the model home and the training offered within it presaged black men's and women's employment in the coming decades. As they moved out of the rural areas and began the Great Migration north, black women entered into domestic service as their primary employment, and black men worked in construction and industrial production. The jobs Washington and Parker were preparing their graduates to engage in— construction and domestic service—would allow them to build and clean the "tasty cottage," but never earn them enough to own one. Neither man proposed a solution to that problem.

Washington understood race, and though women played a prominent role in his plot for achieving citizenship through the home, he failed to comprehend the limits that gender inequality placed on his scheme for racial equality. In general, he paid no attention to gender progress among African Americans as a whole, and, in his model, Washington addressed the female members of the race only as homemaker in the cottage. Many black leaders of the day stood with Washington in that particular oversight.

Nevertheless, black women persisted, often independently and even in defiance of the male leadership. Nannie Helen Burroughs urged men to get out of the way of women so that they could fully participate in leadership roles. Yet despite the urging of charismatic female and male leaders like Burroughs, Ida B. Wells, and W. E. B. Du Bois, early twentieth-century movements for equality of the races seldom fully considered how the so-called private sphere—the home—helped shape and define rights for blacks as they pressed through various means to strengthen their communities and secure their full place in national life.

FINDING A ROLE FOR HOME IN THE STRUGGLE FOR WOMEN'S RIGHTS

Beginning with the struggle for the right to vote, white women chose legal and political parity as their defining marks of equal status with men. In some ways the quest for gender equality and the quest for racial equality operated on parallel tracks, as both groups sought equal access to jobs and education. But measures of gender and racial progress were not identical. There was one critical distinction between the two movements. As it gained momentum, the women's rights movement began to bring attention to a broad range of domestic matters, beginning with a woman's right to own and control her own property regardless of her marital status. Issues associated with home life were included in the meaning of "equal protection under the law," right along with matters involving full participation and fairness outside the home.

Gender rights advocates came to the realization that home is a complicated and sometimes conflicted space. Home is a space that women have pursued both by choice and by compulsion. Home, for all women, has historically been a domain designed to limit our participation in our communities' and country's affairs—even our control over our own bodies. In the 1873 case *Bradwell v. Illinois*, Justice Bradley of the nation's highest court gave credence to such limitations, attributing them to the "paramount destiny and mission of woman . . . to fulfill the noble and benign offices of wife and mother." Due to their "proper timidity and delicacy," women were unfit to "occupations of civil life." "Man is, or should be, woman's protector," and "the domestic sphere" was where she properly belonged.[15]

As the law and social norms increasingly consigned women to the home, they struggled to gain control even there. The image of a drunken husband who came home and abused his wife and children helped energize the temperance movement.

The campaign for women's right to vote was sufficiently popular that an advertiser even linked suffrage with household decisions. Under the banner "Votes for Women," a 1913 ad for Shredded Wheat showed a woman in front of a ballot box and included text announcing that "twenty million women have voted for the emancipation of American womanhood by serving Shredded Wheat in their homes." The ad reflected the sentiments of suffragists, associating the right to vote with women's everyday (shopping) experiences and household routines.[16]

Most matters of the home were thus seen as gender issues and women's (read white women's) concerns. Black women and some black men, namely Frederick Douglass and Du Bois, often struggled along with women for gender equity. But race was a highly contentious subject in women's political and legal struggles, and black women were very often asked to serve in secondary roles in the gender movement.

During the struggle for the vote, white women from the South insisted on upholding their communities' norm of segregation. In what is now considered a turning point in the suffrage movement, during a 1913 parade down Pennsylvania Avenue in Washington, DC, white Northern women acquiesced to their Southern sisters' demands that all black women march at the end of the procession. Ida B. Wells, a Chicago resident who early in her life fought segregation in her native state of Tennessee, was initially shocked and offended that her white friends from Illinois agreed to the last-minute stipulation. According to her biographer, Paula Giddings, Wells was not deterred, nor would she acquiesce. Instead, she waited on the sidelines until the white delegation from her adopted home state came into view. As they approached, she stepped out of the crowd, joined them, and unofficially integrated the parade.

It is worth noting that one major women's organization, which started as an effort to provide homes for girls moving into urban areas, has long included ending racism and empowering women as equal platforms in its official mission. In 1915 the YWCA held its first interracial conference in Louisville, Kentucky. Yet even that organization operated segregated facilities for blacks, whites, and Native Americans.

Despite the restrictions of their social and civic possibilities, African Americans still sought to establish homes—places in their communities—for themselves and their families, and black women were at the forefront of that effort. Black women's desire for a home is not unique, but the route to America becoming our home is different from what Booker T. Washington envisioned.

Sharp lines between public and private spheres and between the political and the personal did not exist for African American women, a large portion of whom worked in some form of domestic service or farm labor. In 1881 Atlanta's black laundresses, who worked out of their own homes, engaged in one of the first labor strikes organized by women. The movement began with just twenty women, but through mobilization in the black neighborhoods, that number rose to three thousand, giving the women a political voice that was unparalleled in the black community or among women workers. There is no clear evidence of what specific concessions the strikers won, but as historian Tera W. Hunter notes, the efforts were "symbolically meaningful." In asserting the value of their skills, the Atlanta laundresses "demonstrated an astute political consciousness by making private household labor a public issue."[17]

In addition, black women had their own ideas about suffrage and its relationship to home. Nannie Helen Burroughs spoke publicly on behalf of women's right to vote. Whereas many of the early white feminists and suffragists sought to use the vote to put in place laws that would help protect them from their husbands' dominance, Burroughs focused more on black women's economic independence from men.

CHAMPIONING THE HOME

Perhaps like no other person of her time, Nannie Helen Burroughs understood that home was emblematic of how women saw themselves, as well as how the world saw them. She was also infinitely pragmatic. The daughter of a maid who often was her family's sole support, Burroughs subscribed to the notion that the vote would mean nothing if women could not support themselves and their families on their own, whether married or single. So in addition to her political activism, she established a school—now Burroughs Elementary public school in Washington, DC—to prepare poor women for civic participation and economic self-sufficiency. In 1909 she brought cooks, laundresses, maids, clerks, and their daughters from all over the country to be educated in Washington. In addition to taking classes in domestic services and dressmaking, Burroughs's students were taught bookkeeping, shoe repair, and agriculture, along with English literature, Latin, drama, and black history. Perhaps inspired by the washerwomen's strike, Burroughs proposed that domestic workers be unionized and that service in homes be elevated to a profession.

The suffragists' approach to the role that home played in political thinking differed from Booker T. Washington's. Each accommodated the prejudices of white male leaders, but suffragists used women's roles in the home as a basis for empowering them with the right to vote. Washington used home—the place— more as a front, a facade of respectability taken on by blacks to win whites' acceptance. Neither denied women's interest in the home, but each wanted something different. Suffragists wanted legal changes; Washington wanted to change the hearts and minds of whites.

To some extent, Nannie Helen Burroughs, a contemporary of Washington's, wanted both, though she was less concerned with the latter. She conceived of home and its role in liberation in yet a third way. Burroughs envisioned the home as a base from which equality would evolve. As the daughter of a domestic worker, she embraced the significance of home in black women's lives but rejected the low status attached to it. Burroughs envisioned the home as a place for intellectual growth as well as a source for professional development. As a rejection of both racial and gender subordination, Burroughs considered housekeeping and child care as skilled labor. She advocated for providers to be licensed and unionized, thus elevating the work originating in the home. Like that of Atlanta's black laundresses, Burroughs's motivation was both economic and political. In the school she established for poor and working-class African American girls, "home" served as the platform for her students' education, economic self-sufficiency, and political engagement.

Nevertheless, Burroughs, a single woman, was criticized by some black male leadership for promoting black women's independence from black men. But this type of rebuke was not new to Burroughs. She had started as an outspoken leader in an association of black Baptist churches, the National Baptist Convention (NBC). Even as the NBC considered racial segregation unholy, it thought gendered restrictions to be biblically demanded. Nannie Helen Burroughs had bucked convention to become one of the most respected speakers in the organization's history. She would use the same resolve and her oratory skills to advocate for equality as she envisioned it, with women as breadwinners and civic partners.

WHO SPEAKS FOR BLACK WOMEN?

Nannie Helen Burroughs was also accustomed to rejection, which she felt was due to her upbringing as the daughter of a domestic worker and her dark skin color. Though those factors were rarely cited as a basis for rejection of her ideas, there was a battle among black leadership as to which black female leader was best suited to represent the "highest type of the race." In 1898 Richard T. Greener, a member of the Washington, DC, black elite, gushed his enthusiasm for a speech delivered to the Women's Suffrage Convention by an African American woman, Mrs. Mary Church Terrell, entitled "Progress of the Colored Women," declaring that racial progress would be achieved through black women's progress.

Also present at the event was Charles R. Douglass, son of abolitionist and suffragist Frederick Douglass, who noted the reaction of other suffragists, including Susan B. Anthony, to Terrell's eloquence. They were "so proud of their new discovery that they fell upon her neck upon the conclusion of her great speech and kissed her. She was covered with floral offerings." Douglass declared Terrell's presentation a success. "Her appeal for the women of her race was a soul stirring effort; and the long continued applause that followed at the close of her remarks attested that she had won her hearers to her."[18]

Mary Church Terrell may have had the blessings of Greener, Anthony, and Douglass to speak on behalf of her race and gender, but others would vie for the role as well. Journalist Josephine St. Pierre Ruffin and educator Mary McLeod Bethune were among the array of leaders who championed the cause of black women. But perhaps no two women were more directly related to the struggles of women trying to build their homes than Ida B. Wells and Nannie Helen Burroughs. Both women were fiery and unapologetic in their quest to move black women and the entire race out from under the dual oppression they experienced. While many of the black women leaders of the day were from educated and relatively wealthy, prominent black families, Wells and Burroughs were not. Wells was the daughter of slaves, and her well-known crusade against lynching gave some blacks hope that the nation would soon put an end to the violence that threatened homes throughout the South on an almost daily basis.

Burroughs championed education for what she called "ordinary" black folks and the professionalization of domestic service. In these ways, her ideas about education were not unlike Booker T. Washington's. "We specialize in the wholly impossible" was her patented response to her critics and others, like Washington himself, who doubted that a school for black women could sustain itself without Northern whites' financial support.

Though her challenge to black religious leaders to address the obstruction of women's progress in the Baptist Church, as well as racism in the larger society, may have put her at odds with church leadership, it aligned her with the efforts of W. E. B. Du Bois, who was viewed as Washington's rival for control of the destiny of black folks. Yet Burroughs's very nuanced take on the political and social future of blacks was closer to the reality of black life than either Washington's or Du Bois's views. Hers were the kind of practical, yet entirely progressive and uniquely multifarious ideas that would pave the way for the majority of black women to imagine equality. She understood the hardships black Americans faced, but had faith in their ability to overcome them and make a home in the country that rejected them.

Despite the apparent challenges, Nannie Helen Burroughs showed her idealistic optimism in a speech she delivered one hundred years ago to the National Baptist Convention:

> A new day is dawning for us. In spite of the fact that we are facing problems more grave and aggravating than any other race in the world and have less of material things to utilize in the solution of them, yet we are abundantly rich in faith and in physical powers to endure the hardships incident to foundation laying. The most hopeful sign is the awakening within to the fundamental needs and a setting in motion of a new force to beat back fanatic race prejudice. We have just seen clearly enough to discover that in the real American is the making.[19]

Burroughs's audience responded with thunderous applause. She would come to be known as "the black goddess of liberty" who dared to posit that black women would lead the way to defining "the real American." The practical side of Nannie Helen Burroughs knew that "foundation laying" for black women had to begin where they were strongest: in the home, whether their own homes or those in which they were employed. She also knew that all Americans had to have a different image of what "home," or at least the work done in it, meant in the public sphere if blacks were to achieve equality through it.

Abigail Adams's arguments for women's legal protections in the home were, for their time, bold and insightful. Women of all races and backgrounds knew that this hallowed space, often thought to be beyond the law's reach, was indeed a place where they could be tyrannized and that any chance they had to live as independent members of society must begin there. And Booker T. Washington knew that African Americans must first establish a place in communities if they were ever to enjoy the state of being at home in America.

Black women's actual control over their homes, like that of all women, has been limited by gender conventions. Throughout history, and even today, economic conditions of most black families have meant that black women work outside the home. They have had to function in both the private and public sphere, without the benefit of protections afforded by race or gender in either. Nannie Helen Burroughs combined the thinking of both Adams and Washington, pursuing recognition outside the home of what women did inside the home. Due to their history and experiences, a safe and secure home for black American women is achieved differently than for black men and other women. Thus Burroughs viewed the home as a unique measure of equality that cannot be divorced from other measures. That perspective, as well as the fundamental social changes that the entire country was embarking on in the twentieth century, would shape how women and men of all races experienced day-to-day life, and Nannie Helen Burroughs knew that well.

All together, Adams, Burroughs, and Washington helped shape thinking about the meaning of equality and how it would be achieved, not only for their times but for the future as well. As the home became the icon of the American Dream through the help of government policies and private actions, those pushing for equality would come to challenge domestic abuse, promote women's rights to own their own homes and to join professional work ranks, and sue on behalf of African Americans' rights to own homes in neighborhoods of their choice.

CHAPTER FOUR

Lorraine's Vision

A Better Place to Live

Home: An environment offering security and happiness.
The American Heritage Dictionary of the English Language

CONSTRUCTING THE AMERICAN DREAM

"That our people should live in their own homes is a sentiment deep in the heart of our race and of American life."[1] Just where this notion came from is unclear, but in the 1920s commerce secretary Herbert Hoover, the man who would one day become president and make that statement, embarked on a strategy to make it a reality. His backing for the Own Your Own Home (OYOH) campaign and open support for the Better Homes movement blurred the line between government policy and private enterprise. Both OYOH and Better Homes promoted home purchasing as the 1920s version of the American ideal.[2] OYOH's coalition of bankers, local officials, builders, and developers, enlisted to help fulfill Hoover's vision of America, promoted home ownership as a symbol of manhood. In the organization's pamphlets, home ownership was credited with placing a man "among the bigger men of your community," and home ownership was equated with "SUCCESS." Flyers and brochures distributed by those in the movement all but promised that a man who buys a house, "whether it be for cash or on the installment plan, secures . . . a happy wife and raises therein patriotic well-educated American children." Not only has he "done the most patriotic and religious thing possible," but he has also accomplished "the most opportune thing for the betterment of human conditions." As the headline in one brochure asserted, "The Man Who Owns His Home is a better Worker, Husband, Father, Citizen, and a *real* American."[3]

Logically, black men who wanted to become "real Americans" would follow the call to home ownership. But in the 1920s, having been locked out of rural land ownership, most "real" African Americans could not afford to own homes in the cities and towns that were growing throughout the nation.

The message of the OYOH campaign was not directed solely at men; the brochures assured women that home ownership carried the potential for better motherhood. Sociologists Paul Luken and Suzanne Vaughan argue that the OYOH campaign was fashioned to order work and family relationships through a vision of home ownership. Luken and Vaughan note that the discourse coming out of the OYOH effort shifted responsibility from social institutions to parents and made women primarily accountable for their children's welfare.[4]

In fact, under the OYOH philosophy, renting an apartment would be near hazardous to women's maternal well-being: "If you are to maintain your ancient, glorious vocation, you need to be a genuine Home Maker, *in your own Home*," an OYOH pamphlet told women. The "walls of a rented dwelling" were "arbitrary"; shelter could be found under the "roof of a real *Home*." Thus the Standard American Home was a single-family dwelling situated in a suburb (or, if in the city, at the very least near a park or some other space that afforded children access to "sunlight, fresh air and a safe place to play"), with appropriately appointed separate rooms for male and female children and parents. Boys' rooms were to be masculine, with hard, durable surfaces, the campaign dictated. Girls' rooms were to be adorned with frilly curtains and painted in soft colors. Both should be sunny and well ventilated. The standard anticipated small, quiet, and dainty girls and rambunctious, active boys. From birth, home was the place that designed masculinity and femininity and gender roles. The ideal of femininity, as represented in the home ownership model in particular, was out of reach for most black women of that era, as the majority of them were more likely to work in someone else's home than own their homes.

But as critical as home ownership was as a social and political creation, it was even more important as an economic instrument. In 1933, with President Hoover's departure from office, President Franklin Roosevelt created the Home Owners' Loan Corporation (HOLC) to help stimulate home construction and stave off the Great Depression's rampant housing foreclosures. Much like the OYOH campaign, the agency, part of Roosevelt's New Deal package, was controlled by prominent real estate developers chosen by the president. In pursuit of the agency's mission, its leadership began mapping out neighborhoods for their potential to support long-term mortgages. Under the HOLC's appraisal standards, suburban, middle-class communities earned the highest mark; they were green zones. Poor neighborhoods were rated the lowest: the red zones.

Race also factored into the agency's appraisal of neighborhood "desirability." The HOLC evaluated communities on the basis of their racial and ethnic homogeneity. Racially homogenous neighborhoods were preferred over mixed-race neighborhoods and thus were more eligible for mortgages. On its face, the term "homogenous" neighborhoods is race neutral. Yet predominantly black and Latino neighborhoods were routinely "red zoned" for loans and investment despite their homogeneity and regardless of the income levels of residents. Neighborhoods with homeowners of various ethnic or racial identities were downgraded, too, regardless of the residents' income levels. And investors, builders, businesses, and buyers got the green light from the HOLC to pour resources into exclusively white neighborhoods, particularly those occupied by wealthy or middle-class homeowners. Thus the United States government gave its financial blessing to segregated neighborhoods.

This government assessment system, coupled with private lending discrimination against individuals, institutionalized racial prejudice in ways that would only begin to be overcome decades later Historian Andrew Wiese makes clear in his book *Places of Their Own* that despite receiving little government assistance, remarkably many blacks in both the North and the South pulled together the resources they needed to create suburbs of their own.[5] Nevertheless, the general landscape of suburban America was segregated, and blacks' access to it was limited.

A PLACE FOR EQUALITY

Just what "race" President Hoover had in mind when he centered home ownership "deep in the heart of our race and American life" is unclear, but blacks were no exception to the desire to own a home. In the 1930s, most rented urban flats. For many, that meant life in squalid conditions that were "virtual slave cabins stacked on top of one another," according to Pulitzer Prize–winning author Isabel Wilkerson in *The Warmth of Other Suns*.[6] In Chicago, a quarter of a million African American families were crammed into a wedge of a community that ran south and west of downtown Chicago. Ironically, the Depression presented an opportunity for a few black families, whose housing needs were increasing and whose incomes in service industries were holding steady, to participate in Hoover's idea of "American life," with or without government encouragement.

By the late 1930s Chicago's once-promising Washington Park subdivision had fallen on hard times. Nevertheless, it would serve as a backdrop for a dramatic civil rights episode, a landmark case that would become the preamble to African Americans' crusade into housing markets previously closed to them. As with many area neighborhoods, the community in this part of the city's South Side was by law off-limits to blacks, except for the janitors, chauffeurs, or house servants who lawfully resided in basements, barns, or garages on the properties owned by whites. All deeds to Washington Park property included a variation of a clause developed by the Chicago Real Estate Board to serve as a model for racial exclusion, following the philosophy of the HOLC and the preference for racially homogeneous neighborhoods. Through the work of the Real Estate Board—which, according to law professor Allen R. Kamp in "The History Behind *Hansberry v. Lee*," sent community organizers to Chicago's neighborhoods to instruct residents on how to write and enforce such restrictions[7]—85 percent of Chicago's communities were off-limits to blacks.

Depression-era financial losses suffered by middle-class homeowners made it necessary for some families to vacate Washington Park residences. Those same losses also meant that few whites were available to buy in the area. Yet the three-by-four-block community still held on to the racially restrictive covenants. This exclusivity, along with its proximity to the park from which the neighborhood drew its name (a sprawling urban oasis designed by the famed landscape architect Frederick Law Olmsted), had once made it a "desirable" place for whites.

In 1937 Carl Hansberry, father of the playwright Lorraine Hansberry, embarked on a mission to change Chicago's housing restrictions by buying a home in Washington Park. He found a white owner desperate to sell to any buyer, regardless of race, who had money to purchase the home he could no longer afford. Hansberry moved his wife and their four children, including eight-year-old Lorraine, into the formerly racially segregated suburb. Determined to keep blacks out of their community, the Hansberrys' new white neighbors terrorized them and vandalized their home. During one incident, Lorraine barely missed being hit in the head with a brick.

Her father was just as determined to stay as his neighbors were to drive the Hansberrys out. When white neighborhood homeowners challenged his purchase, Hansberry sued. He pursued his fight against legally sanctioned racial restrictions on housing all the way to the Supreme Court, where he won his suit on a technicality. *Hansberry v. Lee* led to a landmark Supreme Court decision that allowed blacks to challenge the racial restraints covering Chicago's neighborhoods, ushering in an era of civil rights litigation.

Hansberry prevailed on a procedural issue about how to define the class of sellers who could be sued in such cases. Over a decade later, in *Shelley v. Kraemer*, the Supreme Court would decide a similar case on the merits of the claim brought by an African American who attempted to buy into a restricted neighborhood. In *Shelley*, the court ruled that covenants barring sales on the basis of race were illegal.

After the *Hansberry* ruling, the headline in the *Chicago Defender*, a newspaper owned and read by African Americans, hailed the victory: "Hansberry Decree Opens 500 New Homes to Race."[8] The case also loosely served as the basis for Lorraine Hansberry's trailblazing drama released twenty-two years later: *A Raisin in the Sun,* her blockbuster play about a family's effort to purchase a home in the suburbs. At the drama's end, as her fictional Younger family moves into a home over the protests of their new white neighbors, members of the family seem to put aside their internal differences, and the audience is left hopeful that they are about to secure the home that each member is yearning for. All seems to end well.

The happy conclusion that Hansberry portrays in *Raisin* did not, however, match her own experience as a pioneer in the civil rights struggles. Though she was only eight years old, the experience of moving into the family's new home left a searing impression on Lorraine Hansberry. Indeed, it gave her a chance to see the dark side of the quest for equality. Years later, she wrote about it in a letter to the *New York Times* that the newspaper would not print, but that appeared in her posthumously published work, *To Be Young, Gifted and Black*. Hansberry described the community in which her family resided as "hellishly hostile," where "howling mobs surrounded our home." While her father was battling in the courts in Washington, her "desperate and courageous mother," armed with a loaded German Luger pistol, stood guard nightly over Lorraine and her three siblings inside their new home. Despite the decision in his favor from the Supreme Court in 1940, Carl Hansberry suffered "emotional turmoil" and died prematurely "as a permanently embittered exile." His victory in court was, Lorraine wrote, "the sort of 'progress' our satisfied friends allude to when they presume to deride the more radical means of struggle."[9] The harsh reality of her own experience and the events that occurred in the years after her father's suit are perhaps why Lorraine Hansberry used biting irony in *Raisin* to tell the story of how the home became a battleground in the fight to advance racial equality.

In the 1930s and '40s, blacks would continue to move from rural settings to urban ones, and in moving would continue their quest to be at home in their residences, neighborhoods, and nation. In urban settings, cars replaced wagons, and black women, often leaving their own children, learned to navigate the bus routes past black homes and out of black communities into white neighborhoods and white houses that would be their workplaces and, in some cases, the only source of family income.

Long before Lorraine Hansberry was born, Booker T. Washington was promoting his "comfortable, tasty, framed cottage" as the key to racial equality. Carl Hansberry's actions would serve as a clear marker of the rejection of the accommodation approach to entry into the ideal housing situation that Washington promoted. Both Washington and Hansberry seemed committed to the ideal of the nice house with a yard for the kids, but they disagreed on how it should be achieved. Nevertheless, one can imagine that, had Washington lived to see whites' continued resistance to his idea of residential racial inclusion, he might have been willing to resort to the courts.

But rarely, even after *Hansberry v. Lee*, did blacks migrating into cities have equal access to quality housing. And the entire Hansberry family

paid a price for the challenge that Carl Hansberry waged against segregation. In time, the federal government would accuse Carl Hansberry of
violating the Housing and Rent Act for overcharging blacks for rent in
buildings he owned in Chicago's segregated South Side. Hansberry coun-
tered by suing the city's housing inspectors for defamation. Nevertheless,
the suit against Hansberry raised questions about the conditions of his
rentals and his integrity as a champion of the rights of African Americans. Whether Mr. Hansberry was the victim of retaliation for his civil
rights crusade or a slumlord, as the inspectors alleged, is not clear. In her
unpublished letter, Lorraine Hansberry argued that her father's ill health
and premature death were the price he paid for challenging racism.

By 1959, as inner cities become more and more crowded, the suburbs
appeared more and more as an ideal. For over a decade, with the regulatory and design assistance of the federal government, William J. Levitt
and other builders had been constructing large-scale low- and middle-
cost housing developments throughout the eastern United States. These
suburban utopias were popular with veterans and their families, especially those receiving assistance through the GI Bill for down payments.
By 1960, according to historian Barbara M. Kelly, the population of suburbs exceeded that of rural and urban areas. In *Expanding the American
Dream: Building and Rebuilding Levittown,* Kelly explains how Levitt's
simple four-room design became the emblem of postwar housing policies that affirmed racial segregation and the cult of domesticity. Indeed,
many Levittown residents entered into the same restrictive covenants
that earlier developments had adopted. In 1957 an angry mob in Levittown, Pennsylvania, greeted an African American family moving into the
development.

Resistance from whites notwithstanding, the low cost and relative
comfort of the dwellings must have had their appeal to blacks of that era.
According to the 1950 census, only 24 percent of the minority population
in the country (compared to 64 percent of whites) lived in nondilapidated
homes with a private toilet, bath, and hot running water.

HOME IN FACT AND FICTION

In 1959 civil rights advancements seemed particularly stalled. Against this
backdrop and inspired by her family's experience, Lorraine Hansberry
wrote the play that would become the first drama by a black woman to be

performed on Broadway. Despite *A Raisin in the Sun*'s phenomenal public reception, some critics had difficulty fully grasping its power or masking their condescension toward its author, as suggested by a review in the New York press titled "Housewife's Play Is a Hit."[10] In the decades since it opened, Hansberry's signature work has been hailed in some quarters and dismissed in others, but always viewed as a "race play." Yes, it is a play about a family's struggle against forces outside their home, but what gives it a timeless quality is the author's ability to capture the struggles of the individuals inside the home as each tries to find a place within the family. Hansberry took her title from a Langston Hughes poem that asks, "What happens to a dream deferred? / Does it dry up / like a raisin in the sun? / . . . *Or does it explode?*"[11] Her play deftly articulates each family member's dream—as it is shaped by his or her gender, as well as race—and shows us which dreams evaporate and which erupt.

Clearly, Lorraine Hansberry's family experience moved her to write the play that would become the iconic representation of the yearning for home. Yet any number of events transpiring outside her own family between 1937 and 1959 might have influenced Hansberry's thinking about her experience on the front lines of antidiscrimination efforts and thus shaped the message of *A Raisin in the Sun*.

In 1944, *An American Dilemma*, written by Swedish economist Gunnar Myrdal, warned against overlooking race in conceptualizing our democracy. Myrdal's comprehensive study of the African American experience revealed the fiction of the "separate but equal" doctrine as the best evidence of the inconsistency between the way equality was preached and the way it was practiced throughout the country. The key to his persuasiveness was the case he made for the incompatibility of social inequality with democracy. Myrdal's exposé focused the country's attention on the savagery of racial segregation in the South and the dismal state of race relations across the nation. His solution was not to make blacks conform to white America, but to make the American government live up to the principles of freedom and justice it espoused. Myrdal urged the government that had stepped in to save the world from fascism during World War II to account for its role in maintaining the perverse inequalities that had become the norm of existence for people of all minority races.

Reportedly, Myrdal planned to follow up his report on race with a similar report on gender equality. The Ford Foundation had supported his research on blacks in America, but Myrdal was unable to find funding for an examination of the women of America. What might he have found out about women's lives in the years following the completion of *An American Dilemma*? By 1945 six million women, many of them married, had joined the civilian labor force to do the jobs abandoned by men fighting abroad. Despite being told that the men were fighting the war to protect the women back home, and despite the limited opportunities available to them, another 350,000 women enlisted in the army for war duty. But when the servicemen came home, women were advised to leave their lucrative civilian jobs and military positions to return to married life and have babies. With few employment options, most of the white women then complied. Thus many in the Greatest Generation retreated to what was largely white suburbia and gave birth to the baby boom.

Conformity was an ideal. Marriage was in vogue. Anxious to start families, enlisted men returning from the war urged President Truman's administration to address the housing shortage problem. They favored new buildings rather than refurbishing old homes. Soon the trend toward suburban housing developments took off, with the government's blessing and financial support.

Attracted by better employment opportunities for both men and women, blacks moved to the suburbs too, but separately from and not equally with whites. Housing discrimination limited their residential options, and their own desire to build strong black communities also came into play, as some decided that better housing was a higher priority than integration. Advertisements for homes in black suburban areas extolled the virtues of the nuclear family. In magazine and newspaper spreads, brokers and developers marketed houses equipped with "large, cheerful kitchens" and situated within walking distance of schools and parks, houses where parents could raise their children in a "suburban paradise." Black-owned publications like *Ebony* magazine got in on the act. In a 1945 version of *Lifestyles of the Rich and Famous*, *Ebony* ran articles showcasing the "big, impressive" homes of black suburbia.

Indeed, blacks had lived in suburban Chicago for decades. In Evanston, an affluent suburb north of the city, black neighborhoods had begun developing in the 1920s. Though some of the residents of these primarily black enclaves were professionals and skilled workers, most were maids, chauffeurs, janitors, and others who provided personal services for the whites in Evanston. As the black population in Evanston grew, whites began to draw residential racial boundaries. By 1959 blacks lived mostly on the town's west side; suburban migration had stalled for black professionals and was nonexistent for working-class blacks. Despite the 1948 *Shelley v. Kraemer* decision barring racially restrictive covenants, blacks retained a limited suburban presence. Suburban neighborhoods where blacks resided were by and large segregated, and overall the suburbs were white.

Hansberry had a choice about where to locate the Younger family's search for home and equality, just as her father had. Situating the family in a white suburb was a deliberate confrontation of the racism that she had witnessed growing up, and the play was largely seen as such. Audiences easily grasp *A Raisin in the Sun*'s statement about the relationship between blacks and whites and their battle over space. However, little attention is paid to its clear statement about women's roles in the struggle for equality.

In Hansberry's formative years, gender roles, like racial roles, were well-prescribed. That, too, undoubtedly played a role in her conception of the issues inherent in finding home as she crafted the relationships between the play's central characters. Women in 1959 households were born into an era in which legislators attempted to prohibit married women from working in twenty-six states, and generally women did not work outside the home even where it was legal. The necessities of World War II had changed attitudes about women working, but during the prosperous peacetime that followed, the government's policies reflected prewar sentiments about women's roles. In 1962 *Ladies' Home Journal* found that almost all the young women they polled expected to be married by age twenty-two; most wanted to have four children and to stop working after the first.[12] In a poll taken in 1977, 88 percent of men over the age of fifty-five thought it "best for the man to achieve outside the home and the woman to take care of home and family."[13]

Magazines and television portrayed married, suburban family life as nothing short of a divine experience for women. Magazine layouts showed smiling housewives happily cooking, vacuuming, and doing the laundry. To convince doubters of how easy and enviable their lives were, they performed these tasks in makeup, pearls, and high heels. Beginning in the late 1950s, CBS, NBC, and ABC contributed to the picture of suburban bliss with sitcoms like *Father Knows Best, Leave It to Beaver*, and *The Donna Reed Show*, which aired from 1958 until 1966. Donna Stone, Reed's character—a trained nurse and mother of two married to a physician—was the only one of these sitcom housewives who had any hint of a career.

Television offered one class deviation from the typical sitcom family in the form of *The Honeymooners*, featuring a working-class family headed by Ralph Kramden, a Brooklyn bus driver married to Alice, a housewife. In their small and dreary city apartment, they are not nearly as contented as the other TV families. Many of the episodes' plots center around the couple's shaky finances, Alice's criticisms of Ralph's get-rich-quick scheming, and Ralph's clenched-fist threats to send Alice "to the moon." No one seemed to notice that the show's running gag line involved the intimation of domestic violence. Although the series has become a classic, it ran for only one year. Poverty didn't sell as much soap as middle-class comfort did.

But the poverty Hansberry had witnessed in Chicago's tenements was not unlike that in *The Honeymooners'* New York. It gave her, a woman who had grown up in relative economic comfort, ample ammunition to address not only race and gender as she crafted *Raisin*, but class issues as well. It was against this popular-culture backdrop and the burgeoning civil rights movement that Hansberry set the action of *A Raisin in the Sun*. The Younger family home, which is the setting for much of the play, is more like the Kramdens' cramped quarters than the Cleaver and Stone homes or those featured in *Ebony*.

In the play, the mother decides that the family will escape their crowded apartment in Chicago's South Side by using the proceeds of her late husband's insurance policy to purchase a home in a white residential area. But the trouble in the Younger home is not entirely with the whites who resist their attempt to integrate the restricted neighborhood. Hansberry revealed the Youngers to have internal family conflicts: between Mama and her son, Walter; between Walter and his wife, Ruth; and between Walter and his sister, Beneatha. Mama sees her "family falling . . . to pieces" in front of her eyes. Each member has his or her own

to lift the family, which could be interpreted as the race,
. Walter dreams of getting rich. Mama's dream of own-
e white community with enough space to plant a garden
ostalgic vision recalling her and her late husband's life
it showcases her courage and integrity. Ruth, a domes-
tic, struggles with Walter, a chauffeur, to get him to see her as something
more than a helpmate and producer of his children. She tries to temper
his unrealistic expectations of striking it rich with her own pragmatism.
Beneatha dreams of healing her people—the family and the race—
through education in general, and specifically by becoming a doctor.
When Mama entrusts Walter with money for Beneatha's education, he
invests it in an entrepreneurial scheme that turns out to be a complete
scam.

LOFTY GOALS UNDERMINED BY SEXISM

Despite Hansberry's skillful development of gender dynamics and the
role they play in black advancement, it's no wonder that audiences and
critics responded to *A Raisin in the Sun* largely as a race play. Socially
and politically, the country was much more focused on race than on
gender. In addition to the great struggle for school integration launched
by the Supreme Court's 1954 decision in *Brown v. Board of Education*,
within five years of the opening of *A Raisin in the Sun* the country would
enact its first major civil rights legislation since the Reconstruction era. In
March 1964, President Lyndon Johnson signed into law comprehensive
civil rights protections against discrimination in education, employment,
and public accommodations. A year later, broad protections against voting discrimination were enacted. Within a few years more, legislation for-
bidding the kind of housing discrimination that Hansberry protested in
her play became national policy.

The country also began to address the kind of poverty that *A Raisin
in the Sun* exposed. On a sunny day in May 1964, President Johnson announced his plan to tackle the problem of poverty as part of his Great
Society initiative. The site was the University of Michigan in Ann Arbor,
one of the nation's premier public research and educational institutions.
Reverend Martin Luther King Jr. stood out among the crowd of mostly
white men and a few white women. With the plight of poor people on

the national agenda, all eyes were trained on blacks whose impoverished state was exposed during the coverage of their civil rights struggles. Johnson envisioned a Great Society as "a place where every child can find knowledge to enrich his mind and to enlarge his talents," a vision that rested "on an abundance and liberty for all" and demanded "an end to racial injustice and poverty."[14] Black activists were making a compelling case for antipoverty, civil rights, and education efforts in order to reverse the impact of years of racism. As a consequence, however, over the next few years, poverty imagery would become black, and all black concerns would be linked to the concept of entrenched poverty.[15] In 1965 blacks were largely absent from media poverty coverage. Around the time the Great Society launched, the media shifted its focus from white poverty to black poverty. It wasn't long before 62 percent of the images of the poor in popular magazines were of black people—twice their representation in the population of people living below the poverty level.[16]

What happened to Gunnar Myrdal's caution against making blacks conform to white society? It took a turn he probably could not have predicted when Daniel Patrick Moynihan, assistant secretary of labor, took aim at poverty in 1965 by declaring that black matriarchy had thrown the "Negro" family into a state of crisis that imperiled all of America. Given the prevalence of traditional attitudes about gender roles, it's not surprising that Moynihan's recipe for black family success was emulation of the model nuclear suburban family. He prescribed deliberate and immediate government intervention to put black men back to work and back in charge of their homes and communities. Under the government's proposal, black men would be given economic and educational access if black women agreed to give up theirs, stay home, and raise their children. Patriarchy, Moynihan asserted, would save America from an expanding welfare system, and the "Negro family" from descending into a "tangle of pathology."[17]

Understandably, government-sponsored gender domination held little appeal for many of the women who still bore the scars of government-imposed racial segregation. Moynihan's assessment of matriarchy in African American communities amounted to a stinging indictment of all black women. Unmarried women became community pariahs; the married woman's fate was to be subservient in her own home. Moynihan's plan included no ideas for helping single women provide for their families, instead condemning them to the social and economic disadvantages that his report purported to address. Had he fully appreciated the grip of sexism combined with racism on the black community, he would have proposed policies that promoted the full participation of both women and men. Instead, his devotion to patriarchy blinded him to the fact that gains in the black community could be undermined if bias of any kind reduced black women to second-class status.

To strengthen his case, in his report Moynihan quoted a number of observers of the black experience, but only one of them was an African American woman. Dorothy Height, head of the National Council of Negro Women, expressed many black women's desire that black men be made to feel "important . . . free and able to make [their] contribution in the whole society."[18] Along with Height's observation, Moynihan cited the comments of a white male sociologist who said that "embittered" black wives were "disgusted" with "dependent husbands."[19] Black women had to be recreated in the image of patriarchy, and Moynihan used such comments as endorsements of the concept, suggesting that women should be, and perhaps wanted to be, dependent on strong black men, certainly not vice versa. As the head of one of the oldest and largest organizations of black women, Height later rejected Moynihan's conclusion about the role of black women in the recovery of the black community, but her recantation came too late to be heard in the stir following the report's release.

While some African American women may have preferred patriarchy and others matriarchy, there are good reasons to believe that many wanted communities in which they were equal to men. Two prominent African American women come to mind as proponents of gender equality at the time. In 1965 Aileen Hernandez was the only woman and the only African American named to the newly formed Equal Employment Opportunity Commission (EEOC), the body charged with enforcing the employment provisions of the Civil Rights Act of 1964. When she left the EEOC in 1966, the National Organization for Women (NOW) selected Hernandez as its executive vice president. In time, she left NOW over issues of race. Another pioneer civil rights activist, Pauli Murray, made headlines in 1965 when she urged women of all races to march on Washington to assure equal job opportunities for all. This was not a new idea for Murray. Two decades before passage of the Civil Rights Act of 1964, Murray advocated for freedom from racial and religious discrimination in employment.[20]

Such calls for equality went unheeded as complex historical and social forces, such as slavery, unemployment, lack of education, and crime, combined to make many black women the heads of households. To the extent that it existed, matriarchy was what black women got handed, not what they planned. Whether married or single, black women had a history of family and community leadership. The majority of them worked to help support their families, whatever their marital status. (In 1965, Department of Labor figures showed that 70 percent of black workers were women.) They had learned to be assertive and were more likely than men to pursue an education, in part because of job openings for black women in nonmanagement office positions that were unavailable to black men. Yet they earned less than black men and white women.

Black women's ability to achieve despite the disadvantages of both their race and their gender should have been a model for everyone. Rather than applaud or even recognize their industriousness, the Moynihan report characterized the success of black women as a threat to black men. If they were attain his ideal, they would have to change their roles in the home and community. To support that call for change, Moynihan's report portrayed them as embittered women who made black men feel inadequate. And despite their employment rates, the report painted them as women who chose welfare over marriage. Though Congress never implemented the interventions Moynihan suggested, his rhetoric cast black women in a harsh light that placed them in opposition to black men and to American society as a whole for the next decade.

IN SEARCH OF A NEW MODEL OF EQUALITY

As I was coming of age in the 1960s, few models of the end game of social progress existed, and those that did rarely included a role for black women. I first saw the movie version of Hansberry's play on television as a child. The dramatic portrayal of the Younger family offered me my first inside view of the civil rights struggle, as well as one of my first images of a black family on television.

When *Raisin* premiered on Broadway in 1959, issues of race were being played out with sit-ins and marches aimed at integrating public spaces in the South. Whites opposed to equal rights took the fight into the private and personal spaces where blacks sought refuge—their homes and churches. Two years after the 1961 film version of *Raisin* debuted, the home of civil rights leader Medgar Evers was firebombed. A month later, in June 1963, Evers was gunned down in his driveway. That same year, four African American girls were killed when Klansmen bombed their church in Birmingham, Alabama, as the congregation prepared for Sunday school.

Home ownership in a previously restricted area, in both fact and fiction, was not so much a finale to the procession toward equality; it represented a new chance to work on long-festering issues. Though the passage of civil rights legislation seemed to evidence an understanding that the fates of all Americans were intertwined, that understanding did not hold when it came to the question of whether people of all races should live together in the same neighborhoods. In 1966, when Martin Luther King brought his movement north to take on racism there, he settled into a black neighborhood in Chicago. His mission: to challenge the city's persistent and pervasive pattern of housing discrimination.

In Norman Rockwell's depiction of residential integration, two groups of children—one black, one white—eye each other quizzically, but without apparent hostility, against the backdrop of a moving van. *New Kids in the Neighborhood*—as the painting, which appeared on the cover of *Look* magazine in 1967, was called—bore little resemblance to the confrontation Hansberry faced in real life and portrayed in *A Raisin in the Sun*. Yet it movingly signified a dream that perhaps the artist had for the future—that of America, in the generation of the children he painted, accepting racial integration.

By the mid-1970s the migration of whites from inner cities had changed the populations of neighborhoods in Chicago dramatically. This "white flight" led to the resegregation of neighborhoods and public schools. White rings around black and Latino inner cities became the norm. In 1974, writing in a Supreme Court decision that challenged the school district boundaries in suburban Detroit, Justice Thurgood Marshall lamented that "great metropolitan areas" were being "divided up each into two cities—one white, the other black."[21] The decision the court rendered that day in the case of *Milliken v. Bradley* only encouraged the division of the races, despite Marshall's dissent. In 1954, when *Brown v. Board of Education* was decided, public school integration had promised a new era of racial integration. But the court in *Milliken* refused to allow enforcement of plans that would have combined inner-city and suburban school districts. Thus integration failed, and schools and neighborhoods within and outside major cities became more and more racially isolated.

By 1976, a presidential campaign year, media transformation of poverty into a black and/or a female problem, along with unyielding racial isolation, had paved the way for candidate Ronald Reagan to introduce the public to the Cadillac-driving "welfare queen." Reagan's caricature of women on public assistance linked welfare to dishonesty, laziness, and greed, and it helped turn public sentiment against the impoverished and the government programs designed to aid them. His fictional character was, perhaps predictably, from Chicago's South Side. Despite revelations that the "welfare queen" was not a real person but a composite of individuals who had been caught cheating the system, she became the symbol of more than Reagan's denouncement of welfare. She became the symbol of the "un-American"—the overtly racialized and gendered polar opposite of Reagan's supporters, who viewed government as "the problem, not the solution," as the president himself had put it.

Reagan lost his party's nomination to Gerald Ford, the incumbent. Ford was defeated in the general election by a white southerner, Georgia governor Jimmy Carter, who as a boy had spent many of his summers with a black family in rural Georgia. In 1979 Reagan launched his next presidential campaign in Carter's backyard. In a speech in Philadelphia, Mississippi, where three civil rights workers had been killed in 1964, the year the Civil Rights Act became law, Reagan promised to restore "states' rights"—a rallying cry for 1960s segregationists—and reduce government meddling in people's lives. The reference was better coded than his more blatant welfare-queen allusion, but it too was clearly racial. Moreover, it had the benefit of promising broader policy changes. Even a few years earlier, Reagan might have been dismissed as a carpetbagger for segregationist watchwords; but with the combined support of southerners and middle-class whites, he won the party's nomination in 1980 and went on to win the election. The South soundly rejected Carter, its native son, for

Ronald Reagan, an outsider. Reagan, the Great Communicator, may have sounded more like one of them, even without the southern accent.

By 1983 President Reagan was on his way to a landslide victory over his Democratic challenger, Walter Mondale. He would become one of the most popular presidents in the country's modern history and transform political representation throughout the South and into the border states. One by one, former Democratic strongholds yielded to the allure of the president's new kind of Republicanism. Though some states, like Illinois, remained steadfastly Democratic, my home state of Oklahoma, once represented by moderate and even progressive Democrats like Mike Monroney and Fred Harris, joined the Reagan movement. By the end of the 1980s conservative Don Nickles would lead the state's national congressional delegation as it became increasingly Republican.

From the start of his first term, Ronald Reagan kept his word to states' rights advocates by pushing back on the federal government's role in civil rights protection. Administration officials characterized the integration efforts of offices in the Justice, Education, and Labor departments as examples of government excess. In many corners, "rights" and "rights enforcement" were dirty words. And the stories of the "welfare queen" resurfaced. Through them President Reagan was able to portray black women and the homes they headed as the counter to real American life and aspirations. Blacks were included in the administration, but the successful ones were those who adhered to strict conservative ideology and who were willing to advocate against the welfare system. The first clear illustration that the Justice Department's efforts to enforce desegregation were winding down came in the form of a decision by Reagan's attorney general to support tax-exempt status for Bob Jones University despite the school's written policies that discriminated on the basis of race by prohibiting interracial dating.

That there was a new attitude toward race was evident from the government's civil rights policies, but just how women would fare in the new administration was initially unclear. One of President Reagan's historic acts—perhaps his most compelling singular act—was to name the first woman to the United States Supreme Court in 1981. Sandra Day O'Connor's rise to that position was all the more remarkable because she had been denied jobs in prestigious law firms even though she graduated second in her class from Stanford Law School. When O'Connor was appointed, more than a third of law school graduates were women, in contrast with 3.7 percent in 1963. The number of women law grads had mushroomed in the decades since the civil rights laws were enacted. Despite these increases, and despite O'Connor's credentials as a top law graduate and a member of the Arizona Court of Appeals, her appointment was noteworthy and even politically risky. No other president had made such a move. Don Nickles informed Reagan that he and other socially conservative senators would not support the mother of two and first woman nominated to the court. In the end she was confirmed unanimously, her home life apparently having assured her Republican detractors that she was sufficiently "profamily."

O'Connor's appointment notwithstanding, it became apparent as the Reagan years wore on that the government was not going to mount a rigorous challenge to sexism in education, in the awarding of government contracts, or in any other area. And to be part of the administration, women, like blacks, would have to prove they belonged, that they were not just substantively qualified but ideologically qualified. Under Reagan, women and blacks with a history of advocating for minority or gender rights were eliminated from consideration for government positions.

I would not find my model for home or equality in the politics or law of the seventies and eighties. For a newly licensed lawyer living in Washington, DC, in 1981, that was a profound disappointment. Fortunately for me, America in that decade was more than just Ronald Reagan's America. Through their literary contributions, black women continued informing the country of a different kind of "homebuilding" among African Americans than that portrayed in political circles.

In 1983 African American writer Alice Walker took center stage with a best-selling novel that revealed the twists and turns, the starts, dead ends, and restarts of the black pursuit of a home in America. *The Color Purple*, winner of the Pulitzer Prize for fiction and an American Book Award, told the tale of a young black woman in the 1930s who embraces life and struggles against sexual abuse, racism, sexism, poverty, and illiteracy to find a home. Walker named her protagonist, Celie, after her own great-great-grandmother, a slave who was raped by her owner and gave birth to his son, Walker's paternal grandfather, at the age of twelve.

Walker's efforts to capture the sentiments of Celie resonated with many women who, because of race, poverty, or simply the fact that they were women, felt silenced and powerless even within their own households. The quietly dignified character Celie became a new model of black women's resistance to racial and sexual domination.

In 1985 filmmaker Stephen Spielberg adapted the novel for the screen. Though it received eleven Academy Award nominations, the film won none. Both the novel and the movie had their critics; among them were blacks who found their representations of African Americans stereotyped and sentimental. Walker and Spielberg were both chastised for their portrayal of black men as physically and mentally abusive. One black female critic felt that Walker's Celie was too passive and unlike the many slave women who had resisted their oppression. In sum, *The Color Purple* joined *A Raisin in the Sun* in acclaim and controversy.

In 1983 an estimated two hundred productions of *A Raisin in the Sun* were mounted to celebrate the play's twenty-fifth anniversary. In a review of the Chicago production, *New York Times* critic Frank Rich hailed Hansberry's ability to see "the present and the future in light of the past."[22] Throughout the years, critics have generally praised Hansberry's play. Some commended the universality of its messages about family, human dignity, and materialism. Others hailed the work as a "Negro play" about the triumph of racial pride. Many missed that the play is about home: the home in each family member's dreams for equality versus the real house, a small, three-bedroom dwelling in an unwelcoming neighborhood. *Raisin* is about the home as a location and as a place to belong, and what occurs when these elements misalign. Hansberry's actual experience and the drama she crafted from it show that when the location of the struggle for equality is the home, issues related to marriage, childhood, and family are exposed.

The universality of the themes she explored began to emerge in conversations about the drama, though Hansberry would not live to take part in the discussions. (She died in 1965 after a battle with cancer.) The conflict between Walter and Mama frames the play's debate over materialism and integrity. Walter's materialism, his desire to own a business and strike it rich, as it plays out is easily read as selfishness. In a passage edited out of the 1959 version but reinstated in the 1983 text, Hansberry shows that what drives Walter is not purely desire for himself, but his dream for his son, Travis. Yet she also shows that even that dream is motivated by Walter's view of manhood and the role that he thinks women should play. Walter Younger explains his dream for Travis's education as he imagines his son at seventeen years old "sitting on the floor with the catalogues of all the great schools in America around" him. Once Travis makes his selection, Walter will "hand [his son] the world."

Hansberry's biographer, Margaret Wilson, points out how the passage provides Walter's altruistic justification for his conflict with his mother, wife, and sister. But as Wilson explains, for Walter to realize his dreams he must "buy into a system" of stereotypical gender and class roles. "His image is typical Americana—the independent male who controls the world and around whom the universe revolves. Wife, secretary, gardener, Cadillac, sports car—all are complements to the material universe. His manhood is at stake, he believes, and the women around him with their traditional values are holding him back."[23] It is worth noting that this part of the play is delivered as a monologue and makes clear that Walter's conflicts are not only with his mother. He quarrels with Ruth as he dreams of ways to become wealthy, eschewing more practical choices for the family. Her prize is a sporty car to do her shopping in. His individualism conflicts with Beneatha's notions about the common good of the race. Walter finds a place for Ruth in his dream, but writes Beneatha out of the sequence altogether.

One of the most prescient scenes from *A Raisin in the Sun* brings Beneatha's and Walter's conflict to a head. Beneatha explodes into high-mindedness and contempt for her brother. "I look at you and see the final triumph of stupidity in the world." The fight ends with Beneatha shouting at Walter, who has already left the room in hot pursuit of another path to money: selling the family home to the whites who have offered to buy the Youngers out. Walter rejects Beneatha and the education and kind of knowledge she represents for himself and for her, even though he embraces it for his son.

At the conclusion of *A Raisin in the Sun,* we get a glimpse of Hansberry's vision of how equality could be achieved. As the Younger family put aside their differences, they decide to stay in the home Mama has purchased and turn down the white neighbors' offer to buy out the purchase agreement. The neighborhood representative warns, "I sure hope you people know what you're getting into." One cultural critic, Kristin Matthews, not only sees the Youngers' home as a mirror of black Americans' struggle to find a place in the nation, but also sees the play's ending as promising the family—read the race—"new life as a unified whole." This concept of wholeness on the basis of full race and gender equality might enable us to hear Hansberry's "pluralist call for committed 'builders'—those willing to use their diverse 'tools' in concert to reconstruct vital homes and come closer to realizing the dream deferred: America as 'home of the brave' and 'land of the free.'"[24]

A Raisin in the Sun returned to Broadway in 2004. The success of that production set the stage for an ABC television adaptation of the drama, starring Phylicia Rashad (who won a Tony for her role in the Broadway production), Audra McDonald, and Sean "P. Diddy" Combs. Though it was difficult to envision the famously wealthy Combs as Hansberry's Walter Younger, the presence of the hip-hop icon brought the story up to date even as the play addressed the same issues raised fifty years earlier. Rashad and McDonald, as two black women trying to provide a safe and secure home for their family against the materialism represented by Walter's character, reminded the audience of the hardships that had fallen on black communities in the 1980s and that had brought them so far afield from Hansberry's idealized dream.

A Raisin in the Sun illustrates not only how home became a repository for black Americans' dreams of finding a place in the nation, but also how it symbolizes *all* Americans' desire to belong. It is a story of race and gender and a universal experience of believing in a dream. Hansberry's is a cautionary tale revealing that "a dream deferred" doesn't just "dry up like a raisin in the sun," but as Langston Hughes's poem suggests, instead does "explode." Moreover, the consequences of deferred dreams are not always immediate, often extending decades into the future, with consequences for generations to come.

For over fifty years, Lorraine Hansberry's audiences have focused on African Americans' clashes with the world outside their homes. Her ability to see into the future of conflicts inside the home is just as compelling. Hansberry advises us of the relationship between the problems outside and those conflicts inside. In the years since her play, I have come to fully appreciate how the two work together to enhance or to impede our chances at real equality.

By the 1980s I, like so many people of color and white women, reaped many of the benefits of the advances made during the 1960s and 1970s. But other transformations in society—among them rising materialism, increased violence, resistance to civil rights gains, and a cultural backlash against women—were occurring as well. The suburbs were expanding, and the blueprint of the homes within them grew as well. Inside the home, changes were occurring as more women of all races became part of the paid labor force. The number of law and medical degrees awarded women grew more than tenfold between 1969 and 1979. Women on their own—divorced, single, or widowed—who failed to fit the cultural norm of what "home" and "family" looked like were hit hard. Clashes between the sixties generation of equal rights advocates and their children, who were trending conservative, were escalating and gaining public attention. Though these were all matters Lorraine Hansberry forecast in her play, the ferocity with which they hit by the 1990s caught me by surprise and left many in the black community, in particular, reeling.

CHAPTER FIVE

Blame It on the Sun

Home: An environment or haven of shelter, happiness, or love.
The American Heritage Dictionary of the English Language

In Southern California, a woman named Marla Wyatt had seen the waves of advancement from the days of her youth in the 1960s, but she also knew that women had not achieved the kind of equality that she thought would be hers four decades later. In the years leading up to the new millennium, the dominant model of women as the caretakers of the home and of men as the breadwinners was beginning to be eclipsed by the reality of women working both inside and outside the home. Feminism, which had ensured opportunities for women's employment, moved on to address the difficulties of juggling career, household, and motherhood. By the late 1990s, according to clinical psychologist Harriet Kimble Wrye, young feminists were also moving on to concerns of community: the environment and global violence against women, among others. Certainly not all the goals of feminism had been achieved, but new generations identified evolving issues to tackle, and their emphasis often moved away from the home. For some women, like Marla, though they had jobs and lived in houses of their own, neither the problems of home nor the problems of the global community had been completely resolved.

Marla's struggle to make a home for herself and her children takes place where sunshine, glamour, and the promise of unlimited possibility has long drawn people like moths to a flame. California came to represent the aspirations of so many, and its population doubled from 1960 to 1990. But out of great hope and anticipation often comes great disappointment, even desperation. Nothing could have prepared Marla for the indescribable pain and all-consuming grief she experienced when her youngest son,

Sam, was murdered just blocks from her front door. Nevertheless, Marla continues to maintain her sense of belonging in a place where so many of her dreams have been shattered.

A HOME OF THEIR OWN

They were married in Las Vegas, and Marla, at twenty-four years old, was a young bride for thirty-two-year-old Leonard. But bigger than the age difference was the dissimilarity in their backgrounds. The fresh-faced girl from a midwestern farm had never lived on her own, aside from two years in college; the committed marine from Los Angeles had a failed marriage and two tours of duty in Vietnam behind him. Despite her inexperience, Marla, like most new brides, was sure that she knew what it took to be a wife and mother. Everything about Marla's upbringing left her little choice: a twenty-four-year-old pregnant woman should marry, preferably the father of her child, and start a family.

It was the 1960s, and the young, handsome couple with a baby on the way looked the part of a traditional family. But Marla was no television sitcom housewife, at least not by the stay-at-home June Cleaver standard. Marla worked as a clerk in a nearby bank. Her husband was not a businessman who came home every night to a family dinner; Leonard was away on duty for much of their young marriage.

Though their lifestyle did not match what was portrayed on popular sitcoms of the day, social messages kept Marla informed about her and Leonard's responsibilities. In the decades before Marla and Leonard came of age, the Own Your Own Home campaign had promoted home ownership as the American ideal and encouraged men and women to live out their gender roles, and even their patriotism, by buying a home. In shifting responsibility for children's welfare to mothers and away from government authorities and community organizations, the message of OYOH was that by encouraging their husbands to buy homes, women would be happy and fulfilled, as long as they stayed in those homes and out of the workplace. OYOH slogans declared that the male homeowner was better at just about everything and dubbed him the *"real* American."[1] And even as the Vietnam War death toll among black men climbed, many still saw military engagement as proof that they were "real Americans." Thus the combination of Leonard's military service and home ownership bolstered his patriotic credentials, making his and Marla's a "real American family."

In 1969 newlyweds Marla and Leonard found their dream house: a big living room with a fireplace, a separate dining room, and two bedrooms—just enough room for the couple and one child, which was all Marla intended to have. A yellow-and-black tiled bath, a kitchen with a breakfast nook, and a laundry room completed the floor plan. It was much roomier than the apartment Marla had shared with her older sister, and in many ways it resembled Booker T. Washington's "tasty little cottage." Set on a street with well-tended lawns, the mission-style stucco house with its spacious porch drew Marla outside to untarnished settings. The big backyard, flanked by a two-car garage, had a brick and stucco fireplace that was perfect for the weekend barbecues Marla loved to hold.

The payments on the $18,500 home were much more than a marine earned. In practical financial terms, that meant Marla's and Leonard's salaries were both needed to pay the mortgage. Although a few of her female neighbors stayed home during the day, Marla went to work at the bank every morning. As the years passed, dropping off and picking up her two young children at school and day care became part of her routine, until they were old enough to go home on their own.

Marla and Leonard's wide street bore a striking resemblance to the era's coveted suburban ideal, even if racially, Marla and Leonard did not. On weekends, residents emerged from their tile-roofed homes to trim shrubs, groom lawns, water plants, and visit with each other over fences. Each household was as determined as the next to keep up the appearances of their quiet working-class neighborhood. Marla and Leonard's next-door neighbors were an older white married couple. Nearby, a widowed Latina lived next to a retired wife and husband who were black. A gay couple, white men, lived two doors down, adjacent to a black woman and her children. Marla liked them all. Despite differences in appearance and background, they got along well enough to build a sense of community.

Even after decades of integration, a racially mixed neighborhood in Los Angeles was something of a novelty. By historical accounts, housing segregation and discrimination was as much a problem in California as it was in other parts of the country. Minorities had to contend with those who were reluctant to rent or sell to them and mortgage lenders who refused to give them loans. Those factors combined to uphold racist restrictions that negated many African Americans' dreams of home ownership and relegated most of the rest to specific geographic locations. Rarely did banks grant loans to blacks buying in white neighborhoods, and limited lending in black neighborhoods meant that only a few black buyers had the necessary funds. Wealthy blacks who did not have to rely on the whims of lenders often faced hostility from white sellers and neighbors alike.

Despite their illegality, restrictive covenants, like the one Carl Hansberry challenged in Chicago, had become routinely attached to real estate deeds. In Los Angeles, agreements barring the sale of property to "people of the Negro or Mongolian Race" circumvented the desires and the rights of minorities, as well as white sellers who welcomed buyers of any race. Neighbors who sought to enforce such limitations argued that restrictions prevented sales to "undesirables," which typically meant that nonwhites were unwelcome.

This type of racist behavior simply reflected age-old prejudices; nothing new or surprising was happening in these neighborhoods. Private developers and state and federal governments all played a role in upholding the racial and class hierarchies that impeded black home ownership. Adam Gordon, writing in the *Yale Law Journal* in 2005, argues convincingly that regulations created in the New Deal and carried out by the Federal Housing Administration systemically discriminated against African Americans and gave "whites a generation's head start on accumulating wealth through homeownership."[2] Marla and Leonard's generation was the first to seek federally insured loans without racial restrictions. Nevertheless, the long-term impact of rules that influenced the racial makeup of neighborhoods in cities and suburbs persisted. Marla's heterogeneous neighborhood was an anomaly, even at the end of the sixties.

THEIR CHOICE OF LOCATIONS

Chicago and Los Angeles shared a history of racial restrictions in housing, but Los Angeles had its unique geographical genealogy. In 1949, Nat King Cole and his family were greeted by a burning cross on the lawn after they moved into Hancock Park, an affluent white Los Angeles neighborhood whose first families included some of California's leading industrialists and bankers. The all-too-familiar inferno was attributed to an all-too-familiar source: the Ku Klux Klan, which had been active in California since the 1920s. Although Cole would soon become one of the country's premier "crossover" singers, appealing to multiracial audiences, he apparently did not have the same appeal to his neighbors. The residents in this community of large and small mansions had enjoyed the "privilege" of racial restrictions for more than one hundred years, and they were not about to give it up without some contention. Hancock Park's well-heeled and politically powerful residents had the resources to offer to buy out Cole's attempt to infiltrate their meticulously maintained dominion. When they warned him that they didn't "want any undesirable people moving into the neighborhood," Cole agreed, responding, "Neither do I, and if I see anybody undesirable coming in here, I'll be the first to complain."[3]

Unlike poorer blacks, Cole had the personal financial resources that allowed him to purchase the seventy-five-thousand-dollar, fourteen-room Tudor-style home. Ironically, wealth was what put the Hancock Park residents' racial predilections to the test. Despite the court's ruling in *Shelley*, "gentlemen's agreements" to deny sales to African Americans remained in force, especially in tiny locales. Cole argued that his American citizenship entitled him to take up residence in Hancock Park, saying that "we intend to stay there the same as any other American citizen would."[4] And stay he did.

Nat King Cole's victory over prejudice became the stuff of legend among blacks in Los Angeles, even those who would never acquire the wealth needed to buy a house like his. Restrictions, however, were not limited to high-end real estate markets. Minutes from Marla and Leonard's new home was the suburban city of South Gate, which was made up of a number of working-class communities. The area's open commitment to segregation—born of the southern roots of many of its inhabitants—was notorious. According to historian Andrew Wiese, a local newspaper had once boasted of a community that was "distinctly a white man's town. . . . A goodly percentage of our people were born south of the Mason and Dixon line . . . [and] one of the controlling factors in their choice of a location was the racial restrictions."[5]

Even closer to Marla and Leonard's community was the working-class, previously racially restricted city of Inglewood, California. White residents began leaving Inglewood when its well-paying aerospace manufacturing jobs dwindled, and minorities began to move in. By the 1960s black and Latino residents were not uncommon in Inglewood, but there and throughout the area, the neighborhoods were largely segregated, with people of color living in the poorer areas.

Many Californians seemed intent on preserving racial segregation and furthering the effects of the earlier federal housing policies. In a state referendum in 1964, voters approved Proposition 14 by a two-million-vote margin, amending the state's constitution to make it "the right of any person, who is willing or desires to sell, lease, or rent any part or all of his real property, to decline to sell, lease, or rent such property to such person or persons as he, in his absolute discretion, chooses." Other than the language itself, what made Proposition 14 such a clear rejection of civil rights laws was its timing. Placed on the ballot one year after the enactment of the state's Rumford Fair Housing Act, Proposition 14 went beyond repealing Rumford, which had aimed to undermine discrimination by prohibiting exactly such racist selling and lending behaviors. Approval of the proposition meant that "gentlemen's agreements" to restrict residential sales were legal. Proposition 14 also tied the hands of any municipality that might attempt to pass or enforce fair housing laws in the future, protecting instead the privilege to discriminate as a fundamental right.

It would take another federal challenge, in addition to *Shelley v. Kraemer*, to put an end to the kind of housing discrimination sanctioned by California's constitution. Three years after Proposition 14 went into effect, the United States Supreme Court ruled in the case of *Reitman v. Mulkey* that parts of the proposition violated federal constitutional protections. A year later the federal government enacted the Fair Housing Act, Title VIII of the Civil Rights Act of 1968, which prohibits housing discrimination by lenders as well as sellers. But by then California voters had already shown, by a two-to-one margin, that they accepted segregation as readily as the sunshine the state was known for.

Marla and Leonard's ability to make their home in a racially mixed neighborhood was notable in 1969. The impact of racial restrictions was still being felt decades after the Supreme Court voiced its disapproval of them. Entire neighborhoods had developed around the concept of racial separation and the economic balkanization that went along with it. Just blocks from Marla's home were the congested streets, corner convenience stores, cramped two-story apartment complexes, and outlets for liquor and cigarettes that characterized the urban environments of the 1960s.

ALWAYS FAITHFUL

Home ownership notwithstanding, Leonard never lived up to the ideal of father and husband that the OYOH campaign promised, nor was he the partner and father that Marla and their children, Beth and Marlon, required. For months at a time, Marla experienced what it was like to be a single mother. As she looks back, she realizes that their marriage was never the happy experience she had thought it would be. Marla understood her own responsibilities to the marriage and their home, but she had overestimated Leonard. She had attributed the family's lack of money to his low pay and had suffered silently the humiliation of having to sell soda bottles to pay for groceries. She had overlooked the inconsistencies in Leonard's explanations for why he spent so much time away from the family, convincing herself that absences were the price she paid for being a military man's wife. But all the lies were revealed when she went to pay for the children's school clothes and discovered that Leonard had been taking money from the family bank account to pay for local hotel rooms. The indignity hit her seemingly all at once—the deceit, the loneliness, the lack of money all boiled down to a feeling of immense betrayal. *Semper fidelis*, the motto meaning "always faithful," may have described Leonard's dedication to his fellow marines; it said nothing about his commitment to his wife or his family.

Marla asked Leonard for a divorce. Ten years after she first walked through the door of the house that she and Leonard bought together, Marla learned what it was truly like to be a single mother. Marla's guilt over her failed marriage created a determination in her to make sure that her children would not suffer. Even though the OYOH campaign's promise of marital bliss was unfulfilled in her experience, Marla—knowingly or not—remained dedicated to its child-rearing message: the home, not "the village," would determine her children's well-being.

In the 1970s, the divorce rate in the United States doubled. Conceptually, the target audience of the OYOH crusade was dwindling, and the campaign itself was no longer as viable as it had been when Leonard and Marla were children. Marla's was not the only "happily ever after" story to end in something less. For black women, marriage took a particularly hard hit. From 1970 to 1979, the percentage of African American women who were living with a husband dropped ten full percentage points, compared with a 2 percent drop for white women.

By the time Marla divorced, it was no longer enough for couples to own a home with a yard; parents, whether married or single, were expected to fill those homes with the proper accoutrements to foster their children's growth. As Marla raised her family in the seventies, she saw the positive message of the home's role in raising children being eclipsed by consumerism. Commercials for household products, toy promotions, and the ubiquitous marketing of devices, services, and activities (from trendy games to sugared cereals to expensive sneakers) all claimed to help "normalize" her children's experience and enhance her "family environment." At the same time, government and noncommercial institutional support for families was on the decline. To make matters worse, the gap between women's and men's wages was widening, exceeding what it had been in the 1950s.

Marla was now facing more severe economic difficulties, but she and the children were relieved that they no longer had to endure Leonard's humiliating behavior and abuse, which had come to color the entire family's existence. Marla was happier; Beth and Marlon were calmer. Overall, their lives were more tranquil. Social scientists may have described families like hers as broken and fragile, but she would have none of it. Beth and Marlon deserved the emotional security of knowing that the people living in their home wanted to be there and wanted to be a meaningful part of their lives. Marla refused to see hers as a broken home, no matter how limited a role Leonard played in her children's lives. Indeed, she became convinced that her divorce from Leonard was more of a solution than a problem.

FROM HOME TO HAVEN

Marla knew that her children's emotional security also depended on their staying in the only home they had ever known. The change of the divorce was enough; changing addresses was not an option. In the final divorce decree, Marla got the house, which meant taking responsibility for the mortgage as well as for educating her children, keeping them healthy, and making sure they were safe. In order to keep the house, she could not change her work life. Marla sometimes worked fifty hours a week, which limited her ability to shuttle the children to and from sports practices, music lessons, and other activities. Most nights, when she picked up her children from a babysitter, she had only enough time to set them to their homework and pull together a meal. After Marla put them to bed early on weeknights, she made their lunches and even managed to keep up her daily habit of making an extra sandwich for the man who slept in the alley behind her bank. With the same firmness her own mother had displayed with her, Marla woke Beth and Marlon early for breakfast before school.

Marla was eager to prove to everyone, including the experts who touted the nuclear family as the key to children's well-being, that Beth and Marlon could thrive in a home headed by a single black mother. But she missed having a man in her life. What started out as flirtation with Ernest, a man who repaired her car, turned serious. Other than cars, he seemed interested only in her. Ernest, ten years younger than Marla, got along well with Beth and Marlon and spent most of his spare time with the three of them, becoming a fixture around their home. She eventually agreed that he could move in with them; it seemed a natural progression of their relationship. In retrospect, Marla is not sure whether she saw living with Ernest as a prelude to marriage or just a matter of convenience. What she did know was that five years after her divorce, she did not want to rush into another marriage.

She hadn't planned to have a third child. But once Sam was conceived, she felt she had only one choice. Her two best friends from high school, also working women, each had only one child. But to Marla, her three didn't seem excessive. Ernest was not as certain about becoming a parent as Marla was, but she assured him that if necessary, she would take care of Sam alone, just as she had Marlon and Beth. When Ernest left, Marla bore the responsibility for the day-to-day learning, well-being, and safety of her three growing children.

Sam had been born in 1980. Throughout that summer and for the next year, the city of Atlanta was on edge; a suspected serial killer was on the loose, and many of his victims were black boys. Novelist Tayari Jones was nine years old and lived in Atlanta during the murder spree. Thirty years later, she summed up the fear sweeping the community by saying that one lesson she took away from the ordeal was that "some people are more vulnerable than others. It wasn't ambiguous."[6]

Then in July 1981, the kidnapping and murder of six-year-old Adam Walsh while he was with his mother at a Sears store in Hollywood, Florida, put fresh focus on the dangers that twentieth-century children faced. Adam's death and the deaths in Atlanta combined to change the culture of child rearing in the 1980s. Perhaps this atmosphere of concern for the welfare of children was why Marla grew so protective of hers, especially Sam. Determined to avoid the nightmare of losing a child, Marla became gravely serious about the responsibility of protecting all three of her children. She walked them across the street for play dates with other children. She pestered them to come into the house as soon as it was dark. Once, Marla dreamed that an airplane crashed in her front yard. Two weeks later, a plane fell from the sky into the backyard of a house less than ten miles away. This was close enough for Marla; she read her dream as a premonition—not of the accident that had occurred, but of one yet to happen. Despite her generally laid-back demeanor, Marla grew especially anxious—some might even say a bit neurotic—about her children's safety. For two years after the accident, Marla refused to board an airplane.

But none of her feelings of insecurity could stop Marla's determination to make her house a home. She had raised her children there, planned and financed an addition, scraped and painted cabinets, and even learned to do her own plumbing. Hers was the place where her extended family gathered for Thanksgiving and Easter dinners; Marla had served forty-two turkeys, thirty-five hams, and scores of birthday cakes there. Marla kept her children close. They would have no reason to join the gangs that were growing in the streets and back alleys near her home.

Despite the growing mistrust between law enforcement and black communities in Southern California, Marla knew that it was still the job of the police to control the gangs that were starting to dominate the streets in nearby neighborhoods. But she knew just as clearly that within her home she had to be the law and manage her three active children as best she could. Marla was strong, independent, and determined to prevail with the kind of mothering that was called for in the context of civil unease and increasing street violence.

Marla's older two children took to heart the tough-love messages she sent. Sam, however, preferred to focus on Marla's softer side: his mother's love of poetry and music. Sam shared his with everyone, whether or not they wanted to listen. His most ardent audience was the elderly woman and her daughter who lived across the street. Sam visited them in their home every day on his way home from school. The mother, who was housebound, was perhaps the most appreciative; each day Sam offered a new poem for her to critique, and she was never critical of his performances of verse or his monologues about his favorite television characters, sports stars, or musicians. She was grateful for the time and attention Sam showed her and encouraged him to write more.

Sam had been surrounded by music from birth, so his attraction to it was natural. Through the 1980s, from its origination in neighborhoods very much like the ones near Sam's, hip-hop culture was going global. As early as 1982, inspired by television and movies, youths in places as far away as Denmark formed groups whose musical and dance forms reflected the style coming out of black and Latino neighborhoods in the United States. The style was professionalized and glamorized by Michael Jackson, whose 1982 album *Thriller* was music, dance, video, and fashion all in one. But a peculiar racial phenomenon was happening in the eighties. As Jackson's skin color seemed to turn increasingly lighter, young Japanese men began presenting themselves with regularity at Tokyo dance clubs with darkened faces and dreadlocks, dancing to hip-hop music in rhythmic, interpretive, muscular moves. They were performing their version of blackness. In addition to his remarkable talent, Jackson's broad appeal came from his ability to transcend accepted notions about race and gender, through skin lightening and plastic surgery. His appeal transcended class as well. Jackson made it cool to be a young black man for urban youth, who emulated him and took his dance and musical acumen in new directions. "Popping" and break dancing, forms of hip-hop expression, allowed young men of all races to combine physical agility and a new version of masculinity with their generation's music and texts.

By the 1990s Sam had grown into a teenager with long arms and a slight frame, which might have suited him for dancing. But his lack of coordination (he never even learned to ride a bike) undermined any advantage his physical appearance gave him. Sam loved sports, but he was as unsuited to competitive sports as he was to break dancing. Not only did he lack the physical grace of an athlete, but he also lacked the necessary competitiveness. His older brother, Marlon, delighted equally in hitting a baseball and catching a football. Sam preferred to talk endlessly about sports teams, thrilling games, and star athletes. For Sam and boys like him, rhymes were the readily available mechanism for establishing masculinity. The poetry Sam practiced for his elderly neighbor would develop into rap. Sam's easygoing personality was suited for the combination of rappers' freedom of expression and hip-hop and freestyle rhyme.

In urban settings during the 1980s, rapping had evolved from a musical form to a rite of passage to manhood, the way "playing the dozens" had for a previous generation of African Americans. But to succeed in establishing himself as an artist in the burgeoning musical form—let alone in signifying his masculinity—Sam needed to work on his rhymes. His could not be the poetry that spoke to old ladies; it had to be edgier, angrier, if he were to compete with the rappers whose hip-hop credibility— their "cred"—came from lives on the streets, in housing projects, and as gang members.

Sam had anger to address; his strained relationship with his father had grown more and more contentious. His poetry served him well in that respect. The fact that he had no experience on the streets or with gangs posed a challenge to Sam's musical ambitions. Yet hip-hop was everywhere: in school, on the radio, in the inner city, in the suburbs, and in rural homes across America. The music called Sam, as it did so many youths in the nineties.

But as popular as the genre was, not everyone–certainly not the women of Marla's generation—appreciated its content. In time, the generational and gender battle lines would be drawn in public discussion over the misogyny, violence, homophobia, and materialism that the lyrics arguably promoted in the name of artistry and masculinity. But Marla knew that she would never be able to keep Sam from the music he and many others were drawn to.

Indeed, over time, new and developing communication and entertainment devices have ensured individuals of all races, genders, and ages free access to the words and imagery that many find objectionable. It is absurd to tell those who are offended by the messages to just turn the dial. As Brown University professor Tricia Rose points out, "You'd have to shut down all of your children's and your own investment in MTV, BET, VH1. You would basically have to unplug from society as a whole" to avoid much of the rap that is generated today.[7]

Sam, like many young men, refused to unplug. His finest achievement came when he helped write the music and lyrics for a CD recorded by a group of his friends. Though his contributions went unacknowledged in the liner notes, his role in the production was proof enough for Sam that he had musical talent. He did follow his mother's advice, however, and found other work; he began focusing on his future, preparing for the day when he and his girlfriend would have their own home.

Not only was Sam sure that his poetry would never match that which had become popular; Sam was a pacifist. Growing up, he had heard the stories of boys his age getting involved in gangs and criminal acts and had witnessed gang activity himself in school, but Sam was not a fighter. Through Marla's urging and his own reflection, Sam decided that life on the streets was not for him. On his job, as an aide in a group home for children who couldn't or wouldn't live in their family homes, he saw kids drawn to behavior and places that he had rejected.

William Oliver, a professor of criminal justice at Indiana University, explains the power and allure of the streets, which he describes as a "socialization institution that is as important as the family, the church, and the educational system" to economically marginalized black males.[8] Indeed, the writings of sociologist William Julius Wilson suggest that the streets are in competition with those other institutions. He writes of mothers in poor neighborhoods in Chicago who recognize they have greater social control over their children where strong "churches, schools, political organizations, businesses, and civic clubs," and the resources they need to engage them, are available. "The higher the density and stability of formal organizations," the less influence the streets have on youth.[9] Unfortunately, according to Oliver, the streets are where a small minority of inner-city young men develop ideas about their relationship to the larger culture that promote violent confrontations as a way of asserting power and manhood. And the influences are not limited to those who live by the codes of the streets. In today's cities, even those who don't abide by the codes are hard pressed to entirely unplug from the ubiquitous cultural influences of these alternative urban institutions, which in fact transcend geography. In Los Angeles, infamous for its gang-related activity, the boundaries between the obviously dangerous settings and the protected ones are nebulous and often difficult to delineate.

A PARENT'S WORST NIGHTMARE

Despite Marla's best efforts and even Sam's best intentions to avoid the violence of the streets, that proved impossible. At about six o'clock on a Sunday morning in August 2008, Marla heard Sam as he left to report to his job. That afternoon, anticipating that Sam would return home ravenous after his double shift, she went food shopping. As she unloaded the chicken and vegetables she had planned for dinner, she heard a police helicopter circling overhead. In response to this all-too-familiar sound, Marla said a prayer for the victim she knew was out there. She had no idea that just blocks away, a passerby had found Sam slumped over on a sidewalk, clinging to life.

A few hours later she received the worst news of her life. How she did it she doesn't know, but Marla gathered herself and rushed to the hospital. "He fought so hard," Marla said, but a few days after being shot in the chest at close range, Sam died. Marla was at his bedside.

Tragedy may have visited Marla's home, but hers is not a story of defeat. She has found much-needed but somewhat unexpected allies, including Sheryl, the police detective who is investigating Sam's murder. When she was first assigned to the case, Sheryl assumed that Sam was a gang member. (Among other things, she searched his room for evidence of gang membership.) But Sam was not in a gang. Sheryl could find no trace of Sam in the criminal system, and his murder did not fit the stereotypical "gang member shoots rival gang member" profile. Since Sam had no "usual suspect" enemies, the police force is at a loss for how to solve the crime. Sheryl, the African American mother of a teenage son, remains committed to the case and says she thinks about Sam every day. To Sheryl the mother, Sam was one of the kids who were supposed to escape that fate. To Sheryl the police detective, Sam is an enigma. She is willing to use whatever resources are available to find who killed Sam and has petitioned the city to put out a fifty-thousand-dollar reward for information leading to an arrest in his case. No one had collected it yet. Sam's murder remains unsolved.

Ferroll is another of Marla's allies. She, like Sheryl, is devoted to justice, but pursues that ideal through healing and educating grief-stricken survivors of violence. Ferroll started her counseling service, Loved Ones Victims Services, after working directly with police officers as they investigated homicide scenes. Nine years into her counseling work, her own brother, on the verge of becoming a lawyer, was killed by a robber. Ferroll's effort to channel the anger and pain of loss into healing and positive action is directed to the eighteen hundred families she has served, as well as to the city itself. Every Angeleno suffers the effects of violence, whether it occurs in her own backyard or in streets miles away. For Ferroll, no neighborhood is immune from violence—it happens in wealthy and poor communities. Thus the responsibility for ending violence is both individual and collective. Ferroll and her network pursue the city's and families' healing with the same tenacity that Sheryl demonstrates in searching for Sam's murderer.

Some days Marla wakes wanting to think only of Sam, to fix him in her mind and hold on to his laughter. On other days Marla cannot bring herself to think of him, lest her imagination go to the fear her child must have felt standing defenseless, face to face with his assailant. In her mind, Marla was there with him—and just as powerless.

Often Marla wonders whether she had ever really been able to protect her children or whether she had been helpless all along. But each day, even after a sleepless night, she rises and shakes her fist at the sun, perhaps as much an expression of anger as defiance. Marla, the retiree, would rather sleep in, but cannot bear to become "one of those people," so overcome with grief as to fear facing the day. She doesn't see herself as the helpless victim. Marla knows how hard she fought, but she also knows that her best chance of winning was to fight within her home. She did that, and she won the battle to convince her children that their own dreams were bigger than a life of violence, but she was no match for the streets.

As Lorraine Hansberry's Mama explained in *A Raisin in the Sun*, "I—I just seen my family falling apart today. . . . We was going backwards instead of forwards. . . . When it gets like that in life—you just got to do something different, push on out and do something bigger." And so Mama made the decision to buy a home for her black family in a predominantly white suburb. Women like Mama Younger have chosen to "push on out" from neighborhoods for a variety of reasons. Whether the talk about killing and "wishing each other dead" refers to violence within the home or in the communities, the impulse is the same. Sometimes you have to push out of the place where devastation hits.

But Marla, like so many women whose children have been killed, remains. During his life, Sam had made their house more of a home to Marla. She would not allow his death to take that away. And so Marla pushes out by volunteering each year for her community food and clothing drive. During their 2011 event, Marla stood at her post for eight hours as more people than the previous year came, even though fewer goods were available than her group had been able to collect in 2010. In the face of increasing neighborhood hardship, the urge to move on is strong, but staying is often the best option. The unexpectedly single working mother is determined to remake the house where she has lived for more than four decades, raised three children, and watched her youngest's life come to an end into the home it once was—not for herself alone, but for her children and now her grandchildren. And for the first time in her life, Marla has accepted that she needs help. Granted, she is not like the many neighbors and friends who have lost their homes in the housing crisis, and for that she is grateful. Yet she still struggles to feel secure, sheltered, and happy in her own home. In reaching out to Ferroll and Sheryl, Marla—thankful for the place that is her home—is restoring home as a state of being.

I learned a lot from listening to Marla. The idea that the safety of the family depends on the individual homes we build today is a recipe for isolation and disappointment. Making a home in Los Angeles is impossible without a shared sense of responsibility and connectedness that extends not only to Marla's immediate neighborhood, but to the impoverished one around the corner, where Sam was shot—and even to wealthy Hancock Park, miles away. In all these neighborhoods, families struggle to stay together, safe and secure. And in each there are women like Marla, Ferroll, and Sheryl who, in the words of Nannie Helen Burroughs, are committed to the idea that we are "real Americans" and committed home builders. They are joined by kindred souls whom they will never meet, whose struggle is not only to keep their communities safe, but to find and keep homes within them.

CHAPTER SIX

Lessons from a Survivor

Anjanette's Story

Home: The place where something is discovered,
founded, developed, or promoted; a source.
The American Heritage Dictionary of the English Language

On Sunday, December 14, 2008, the *Boston Globe* featured as its home of the week an 1895 Victorian cottage. With four bedrooms, a small library, and a large porch flowing to a landscaped garden, it was much like the tasty little cottage Booker T. Washington imagined and built. The asking price was $719,000. With a down payment of $70,000, the monthly payment on a thirty-year fixed-rate mortgage at 6 percent would be more than $4,000. Especially in today's conservative lending climate, in order to qualify for a mortgage of $650,000, a potential buyer would need to show nearly $175,000 in annual income. The median income of the inhabitants of the Greater Boston area is $62,000. Women in Massachusetts earn on average less than half of that, $30,300 annually, as 55 percent of them work in low-paying domestic and professional service jobs.

If Washington's cottage was out of reach for most black Americans when he first proposed it in 1895, it was no less so over a century later. Owning a home, and thus acquiring this piece of the American Dream, had become increasingly difficult for people of color and single women. Indeed, realistically, this way of showing one's belonging and civic participation remains out of reach for many of them and millions of other Americans today. But over the last two decades, pragmatic assessments of the housing market didn't stop the real estate industry and the government from aggressively pursuing policies that promoted home ownership. These policies affirmed the centrality of the idea of "home" in the American imagination. But for millions of Americans, the reality of purchasing and paying for a home would become the stuff of nightmares, not dreams, as predatory and subprime lenders joined the campaign.

A SURVIVOR'S TALE

In January 2008 the mayor of Baltimore, on behalf of the city of her birth, filed suit against Wells Fargo Bank. Citing the possibility of nearly half a million home foreclosures, mayor Sheila Dixon alleged that Wells Fargo had engaged in "reverse redlining," a practice banned by the Fair Housing Act. The complaint accused Wells Fargo of targeting African American communities in its marketing of deceptive and predatory lending options and then disproportionately foreclosing on the residents of those communities.

The same month, a front-page article in the *New York Times* told the story of Anjanette Booker, a black woman in Baltimore. "Four years ago, Miss Booker bought a brick row house for $130,000, taking a subprime mortgage because she had a low credit score. Her initial payments were $841 a month. . . . After two years, her mortgage payments shot up to $1,769." Though she borrowed money from her former husband and from friends, she could no longer keep up with the payments.[1]

The divorced mother of a teenage daughter, Anjanette Booker operates a beauty shop called Vixxen in a mostly black neighborhood of Baltimore. In early 2008, as she was facing the reality of losing her home, many of her customers were confronting the same problem. A year later she proved to be one of the fortunate few who had survived the housing crisis. She still had her beauty shop; she still had her home. She said she had no regrets, avowing that owning her home was worth everything she endured to keep it. As of January 2009, the City of Baltimore was still embroiled in litigation with Wells Fargo, which by then had received $25 million in taxpayer funds from the federal bank bailout that Congress approved late in 2008.

The world will recall 2008 for a series of catastrophic events. First the housing market crashed. Then we learned that the banking industry was in deep trouble and that American car manufacturers, long in distress, were on the brink of bankruptcy. Individuals from every walk of life and in every part of the United States lost homes and jobs, and often any pros-

pect of getting either back. But for Anjanette Booker, 2008 was just another chapter in a tumultuous life defined more by her resilience than by
her trials. When I spoke with her on a Sunday afternoon in January 2009,
she had just come home from church. To my surprise, she laughed easily,
even as she described some of the hardships and sacrifices of her life and
the lessons she learned from them.

As a child, Anjanette was orphaned by parents who died in their
twenties. Like so many casualties of the drug and alcohol culture of the
sixties and seventies, they were bright young people who made devastat-
ingly bad choices. In the case of Anjanette's mother, a poor upbringing
was not available as an excuse. In 1963 Anjanette's maternal grandparents
moved their family from South Carolina to Baltimore, where there were
better opportunities: better schools for Anjanette's mom, who was sixteen years old at the time; steady construction work for her grandfather;
and work in the households of two affluent Jewish families for her grandmother. They bought a home in a middle-class neighborhood and began
to live out the dreams that had prompted them to leave South Carolina.

In 1965 Anjanette's mom met a local man, three years her senior and
much more familiar in the ways of city life in general and Baltimore in
particular. They married. But neither the stability of her parents' good
home nor the birth of two children, Harry and Anjanette, was enough to
keep the young woman from South Carolina from the drugs that her husband encouraged her to use and that were readily available in Baltimore.
By the time Anjanette was born, her father had become addicted to drugs
and alcohol. Her mother would follow suit.

Heroin, a drug that was in vogue among middle-class whites at the
turn of the twentieth century, came into wide use among working-class
immigrants in the 1920s. African American urban youth discovered it in
the 1950s and 1960s, though it was rarely the drug of choice for white suburban youth. Addiction to the opiate remains widespread in Baltimore,
which currently has the highest per capita rate of heroin use in the United
States. The city where Anjanette and her father were born has become
something of an urban laboratory for antiaddiction research, but that
came years too late to save Anjanette's parents.

Her father died first, and soon after, her mother. Anjanette and her
brother Harry went to live with their grandparents. They gave them a

home, and along with it the safety and security they needed as orphans. "We went to church every Sunday, and after church we went to my uncle's house," Anjanette recalls. "He didn't go to church, so after service we took the church to him." When the "two services" were over, Anjanette, her brother, and her grandparents went home for dinner. Throughout her childhood and into her early adult life, Anjanette's grandparents were "always there, every step of the way. They worked hard to make sure I had whatever I needed," though her grandmother took pains to make it clear that "I'd have to stand on my own two feet."

Anjanette did. When she married, she and her husband, both cosmetologists, opened their own beauty salon. After renting an apartment for a year, they decided to buy a house, which made more sense than putting their money into a rental that cost too much and meant "you always had someone living over you or under you." A mortgage broker helped them find financing, and their mortgage payment was roughly the same as what they had been paying in rent. Things were going well for Anjanette. With her grandparents' guidance, she put her parents' death in perspective and moved into adulthood strong and whole.

But tragedy struck again. This time Anjanette's grandparents were the casualties. Ironically, the work that had enabled them to live their dreams turned on them. First her grandfather learned that years of toiling at one construction site after another had exposed him to toxic levels of asbestos. Years of washing her husband's work clothes had exposed Anjanette's grandmother as well. They were both diagnosed with asbestosis. Her grandmother died first, and her grandfather's will to fight his own illness steadily evaporated. Within months he was dead too.

They left Anjanette the family home in Baltimore and some property in South Carolina. She rented out the house and kept the taxes up on the South Carolina land. She and her husband earned enough from their beauty salon to pay their mortgage and send their daughter to private school. "I tried the public schools, but they were just terrible—fighting and old textbooks, lead in the water, heating systems don't work, teachers aren't trained."

At this point, Anjanette might have begun to believe that her troubles were coming to an end. Despite all the bad fortune she had experienced, she was doing relatively well. She and her husband were proud parents.

They had a successful business that kept her in touch with the community. But a few years after her grandparents died, Anjanette came to the realization that her marriage was over. She and her husband agreed they should get a divorce, dissolve the business, and live separate lives.

A PLACE TO CALL HER OWN

Anjanette went back to the same mortgage broker she and her husband had used when they bought their house. This time she went alone, but with her grandmother's steely resolve and her husband's advice in the back of her mind: be sure you get a fixed rate. She left the broker's office with a $130,000 loan for the home she'd chosen in a mostly white neighborhood. Two years later, when her monthly payment of $841 more than doubled, she realized for the first time that she had signed up for an adjustable-rate mortgage.

In the not-so-distant past, home buyers were typically married couples. Nowadays more and more unmarried, widowed, and divorced women, with and without children, are making the choice to purchase a home. Women on their own have become a key component of the real estate market. In Baltimore, 40 percent of all home sales made in 2006 were to single women. Across the country, single African American women account for half of the home purchases made by black people. For many of them, purchasing a home is an affirmation of independence, as it was for Anjanette Booker. Home ownership meant that she could stand on her own, without her grandparents and without her husband.

MORE LIKE A MAN

In December 2006, a year before Anjanette Booker's story appeared on the front page of the *New York Times*, the Consumer Federation of America tried to alert the nation to the fact that subprime lenders were targeting women. A twenty-four-page report on lending practices in the year 2005 gave plenty of details about the disparate treatment of male and female borrowers but got very little attention from regulators or from the public in general.[2] Newspapers across the country picked up on the research and began to hint at the possibility that there might be racial and gender discrimination in this lending market. In November 2007 a *New York Times* story on subprime lending raised the question "What's Behind the Race Gap?" but gave no definitive answer.[3] An Associated Press analysis of 2007 census data showed that the impact of the historic real estate bust that began that year had fallen disproportionately on Latinos, blacks, Asians, and other minorities.[4]

Researchers were skeptical of the subprime lending market long before the public took any interest. Elvin Wyly, a professor of urban studies at the University of British Columbia, began measuring racial disparities in subprime lending during the crest of the housing boom. He found that from 2004 to 2006 these disparities actually grew, even though there was no decline in the credit ratings of minorities during that period. Though Wyly did not run the numbers on gender disparities, he noted that if "there is an overlapping of race and gender, it's a good bet that one would find a very strong relationship."

Why would a woman commit herself to the uncertainty of a subprime loan? Why would Anjanette Booker and so many women like her get themselves into such a financial predicament? Questions like these filled the media in the wake of the housing crisis, and it's not much of a stretch to hear underneath them the question memorably asked by the "eternally noble" professor Henry Higgins in *My Fair Lady*, a musical about his attempts to transplant his psyche into the mind of the unschooled Cockney flower girl Eliza Doolittle: "Why can't a woman be more like a man?" Higgins, the tutor, accuses Doolittle and all women of constantly fixing their hair and neglecting their flawed ways of thinking.

Our imagination for the "proper" way for women to act is often as limited as Higgins's. When women face financial trouble, our default response is to blame it on their bad or foolish behavior. When things go badly for a woman, as they did for Anjanette Booker when she couldn't make her mortgage payments, we expect her to presume that she needs to fix herself rather than question the system. We want her to ignore the history of bad credit experiences that she and other females have lived with.

In fact, despite the 1974 Equal Credit Opportunity Act—giving women, whether married or on their own, the right to obtain credit in their own name and protecting against other kinds of credit discrimination—there is evidence that even today, women seeking loans are treated differently from men. Women borrowers are overrepresented in the subprime lending market, according to studies done by both the Consumer Federation of America and the National Community Reinvestment Coalition. Across the economic spectrum, women receive less favorable terms than similarly situated men on home purchase, refinance, and home improvement loans, and the gap between women and men who get subprime loans actually increases at higher income levels.

Elderly women are prime targets of refinance and home improvement subprime lenders. Women on average live longer than men and have a greater chance of living alone. Rising property taxes and medical expenses make older women on fixed incomes particularly susceptible to lenders who promise money for necessary repairs but charge huge fees and inflated interest rates.

Rather than asking why women don't behave differently, the better question is why women are overrepresented in the predatory and subprime markets. As one woman put it, "I think so much of this is targeted into the inner city, you know? Do they go after us because we are black or poor? How do they find this out?"[5] There is ample evidence that certain loan applicants are marks. As a former loan officer testified under oath, "If someone appeared uneducated, inarticulate, was a minority, or was particularly old or young, I would try to include all the [extras at additional expense that] CitiFinancial offered."[6] Not until 2004 did the Federal Reserve require subprime lenders to provide any specific data on their loans. Even today, subprime lenders resist any effort to provide information about the risk profiles of borrowers. And as Elizabeth Warren, an adviser to the president on the establishment of the Consumer Financial Protection Bureau, told me in a 2007 conversation, what we do know is that many women who qualified for conventional loans did not get them and that "they and others were being fleeced." Warren, seemingly unlike most policymakers, has the uncanny ability to put herself in the place of female debtors with limited options, perhaps because in 1978, as a twenty-nine-year-old divorced mother, she was one.

GENDER, RACE, AND CREDIT

For thirteen years I taught a case called *Williams v. Walker-Thomas Furniture Company* in my first-year contract class at the University of Oklahoma's law school. The plaintiff, Ora Lee Williams, was a mother of seven living in Washington, DC, in 1962 on a monthly government stipend of $218. I don't know whether she was black, but she lived in a predominantly black neighborhood in a predominantly black city. The students often assumed she was black because of where she lived and her economic status.

The course was required, and the students were randomly chosen for my section. Like the school's student body in general, they were mostly white and middle class, with a few black and fewer Native American middle-class students. Typically the men outnumbered the women, but only slightly. Their average age fluctuated from year to year, but most of them were twenty-somethings fresh out of college. Over those thirteen years, I taught the case to nearly one thousand students, and I never had one who matched the profile of Ora Lee Williams, though some may have had family members who did. Once I did have a student who was the mother of four children, but she and her husband were financially very comfortable.

Between 1957 and 1962, Williams purchased a range of household goods from Walker-Thomas Furniture. All the items, including sheets, curtains, rugs, chairs, a chest of drawers, beds, mattresses, a washing machine, and a stereo set, were bought on an installment plan. The lawsuit was occasioned by the terms of that plan, which kept a balance due on all items purchased until every item was paid for in full. Williams signed this type of agreement not once, but as many as fourteen times over the course of shopping at Walker-Thomas.

To all outward appearances, Ora Lee Williams was a reliable Walker-Thomas customer. She bought most of the items, including the $514.95 stereo set that was her final purchase, from a salesman who came to her home. Walker-Thomas salesmen kept coming back to sell her items large and small, and until the spring of 1962 she made her payments on time. When she defaulted on a payment shortly after she purchased the stereo set, Walker-Thomas sought to repossess all the items she had purchased since 1957, or what was left of them. Given that she had seven children, there must have been some wear and tear on chairs, chests of drawers, and mattresses, not to mention the washing machine. The resale value of these items was undoubtedly minuscule, but the furniture company went to court to get them. Williams, with the help of the Legal Assistance Office, fought back.

My classroom was always buzzing when *Williams v. Walker-Thomas* came up for discussion. And every time I taught the case, I felt a monumental challenge to get the students to overcome their prejudices and see the plaintiff as a real person not unlike themselves, and then to see themselves in her shoes. Each student had an opinion and eagerly shared it. The students easily grasped the legal basis for the court's final decision to undo the contract, and were pretty evenly divided on whether it was correct or incorrect, but the discussion didn't end with the merits of the legal opinion. The budding lawyers were much more interested in the case as a morality tale whose lessons they directed mainly at Ora Lee Williams, placing the burden of better behavior disproportionately on her.

"Mrs. Williams should not have bought such an expensive stereo set." None of my students could ever tell me what a stereo set at a credit furniture store should have cost in 1962 or what she should have spent on one. "Mrs. Williams should have read the contract more carefully." "Mrs. Williams should never have signed the contract." "Mrs. Williams should not have had seven children." I don't have any children, but it doesn't take much imagination to think of reasons a mother of seven might want to fill her home with music. Yet even though most of my students confessed to owning stereo systems of varying costs, they considered that kind of expenditure a luxury for Ora Lee Williams.

Was the stereo a necessity? Does it matter? What my students might have considered was that Mrs. Williams raised her seven children in Washington, DC, at a time when the public schools were in terrible shape. In 1954 the Supreme Court had ruled in favor of parents who sued to end racial segregation in the District of Columbia. Activists who sided with the plaintiffs believed that integration would push school officials to eliminate the overcrowding and part-time classes that were pervasive in black schools under the segregated system. But the poor condition of the schools in Washington, DC, persisted. With white flight from areas like the one where Walker-Thomas Furniture was located, the schools became even more segregated. In 1958 the DC board of education put a tracking system in place. Some important innovations were instituted under the system, like special reading programs for poor children, but poor black students were more likely to be put on a track where their exposure to advanced academic courses, preprofessional programs, and the arts was limited.

Would it matter that the home may have provided the only opportunity for the Williams children to be exposed to music? Would it matter if one of the children was interested in music? Would it matter if the stereo was Mrs. Williams's valiant attempt to keep her children off the streets after school? What is a necessity? Would our opinion change if we learned that one of the Williams children went on to become a world-famous music critic or violinist? We don't know why Mrs. Williams wanted a $514.95 stereo, but we do know that in the companion case, *Thornes v. Walker-Thomas Furniture Company,* the plaintiff had agreed to purchase a used refrigerator on credit for $305. We can easily understand that a refrigerator is essential, but would the law have us make a different rule for Mrs. Williams than for Mr. Thornes in the companion suit?

Interestingly, the higher on the policymaking scale I took the students—the more removed from Mrs. Walker—the less likely the students were to empathize with her. The furniture company was the target of some of my students' admonitions, but usually in more general terms: "Walker-Thomas shouldn't be allowed to cheat people." The students were never clear as to where they would draw the line between cheating people and making money from selling expensive (overpriced) stereo units to poor people. When it came to the role of the courts and any legislative oversight of practices like Walker-Thomas's, the students were even vaguer: "The court has to exercise caution." "Legislatures have to balance a lot of different interests." When I asked them whether they thought there were judges and legislators with life experiences similar to those of Mrs. Williams, they were willing to bet there were none. At the same time, they were sure that the decisions of hypothetical judges or legislators who had been poor or had lived in Mrs. Williams's neighborhood would be informed by those experiences and might well be different from the decisions of those who had not.

In teaching the case, I asked my students to step out of their roles as lawyers representing a client and try on the role of a judge or legislator. This was not so difficult. The students enjoyed seeing themselves in positions of power over the process by which justice is served or law is made. The real challenge was to get them to see Mrs. Williams's choices as not so different from their own. I found that the finger-wagging usually became much less pointed when I shifted the discussion to credit card debt. Many of my young students were already beholden to MasterCard and Visa, and they were much more inclined to put the responsibility for better behavior on the banks that loaned the money. When the lender was a bank and not a furniture store, they were much better able to understand how borrowers could be fooled into thinking they were getting one rate and end up with a higher rate. The nature of the purchases had little impact on their ability to empathize. Whether the debt was incurred for a necessity like a mattress or a luxury like an expensive stereo, credit card holders like themselves were somehow less responsible for bad deals than holders of furniture store credit accounts like Mrs. Williams.

Over the years, our class discussions varied; but generally, in analyzing *Williams v. Walker-Thomas Furniture*, my students were quick to focus on Mrs. Williams's personal choices and pass judgment on them. In this way, I suspect, first-year law students are like most humans. (And even to the most ardent lawyerphobe, they still are human at this phase of their legal training.) I haven't taught Anjanette Booker's case to a class, but I imagine that the conversation would be similar: "Ms. Booker should have read the contract more carefully." "Ms. Booker should have found a house she could afford." "Ms. Booker should have rented and not tried to buy." "Ms. Booker should have lived in the home her grandparents left her." "Ms. Booker should have gotten a regular job and not tried to run her own business."

When stories like that of Anjanette Booker first started to come to light, there was a widespread presumption that the victims of the mortgage crisis were to blame for their troubles. A CNN poll taken in December 2007 found that 51 percent of the public believed that the housing woes chronicled in newspapers and on television were the fault of borrowers. In an opinion column written for the Bowling Green University paper, a student put the sentiments of that 51 percent crassly, showing an eagerness to associate foreclosure with deviance:

> Very little of this problem can be assessed to lenders since they already have to fully disclose everything and have scores of federal and state laws to follow.
>
> But a large amount of responsibility rests at the feet of the homeowners themselves. What kind of person gets into mak-

ing one of the biggest investments of their life without knowing what's going on?

Ignorance of how credit and debt work is not an excuse to cause financial havoc. We don't tell crackheads that it's OK that they did not know about the effects of smoking crack when they started smoking.[7]

To help answer the question of how the writer so easily made the leap from mortgage default to drug addiction, let's look at the early portrayal of those caught in the subprime debacle. "What kind of person" entered into these toxic credit agreements? How did women like Anjanette Booker become "predatory borrowers" and social pariahs?

The term "predatory borrowers" was reportedly first coined in 2001 by Senator Phil Gramm in a speech to an appreciative audience of bankers who greeted him like a conquering hero.[8] In the years that followed, Gramm, a former professor of economics, was called upon to respond to the meltdown of mortgage. He succeeded in creating the perception that people over their heads in debt were there because they had taken advantage of poor, defenseless lenders. A spin on the homeowner crisis had been born.

The housing market collapse initially manifested itself in poor black and Latino communities. Instead of urging the public to question the legality of subprime lending practices on grounds of discrimination, press stories simply gave the problem of subprime lending a race—black—and a gender—female. Media coverage of the foreclosure crisis calls to mind what happened with poverty and Aid to Families with Dependent Children (AFDC) policy in the 1980s. Just as women receiving assistance under the AFDC program became "welfare queens" in the political parlance of decades past, defaulters on subprime loans became "predators."

By 2007 the kind of over-the-top commentary typical of student writings was appearing in mainstream news sources, tabloids, the blogosphere, and just about everywhere else the mortgage crisis was discussed. Few commentators took the time to distinguish borrowers who were victims of predatory lenders from those who got loans by supplying false information. People who were trying to get rich quick by flipping property, people who were simply trying to house their families, and the many who were somewhere in between were ultimately all branded with the same label.

It was in this atmosphere that Anjanette Booker found herself trying to make a monthly mortgage payment that had ballooned from $841 to $1,769. With her finances spinning out of control, Anjanette felt the pain of her grandparents' deaths all over again. The absence of the two people who were always there for her loomed larger than ever, but she was determined to stand on her own two feet, just as her grandmother had preached, though not just to honor her grandmother's memory. She had a living, breathing person who looked up to her as she had looked up to her grandmother. She didn't want to be the disappointment to her daughter that her own mother had been to her. She was determined to save her home.

Many lenders might have looked at a small-business owner like Anjanette Booker and seen little chance that she could earn a steady income in a faltering economy. But perhaps Anjanette's lender understood something about women that Henry Higgins did not when he dismissively declared, "Straightening up their hair is all they ever do." Perhaps the lender understood the role of hair and beauty salons in the lives of black women and the black community.

In terms of the credit market, Ora Lee Williams and Anjanette Booker were very similar. Granted, Mrs. Williams's and Mrs. Booker's life situations were different. But the kinds of credit choices available in the 1960s to Williams and those available to Booker in 2004 were comparable. And even as Ora Lee Williams's life and unpaid labor were based in her home, Anjanette Booker's work was an evolution of labor that started as domestic work and moved into the paid labor market. Work—including child care, home health care, private and institutional housekeeping, and even garment making and hairstyling—with origins in women's "traditional" domestic activities is undervalued in the paid labor market. And by some estimations, over 50 percent of women workers occupy those jobs. The percentage of working women of color in those jobs is even higher. Even with changes in the law's protection of women's credit rights, based on occupations alone, a large portion of people in the United States are disadvantaged by the market's evaluation of their worthiness.

Nannie Helen Burroughs was right. Women's work in the home was their point of entry into the marketplace. What never happened was Burroughs's goal of getting the market to appreciate and value women's work. The problem is not the often tedious and sometimes brutal work, but the view that society has of it and the years of gender discrimination that lessened its marketplace value and continues to impact it.

So how did Anjanette save her home? It helped that she had a cooperative lender. When she called to discuss her loan, Anjanette was pleasantly surprised to learn that her original lender still held it, and even more pleasantly surprised by what the loan officer told her next. "We don't want this house back" was not what she had expected to hear. She was able to negotiate a loan modification that kicked in after she made the higher payment of over $1,700 for six months.

Anjanette got the income she needed by sticking with her trade, hairstyling. Hair has been a source of income for black women for more than a century. In the early part of the twentieth century, Sarah Breedlove, a.k.a. Madam C. J. Walker, built a fortune around "fixing up" women's hair. In smaller, more intimate enterprises than Walker's operations, hair is also a source of shared experiences.

As is common among black women my age, my first hairdresser was my mother, in our family kitchen. My first professional hairstyling experience was at the hands of my cousin Juanita Taylor, Great-Aunt Sara's daughter. I don't know if she had been professionally schooled in the style of Walker, or if she had any training at all, but Juanita Taylor had exceptional skills. She got her business started with seed money from her common-law husband, Fred. With it she built a shed on the back of her mother's home and furnished it with a salon chair and a sink. Even though the floor dipped when too heavy a customer entered, Juanita's beauty shop had two important things going for it: plenty of air and light. It was hers; it was a source of income for Juanita, her eight children, and her mother, and it was a foundation for Juanita's independence.

I saw Juanita only on special occasions, but I knew each time that I would leave with a hairdo that neither heat nor humidity nor hard work could penetrate. That was her reputation, and she never disappointed. She locked in a "press and curl" in such a way that hair never "went back" (became kinky) before you had a chance to get back to her shop. Standing for hours over a hot gas burner, Juanita Taylor earned every dime of the money her customers paid her. She was as good-natured as she was hardworking. Every customer was "baby": "How ya doin', baby?" "Ya still in school, baby?" "Hold your head down, baby." "I'm almost finished, baby." Her greetings, instructions, and assurances were always delivered in the same interested, soothing tone of voice, and we, her happy customers, kept coming back for the chance to get our hair "fixed" and feel good about it, or at least not worry about it.

VALUING WOMEN AND THEIR WORK

Admittedly, hair is a complicated concept. Hair issues are rooted in race and gender and are certainly not confined to black women. All the advertisements for hair growth products directed at men of all races attest to a preoccupation with hair. One could write an entire book on the identity politics of the stuff on our heads. This is not that book or chapter. Instead, I hope to understand fully Anjanette Booker and others like her and what they mean in the black community. Anjanette Booker has been successful because she found spaces for her enterprises: the beauty college—a gendered space—and the Vixxen salon, a racialized and gendered space where black women with their own authentic (as they define it) hair can be at home. A similar observation can be made about beauty salons' counterparts in black neighborhoods: barber shops.

Salons like Anjanette Booker's Vixxen and her nearby competitor, Hair Vysions, are often social and economic anchors in black neighborhoods. They are also racialized and gendered because of what takes place in them and where they are most likely located. Since Madam C. J. Walker made black women's hair an industry, thousands of working-class black women have increased their incomes in the hair business, mostly in small shops located in black neighborhoods. As places where black women gather for hours, these small salons are a community resource as well.

Despite all the odds, Anjanette's ability to style black women's hair allowed her to save her home. She may have been at a disadvantage in the lending market, but in the hairstyling market she was superbly positioned. There were times when the chairs in Vixxen sat empty, but she kept the shop operating. She adjusted her schedule. To supplement her income, she taught at a cosmetology school five days a week and moved her salon appointments to the evenings. Her daughter spent some of those evenings with her father, Anjanette says, and some in the shop "doing what she's supposed to do"—her homework—while watching her mother "do what parents are supposed to do." Anjanette's clients began to adjust as well. They returned to their weekly appointments, saving money by making their own lunches or spending less on clothing. The regular hair appointment was more important than going out to eat or buying a new sweater. At the salon they could socialize, discuss their financial woes, share their problems, and trade information about how to resolve them.

Like so many other black neighborhood businesses, black beauty shops developed specifically as alternative spaces. Historically, black businesses were places where black people could go to get the goods and services they required without having to adapt to or respond to racial prejudice. But beauty shops are unique even among black businesses. They have remained in place in black neighborhoods years after black banks, grocery stores, dressmakers—all viable enterprises during segregation—disappeared. They have remained because they provide services that are not reliably available in white neighborhoods.

When I moved to my current neighborhood, which is predominantly white, my young white real estate agent, in an effort to help me feel more at home, provided me with the name and location of a salon where he said I could have my hair done. The salon was owned and run by black women in a black neighborhood. He did not give me any tips on other black businesses.

Black beauty salons are more than places where black women go because they can't go to white beauty salons, and even more than income bases for many black women. They are places that affirm our identity and value, sites for socializing, and conduits of information. In recent years there has been increasing recognition of the pivotal role of black beauty shops in black communities. Public health officials are now realizing that styling salons can be locations for dispensing important medical information about diseases like cancer and AIDS. In the 1990s the notion first occurred to Dr. Georgia Sadler, a nurse and epidemiologist with an interest in breast cancer prevention and community engagement. Her effort to encourage black women in San Diego to perform breast self-examinations, have regular mammograms, and seek medical help if they found suspicious lumps was successful only after she recruited black hairdressers to talk to their clients about the procedures.

After Malcolm Gladwell wrote about Dr. Sadler's innovative thinking and her remarkable success in his 2000 best seller *The Tipping Point*, people took note. In a 2001 address to the Society for Business Ethics, John Dienhart, the organization's newly elected president and a professor of business ethics at Seattle University, asked the question "Who are *our* hairdressers?" as a way of expanding on Sadler's community engagement approach as a model for ethical business organizations. Dienhart proposed a multilevel framework that moved from the personal to the national, starting with individuals and ascending to families, organizations, markets, and social institutional frameworks such as regulatory agencies. Instead of simply asking how individuals influence business organizations, he asked how individual behavior could influence the actions of, say, mortgage lenders or agencies like the Federal Reserve.[9]

When I spoke with Dienhart, he was quick to remind me that relationships between lenders and borrowers are often based on the borrower's trust. That was precisely the case for both Ora Lee Williams, who bought from a salesman who came to her home, and Anjanette Booker, who got her mortgage from a broker who helped her buy her first home. Dienhart urges business people to get to know the people to whom they market their products, in order to respond to them in a way that is not only profitable but ethical. He proposes looking at who women like Anjanette Booker are as a means of understanding how to change business behavior. He even suggests that knowing who the "hairdressers" are is the first step in changing the way health care systems and insurers operate.

Dienhart's framework is another way of expressing what I wanted from my students when I asked them to consider how legal systems should react to people like Ora Lee Williams through the vehicle of courts and act on their behalf through the vehicle of legislatures. The students found it much easier to censure Mrs. Williams's behavior than to work out how the law should respond to the lack of personal choices available to her. And the larger point that they routinely missed was that by making better law for Mrs. Williams, judges and legislators would be making better law for my students and people they saw as more like them.

If I were to teach the case of Anjanette Booker, I would require my students to study hair. No doubt many would object to the subject as superficial, if not frivolous, and I would have to explain that if they didn't understand hair, they wouldn't understand why Anjanette's chances of succeeding were so good. They might misread her original loan application as a case of predatory borrowing or her mortgage lender's renegotiation as a bleeding heart mistake. In their future professional lives, they might miss a chance to keep one more woman and her child in their home. But I also want my students to know who the day care worker or home health provider or teacher's aide seeking a loan really is. As much as anything, I want my students to understand how our persistent devaluation of those things black and those things female undermines our communities and our country, culturally and economically.

With her home safe and her income steady, Anjanette Booker decided to go back to school to get a degree in business. Baltimore City Community College offers a program with classes she can take online. She meets with her classmates occasionally to work on group projects, which is hard because "everyone has a busy work schedule." She's set a goal for herself: "I want to finish college before my daughter graduates from high school." She sees this as her happy ending and enough to make her "very thankful."

But here I would caution my students: do not think to use Booker's story as a testament to rugged individualism or an example of how government should "get out of the way" and let people take care of themselves. It is a very American story, yes, but it is not a modern version of the Horatio Alger myth in which, through hard work and determination, a woman faced with adversity is able to achieve the American Dream. To read her story in such simplistic terms is to ignore the racial and gender reality of her experience. With so many people in danger of losing their homes, the jury is still out on whether Booker was targeted for a subprime loan because of her race and gender; but it is undeniable that at numerous points in her life, race and gender exacerbated her problems.

Very few of my students could ever be cast as the lead in the story of Anjanette Booker's life. Too many elements would have to be changed to make them believable. If you have any doubt, switch the race or gender of the players in Anjanette's life. Her grandparents' move from South Carolina to Baltimore for better job opportunities is an American story made all the more powerful and poignant because of their race. The change in her financial status coming out of a divorce is an experience that many women share. The way she was able to recover financially and regain her sense of self through her ability to style hair is a story of both race and gender and what generations of black women have done at home.

With a steady flow of income from her teaching, her salon, and the rent from the property her grandparents left her, Booker prevailed. She told me that in early 2008, when she looked out her living room windows she could see five homes with "For Sale" signs out front. A year later, the neighborhood no longer has the "ghost town" appearance she described. Her neighbors, too, have been able to renegotiate their loans, she presumes. The "For Sale" signs are gone.

A SYSTEMIC SOLUTION

Unfortunately, many of Ajanette's clients from other neighborhoods have not fared as well as she has. Some have lost homes in the housing crisis; others have seen Baltimore neighborhoods ravaged. In response, the mayor and city council sued Wells Fargo for economic losses they attributed to the bank's lending practices, which were described as a "subprime lending spree." If the city's projection of nearly half a million home foreclosures is correct, then Baltimore is in dire straits. To Mayor Sheila Dixon's credit, she saw the city's responsibility to Baltimore's citizens. The problems that lay in the wake of the credit crisis were not going to be solved by individuals, even those as determined as Anjanette Booker. The problems were structural, with impacts that were citywide and thus deserved a systemic solution. In January 2010, U.S. District Court judge J. Frederick Motz, himself a Baltimore native, dismissed the city's claim in a decision that allowed the mayor and city council to refile their complaint against the bank.[10]

For five seasons, ending in early 2008, the city's conditions were played out in *The Wire,* an HBO television series created by a former *Baltimore Sun* reporter, David Simon. The program's content—impending crises in education and housing, corruption, capitalist greed, crime, drugs, high rates of AIDS, racial unrest—foreshadowed Judge Motz's appraisal that Baltimore's troubles went well beyond Wells Fargo's actions.

I was nearing the tenth anniversary of my home purchase in Massachusetts when the news of Baltimore's legal response to the foreclosure crisis came to light. Fortunately for me, my neighborhood remained stable throughout the period when many in the state were in distress. As a woman who had bought my home on my own, I was troubled about the number of single women whose savings and dreams had been lost when the housing market collapsed. As a civil rights advocate, I was encouraged by the use of civil rights law to bring some justice to the communities that appeared to have been targeted by unscrupulous lenders. As a professor, I was anxious to use the Baltimore case in my class at Brandeis University, where I taught graduate students about the role of law in advancing social justice.

My students found the case intriguing as well. But as young people raised in an era after the gender and civil rights laws revolutionized individuals' ability to purchase homes, they were more skeptical than I was. The critical question they raised, and which has not been satisfactorily addressed, is whether any of the individuals who had suffered at the hands of lenders would benefit from an award of damages to the City of Baltimore. In reality, the true losers in this conflict may have left the area entirely, and many who remained are unlikely to be able to buy again, assuming the city reinvests in neighborhoods. They didn't blame the residents for not suing the bank themselves. If those buyers were too destitute to afford their mortgages, they were unlikely to have the resources to sue one of the largest banks in the country. Yet how effective successful individual litigants might be in encouraging systemic change is uncertain.

I was struck by the hard reality my students' questions brought me to confront. That reality led me to yet another question about the adequacy of laws to establish and protect rights. Though critical, the protections against racial discrimination in lending articulated in the laws were not enough to protect the individuals in Baltimore, and possibly not even their communities. Though Baltimore was indeed working to restore its neighborhoods, these buyers' inability to find a place they could call home preceded the "subprime lending spree."

Moreover, as a country, we cannot continue to urge home ownership as a path to citizenship and equality without directly addressing the disparities in women's income, as well as the problems Judge Motz highlights. The crisis is not limited to Baltimore, nor to African American women, and its reach is broader than communities of color throughout the country. It is a catastrophe whose roots are deeper than the recent housing market meltdown—it is a crisis in the meaning attached to home itself, for millions of people who have lost their largest tangible asset and even for many who have not. And resolution of this larger dilemma requires us to examine our fundamental understanding of what it takes to make sure people are able to enjoy home as both a place and a state of being.

CHAPTER SEVEN

Home in Crisis

Americans on the Outside of the Dream

The American Dream: A dream of a social order in which each
man and each woman shall be . . . recognized by others for what they
are, regardless of the fortuitous circumstances of birth or position.

J. T. Adams, *The Epic of America* (1931)[1]

In the months, now years, since the 2008 front-page story chronicling
Anjanette Booker's troubles, the whole world has come to understand and
appreciate the depths of the financial crisis that Booker's situation fore-
told. Throughout that year, headline after headline described the growing recession, then warned against a possible depression with potential
to match the one that followed the 1929 stock market crash. In time, the
intensity of the reporting leveled off, as financial institutions were bailed
out and salvaged and the structure of our system was restored. By the end
of 2010 many market economists were satisfied with the assessment that
the financial industry had rebounded. And even if labor economists were
not so sanguine about the fact that unemployment was well above the
levels of a healthy economy, they were hopeful that with the right policies
and public investment, jobs would return. But one large piece of the economic puzzle—housing—remained in jeopardy. Indeed, Dean Baker of
the Center for Economic and Policy Research posited that it would take
twenty years torecover the six-trillion-dollar loss in housing wealth that
occurred between 2005 and 2010.

For me, that revelation spells more than a crisis in the housing market; it signifies a crisis in home, one that threatens our country's belief
in its promises of fairness and prosperity for generations to come. At the
heart of the crisis is the ideological disconnect between home as a basic

element of the American Dream and pathway to equality, and home as a market product. This disconnect is not new. In fact, it has arguably existed since President Hoover enlisted bankers and developers to help promote home ownership as a route to citizenship. Nor does the philosophical dissonance fully explain the disastrous consequences of the housing market collapse. But in the turn-of-the-century housing market, that discord was combined with the human disconnect between borrowers and financial speculators. The market responded by introducing complex, and ultimately valueless, mortgage-based securities that were entirely removed from the houses themselves and even from the basic mortgage instruments that secured them. In short, for many, the American home—along with our dreams for it—was bundled and reduced to what turned out to be worthless paper.

Before the collapse of what the congressionally empanelled Financial Crisis Inquiry Commission (FCIC) called the "mortgage security pipeline," the nation's leading financial institutions created increasingly complex forms of mortgage-backed securities that they sold to pension fund managers, among many other investors in this country, and ultimately to buyers around the globe. According to one executive testifying before the FCIC, the pipeline "functioned fine until one day when it just didn't." That is to say, "speculators who flipped houses . . . mortgage brokers who scouted the loans . . . lenders who issued the mortgages . . . [and] financial firms that created the mortgage-backed securities" all profited, off-loading the risk to the next person in line, until the bubble burst and homeowners could no longer pay their mortgages.[2]

Between now and the end of the twenty-year recovery period that Dean Baker predicts, there will doubtless be numerous reports on financial market disconnect between home loans and collateralized debt instruments. In fact, a 576-page report issued in January 2011 by the FCIC casts blame on presidents Bill Clinton and George W. Bush, financial regulators, and Wall Street for what it is calling an "avoidable" disaster. There are likely to be calls for more, less, and different forms of regulation of the banking industry. But what should not be lost in the policymakers' ensuing conversations is the human and ideological disconnects that are central to the tragedy and that, in part, explain why the "subprime meltdown" could not be contained. A glimpse inside the string of lawsuits filed against banks provides us with a picture of how that human and spiritual antipathy resulted in an enormous crisis of home as a place and a state of being.

"THOSE PEOPLE"

As the mortgage meltdown went into full force, hundreds in Baltimore saw their American Dream vanish. Hundreds of homes went into foreclosure, and a host of associated costs began to pile up. Nevertheless, United States District Court Judge J. Frederick Motz viewed with skepticism the city leaders' lawsuit aimed at recovering some of Baltimore's losses. In January 2010, Motz, a Baltimore native, dismissed the claim, citing "other factors leading to the deterioration of the inner city, such as extensive unemployment, lack of educational opportunity and choice, irresponsible parenting, disrespect for the law, widespread drug use, and violence."[3] Judge Motz's critics would attribute his remarks to his background in law enforcement or what many had long perceived as conservative, probusiness leanings. Over the course of his career in the legal profession, Motz had served as both assistant U.S. attorney and U.S. attorney for the District of Maryland. President Reagan had appointed him to the federal bench in 1985. As a judge, he had heard a number of high-profile cases involving the likes of the Microsoft and Wal-Mart corporations. His "probusiness" label came from a decision he rendered in favor of the latter in a case that challenged Maryland's legislative attempt to require large employers to provide health care for their employees. Motz's choice of language in the Wells Fargo case echoed the political rhetoric of the man who put him on the court.[4] The federal judge concluded that the bulk of the problems alleged in Baltimore's litigation against Wells Fargo Bank were due not to the bank's actions but to flawed government policies ("lack of educational opportunity and choice"), individual neglect ("irresponsible parenting"), or criminal activity ("widespread drug use, and violence").

Judge Motz's observations can't be chalked up to politics entirely. As a prosecutor and a judge, he was perfectly positioned to observe what happened in the city. Frederick J. Motz had lived in Baltimore most of his life. For eight years, during some of the city's most troubled times, he had been a member of the advisory commission for the City of Baltimore's Department of Social Services. Judge Motz, like *The Wire* creator David Simon, portrays a city that few could love.

Mayor Sheila Dixon, a former public school teacher and Baltimore native, knew her city as well as either the judge or the television writer. Dixon's website described her as a "champion of neighborhoods," and she ran for office as a promoter of gender equality. During the first year of her term as mayor, she carried out her vision for the city with the help of individuals, community organizers, business people, and developers who shared her "passionate interest in improving" Baltimore's livability.

Dixon appeared undaunted by the small-screen version of her hometown when she brought the suit against Wells Fargo. But a year later, Dixon's own legal troubles surfaced. In December 2009 a jury convicted Sheila Dixon of embezzlement stemming from her personal use of six hundred dollars' worth of Target and Best Buy gift cards that had been donated by a prominent local developer for the use of impoverished residents. In a year that saw a number of political figures embroiled in sex scandals, it may come as no surprise that the local developer, who agreed to testify against the mayor, and Dixon—both single—were once romantically linked. None of this served the image and reputation of Baltimore or its inhabitants, many of whom supported Sheila Dixon throughout her trial. Following her conviction, Dixon resigned as mayor. In February 2010, veteran politician Stephanie Rawlings-Blake took over the job of leading the troubled city. Baltimore had taken a blow and was in recovery with Rawlings-Blake at the helm.

Baltimore's leadership was stable, but the challenges the Wells Fargo lawsuit exposed were not so quickly resolved. The foreclosure nightmare continued. Judge Motz had concluded that the collapse of the housing market in the city was the inevitable result of years of urban decline. Motz's words amounted to a sweeping pronouncement that Baltimore's black neighborhoods were destined to fail. Indeed, for decades prior to the subprime era, many Baltimore neighborhoods were notorious for high crime rates and communicable disease outbreaks. Some would declare them dysfunctional. Yet they had never completely collapsed as they did under the weight of the mortgage meltdown. Was it realistic to believe that such massive disintegration could be attributed to preexisting conditions in a few neighborhoods? Presumably, homeowners held titles to structures with some market value; landlords still collected rents; and the city continued to assess taxes on the properties in even the most troubled areas. And neither any of the city's leadership problems nor the decline in Baltimore neighborhoods should have given Wells Fargo a free pass to exploit Baltimore's residents.

One might read Judge Motz's assessment as an attempt to distinguish blighted neighborhoods from other Baltimore communities that still had some chance of weathering the foreclosure storm. Taken in this light, in giving the city leave to refile against the bank after dismissing the first complaint, Judge Motz may have been engaging in a bit of judicial triaging, encouraging the city's legal counsel to narrow its claim to neighborhoods whose circumstances were less notorious. But in its second amended complaint, the city chose another route. In essence, the new pleadings alleged that Wells targeted poor black men and women in distressed communities *because* they were in the throes of crisis and were individuals desperate for credit. The attorneys set about to convince the court that Wells Fargo had siphoned off the equity left in the residences of down-and-out neighborhoods and left those communities to perish along with the rest of the municipality.

The City of Baltimore's attorneys reasserted that "Wells Fargo's discriminatory practices, and the resulting unnecessary foreclosures in the city's minority neighborhoods, [had] inflicted significant, direct, and continuing financial harm on Baltimore."[5] This time the city's claims were more circumspect, but its allegations of deliberate bank wrongdoing directed at black neighborhoods were still detailed and damning. Baltimore introduced into the record statements from former bank employees about training they had received that helped them sell loans in poor, primarily African American neighborhoods throughout Maryland. One *New York Times* article quoted a Wells Fargo bank officer, Elizabeth Jacobson, describing the bank's "emerging-markets unit that specifically targeted black churches, because it figured church leaders had a lot of influence and could convince congregants to take out subprime loans."[6] In her affidavit submitted by the City of Baltimore in its amended complaint, Ms. Jacobson attested to a consistent pattern of steering black loan applicants to subprime loans, even though they may have qualified for conventional loans at lower interest rates. Jacobson even admitted that loan officers would tell the bank's underwriting department that applicants who had been steered to subprime loans did not want to file proper documents that would qualify the customers for prime rates.

In the heat of the meltdown, commentators would question what kind of individuals enter into potentially disastrous loans, loans that they could not possibly repay once teaser rates expired. As I read the allegations in the Baltimore suit, I began to ask what kind of persons would *market* these kinds of products to homeowners. But that approach puts undue emphasis on the individual participants. Although it is admittedly tempting to demonize Jacobson and her fellow agents, the problems that led to the lawsuit were systemic. The more revealing inquiry looks into the atmosphere that existed inside banks and the banking industry as the subprime crisis brewed. The environment was one that, from top to bottom, fostered detachment. And my conclusion is that there were agents who were given financial incentives to make high-risk loans while simultaneously being encouraged to disengage from borrowers and the neighborhoods in which the borrowers lived. Reportedly, Wells Fargo also gave lavish gifts and trips to successful subprime loan officers.

Parts of Jacobson's declarations and those of Tony Paschal (another Wells Fargo employee) read like instructions for how to marginalize customers based on where they live and skin color. The two reported that "subprime loan officers described African-American and other minority customers by saying 'those people have bad credit' and 'those people don't pay their bills,' and by calling minority customers 'mud people' and 'niggers.'"[7] Paschal reported hearing fellow employees refer to "loans in minority communities as 'ghetto loans.'"[8] Elizabeth Jacobson was an extremely productive lender: in a span of three years, she reportedly sold more than fifty million dollars' worth of subprime loans in Baltimore's black communities.

Wells Fargo also relied on brokers, who would take loan applications from potential borrowers and shop the papers to a number of lenders. These independent brokers sometimes earned as much as $15,000 in commission on $130,000 loans. Even when brokers knew the borrowers or knew the neighborhoods, they rarely had any idea of the terms the lenders ultimately offered Baltimore residents. Brokers never evaluated borrowers. Their job was to fill out the forms, and Wells Fargo exercised stunningly little oversight over how they accomplished that task.

And just what were the consequences of the bank's purported "subprime lending spree"? According to the lawsuit filed by the city, subprime loans led to foreclosures, and foreclosures led to abandoned properties. Baltimore's housing department has had to board up scores of vacant homes, stabilize properties that threatened public safety, and condemn some others that could not be boarded and stabilized. The crisis has strained public safety resources, as police and fire departments have had to step up efforts to respond to incidents related to unoccupied homes. It is clear that the fallout is citywide, not limited to geographically or racially distinct neighborhoods, when public safety costs and losses in tax revenues attributed to the foreclosures are taken into account. Although Baltimore was once nicknamed Charm City, if the projection of nearly half a million home foreclosures is correct, its lure may be a long time returning. And sometimes lost in the talk about lost tax revenues and police and fire department expenditures are the individuals who had no part in the subprime market debacle but are left behind in impacted neighborhoods. Some remaining residents are at the mercy of squatters who take up residence in foreclosed and unsellable properties as close as next door.

BEGINNING TO SEE A PATTERN

Skeptics might conclude that the situation in Baltimore was an anomaly. And even with the evidence against Wells Fargo, it's uncertain exactly what part of the problem in Baltimore was the fault of that one lender. Judge Motz dismissed the City of Baltimore's second complaint against Wells Fargo too. "Theoretically, the city does have viable claims if it can prove property specific injuries inflicted upon it at properties that would not have been vacant but for improper loans made by Wells Fargo," he wrote. " In the interest of justice," Judge Motz gave the city "leave to file a third amended complaint."[9] Nevertheless, the dismissal casts doubt on whether Wells Fargo will ever be held liable for the problems in Baltimore.

But when other public officials began raising claims, questions about Wells Fargo's behavior got more intense. Were the practices alleged in the Baltimore lawsuit the product of rogue loan officers, or of local—

or even headquarters—Wells management, or were they the way business was done throughout the industry? In March 2008, Illinois attorney general Lisa Madigan gave two lenders, Countrywide and Wells Fargo, a chance to explain what she described as the "alarming" disparities "between the home loans sold to white borrowers and those sold to African American and Latino borrowers."[10] Madigan's investigation looked into disparities in the issuance of "high-cost" loans—those that were three percentage points above the U.S. Treasury standard—which performed in ways similar to subprime loans. The attorney general had been tipped off to the problem by an investigation conducted by the *Chicago Reporter*, a monthly investigative news magazine. In a study of loans issued in 2003, the *Reporter* found that African Americans, even those with six-figure salaries, were far more likely to get subprime loans than whites or Asians and that the preponderance of those loans were given out in black and Latino neighborhoods. High-cost loans made up 64 percent of all the loans Wells Fargo made to blacks and 50 percent of the loans Countrywide gave to blacks. Comparable figures for Wells Fargo's and Countrywide's white borrowers were 17 and 20 percent, respectively.

In October 2008 Madigan's office settled with Countrywide, which by then had been bought by Bank of America. The State of Illinois was granted both injunctive and prospective relief, including an agreement that qualifying borrowers might have their loans modified. In July 2009 the attorney general announced a lawsuit against Wells Fargo Bank. The bank was once again accused of targeting black communities. And in the Illinois case, Latinos were also allegedly preyed upon for subprime loans. "As a result of its discriminatory and illegal mortgage lending practices, Wells Fargo transformed our cities' predominantly African-American and Latino neighborhoods into ground zero for subprime lending," said Madigan. "The dreams of many hardworking families have ended in foreclosure due to Wells Fargo's illegal and unfair conduct."[11] This lawsuit continued even after Madigan's office settled another claim against Wells Fargo over allegedly deceptive marketing of extremely risky loans. The costs of foreclosures in Chicago specifically are social and economic, with borrowers, their neighbors, local businesses, and the city all paying a price.

Where the complaint in the Baltimore suit gives one a sense of sub-prime lenders' predatory assaults on the African American community, the Illinois complaint does that and more. It chronicles the growth of sub-prime lending practices nationwide and the parallel expansion of Wells Fargo's role in it. Madigan's filing gives insight into how the subprime mortgage market grew—both because of larger immediate returns and because bankers assumed that securities backed by subprime mortgages would perform in the same way as those backed by prime mortgages. The court documents state that Wells Fargo undertook an aggressive growth strategy and, according to one bank employee, "wanted to be the number one lender in all markets it served and wanted to serve all markets."[12] One employee maintained that Wells Fargo's goal was to have the subprime lending division cover the fixed costs of all the bank's operations.

In time, as the company vigorously pursued its fast-paced growth, the market for subprimes grew. According to the Illinois complaint, subprime mortgage lending increased from $35 billion to $625 billion between 1994 and 2005. By 2003 Wells Fargo's subprime lending totaled $16.5 billion, and by 2007 Wells was the eighth largest subprime lender, by loan volume, in the nation. At roughly the same time, Wells Fargo was the Chicago area's second-largest lender by volume, making over twelve thousand high-cost loans. The complaint suggests a culture inside the bank that was dominated by subprime loans. The bank set quotas for the number of subprime or high-cost loans "every area had to close" and "kept scorecards" that recorded managers' subprime loan tallies.[13]

In 2009 the City of Memphis filed a suit against Wells Fargo Bank. Allegations mirror those in the cases coming out of Baltimore and the State of Illinois. Wells Fargo denies the allegations of the plaintiffs in these suits. In addition to existing urban woes, they blame the foreclosure problem on borrowers themselves.

Indeed, by 2000 a number of cultural and economic factors had fueled a passion for home ownership among single black women. In the popular press, *Essence* magazine ran a campaign for home ownership. Even the *Economist*, a magazine that caters to middle-class and business readers, promoted owning a home as a way for black women to live the American Dream. In fact, since the mid-1990s, even the gap between black and white unemployment rates, a historically persistent and seemingly intractable problem, had been shrinking. Apparently unaware of the dramatic rise in subprime lending, the *Economist* reported:

> The growth in home ownership both drives and feeds off continued gains in wealth. The University of Georgia's Selig Center for Economic Growth says that black buying power has increased steadily across the country, from $318 billion in 1990 to $723 billion in 2004 and a projected $965 billion in 2009. At a time when every American seems to be paying for his credit-card debts with home-equity loans, blacks have (for better or worse) joined the party, helped partly by the fact that many mortgage firms now rely more on color-blind computers than on sniffy clerks to check up on applicants.[14]

But when lenders began targeting black and Latino communities for subprime loans, the positive effect of computerized processing went out the window. Race and ethnicity were reembedded in the process in a way that no computer could deflect.

In 2006 Corey Booker, the dynamic and popular mayor of Newark, New Jersey, advocated home ownership as "a critical step, especially [for] those [families] headed by a single parent, in breaking the cycle of violence and poverty."[15] Not-for-profit agencies set up seminars in Newark to show women how they could make home ownership a reality despite high interest rates and poor credit ratings. And why not? At the end of an era when the political message to those in poverty was to take personal responsibility, how better to evidence responsibility than to invest in their own neighborhoods and put a roof over their children's heads. In the mid-1990s President Bill Clinton had used the rhetoric of personal responsibility and economic prosperity in reforming welfare and in his National Homeownership Strategy, which was introduced by a document subtitled "Partners in the American Dream." Following in Clinton's footsteps, President George W. Bush and Alan Greenspan, the longtime Federal Reserve chairman, also promoted the idea of home ownership in both rhetoric and policy. In 2003, when housing prices were beginning to spike, Bush introduced the American Dream Downpayment Initiative, promising that the law would help Americans realize the dream of home ownership and help close the gap between "minority households and the rest of the country" in that regard.[16]

Nevertheless, none of the leaders, conservative or liberal, seemed aware of what was happening in the financial industry. Bush and lenders encouraged potential purchasers to "buy high" with the promise that housing values would continue to climb. Builders and developers responded. The average size of new single-family homes increased from around 2,000 square feet in 1992 to 2,241 square feet in 1999, then to over 2,500 square feet in 2006. Understandably, buyers spent more on new homes. The average-size home in 1999 cost $195,600. By 2006, in order to get the average home a buyer would have to come up with $305,900. Average household income enjoyed some growth, but it wasn't steady and didn't keep pace with the cost of housing. During this period of steeply rising home costs and inconsistent income growth, the number of subprime and high-cost loans spiraled upward.

Whether Baltimore or Memphis or the State of Illinois will be able to prove that Wells Fargo or any other bank targeted minority neighborhoods and violated fair housing laws remains to be determined. Nevertheless, the U.S. Department of Housing and Urban Development's analysis of data available under the Home Mortgage Disclosure Act (HMDA) suggests that in the late 1990s, a potentially calamitous situation existed in black neighborhoods. HUD's analysis of the situation in Baltimore, for example, pointed out the following facts:

1. As reported in HMDA, the number of subprime refinance loans originated in Baltimore increased over ten-fold between 1993 and 1998. . . .
2. Subprime loans are seven times more likely in low-income neighborhoods in Baltimore than in upper-income neighborhoods. . . .
3. Subprime loans are six times more likely in predominantly black neighborhoods in Baltimore than in white neighborhoods. . . .
4. Homeowners in middle-income predominantly black neighborhoods in Baltimore are almost four times as likely as homeowners in middle-income white neighborhoods to have subprime loans. . . .

5. The findings are similar when borrowers (rather than neighborhoods) throughout the Baltimore metropolitan area are examined. . . .

6. Like originations, the subprime share of foreclosures is highest in low-income and predominantly black neighborhoods.[17]

In the HUD's own words, Baltimore's African American residents bore an "unequal burden" of the burgeoning high-cost and subprime mortgage product market. Baltimore's attorneys have filed for the third time in the suit against Wells Fargo in an effort to persuade the court of the merit of the discrimination claim. Will the numbers ultimately speak for themselves? An attorney in both the Baltimore and Memphis suits explained to a Memphis newspaper why the data reveal disparities that are, absent racial targeting, hard to explain: "Wells [Fargo] is getting it eight times more wrong in the black community than in the white community [in Memphis]. . . . That just can't happen in and of itself. What it means is they're making loans they know at the time can't succeed. Or they're pricing people beyond their means or too high."[18]

AN INDUSTRY ICON

As a consequence of the lawsuits, borrowers in Baltimore, Memphis, and Illinois have come to represent one end of the spectrum in the human drama of the subprime market. Agents like Jacobson and Paschal fit somewhere in the scheme, as do their supervisors and brokers, in some instances. However, if the bank could be reduced to a symbol of one person, it would have to be Wells's former CEO, Richard M. Kovacevich.

Kovacevich began his ascent in the banking world from an executive position in consumer operations at Citibank. From that spot, he went on to become second-in-command and then CEO (in 1993) at Norwest Corporation, a Minnesota banking operation with a large mortgage subsidiary. In 1998 Norwest, which was already a national player in the mortgage lending and consumer finance markets, merged with Wells Fargo, the nearly 150-year-old California corporation. Kovacevich called it the "most successful large merger in banking history."[19] Although by some reports the Minnesota company acquired Wells Fargo, Norwest took the Wells Fargo name.

With the merger, Kovacevich climbed from number 206 in *Forbes* magazine's annual ranking of executive pay in 1999 to number 7 in 2004. In 2005, during the apex of subprime and high-cost lending, his total compensation was $53.1 million, which put him in the number 12 spot on the Forbes list of all executives and number 1 among his banking peers.

While Kovacevich was the banking world's top money maker, the financial industry traded in more and increasingly risky credit products, including over-the-counter derivatives, which financial wizard Warren Buffett viewed as "financial weapons of mass destruction" and "time bombs, both for the parties that deal in them and the economic system."[20] A Brookings Institute paper concludes that 2005–2006 was the period when the bulk of the precarious loans were issued to consumers.[21] The following year, although his *Forbes* ranking dropped, Kovacevich garnered $7 million in bonuses. When he resigned, precipitously, as chief executive in 2007, handing over the reins of Wells Fargo's "stagecoach" to John G. Stumpf, Richard Kovacevich was considered one of the top bank executives in the country.

Early in October 2008, Kovacevich, as chairman of Wells Fargo's board of directors, announced the bank's intent to acquire Wachovia, proclaiming the agreement as an "outstanding opportunity" for, among others, "the U.S. government and the banking industry." In his words, Wachovia's "outstanding customer service and their highest standards of community leadership are identical to [Wells Fargo's] own values." Less than a month later, Wells Fargo, on the brink of collapse along with other major banks, received $25 billion in assistance from the federal government. Within weeks the Wachovia merger was finalized, creating, as the heading on the firm's news release proclaimed, "North America's Most Extensive Financial Services Company, Coast-to-Coast in Community Banking."[22]

On October 21, 2008, just days after Congress voted to bail out Wells Fargo, Richard Kovacevich spoke to the Commonwealth Club in San Francisco about the era of banking that matched his career. He explained to the audience, almost apologetically, that his remarks had been prepared before the collapse of the banking industry. By his own admission, what Kovacevich had to say reflected the industry's boom mentality. He described the banking business before 1985 as boring: bankers paid

3 percent interest on deposits, charged 6 percent for loans, and were "on the golf course by 3:00 p.m." According to the former bank executive, an "exciting" industry period followed, marked by "unprecedented" growth enabled by deregulation, technology, and nonbank competition.[23]

During this lauded period, bank assets rose from billions to trillions. And why not? President George W. Bush touted the country's economic growth as a defining feature of his presidency. Not only was home ownership thought to be good for business—the banking business in particular—but it may also have been considered to have political benefits, as homeowners were assumed to prefer more conservative policies than renters.

Years earlier, Greenspan had revealed his inclination to allow unfettered economic expansion. Along with Clinton appointees Robert Rubin and Lawrence Summers, the fed chief publicly rebuked Brooksley Born, chair of the Commodity Futures Trading Commission. Born had proposed that her agency reexamine the way it regulated over-the-counter derivatives, the devices that ultimately enabled the industry's explosive growth. In a bold move, Greenspan, Rubin, and Summers convinced Congress to strip Born's agency of its authority to investigate, let alone regulate, the derivatives market. Even the independent watchdogs seemed to have caught the fever. Independent rating agencies Moody's, Standard & Poor's, and Fitch put "their stamp of approval" on the uncertain deals, the Financial Crisis Inquiry Commission later said. And media watchers have since accused the business press of being too cozy with the financial institutions that ultimately brought about the financial crisis. Even in the down market, the reality television show *Flip This House*, which premiered in 2005, declared that "flipping houses is the most tried-and-true way to make a fortune in real estate."

In his presentation to a relatively friendly crowd, Kovacevich, the retired executive, spoke volumes in what he said and what he didn't say. Missing from his prepared remarks was any mention of the human factors that came to play in the rise of banking in the country, especially as they related to the mortgage industry in which Wells Fargo was a major player.

Kovacevich was only slightly more reflective a few months later when, in reference to the financial crisis, the organizers of his 2008 Commonwealth talk asked him to explain, as he put it, "what the hell happened."

Without pointing the finger in the direction of any one person, he laid the blame on greed, unchecked by regulatory authorities or the safety valves that rating agencies were suppose to provide. Kovacevich's abstract appraisal still made no mention of the human costs of the industry's transgressions or the monetary impact on communities and cities, as alleged by the three suits that Wells Fargo was defending against. To his credit, Kovacevich acknowledged the tragedy. But his lens still focused on the industry. Perhaps a banking executive who drew millions in bonuses lacks perspective in formulating a solution for those who lost homes. His mea culpa still demonstrated the financial world's lack of affinity with its first-line customers and even its sales force.

Don't think for a moment that Wells Fargo was the only participant in the fleecing of borrowers. Brian Kabateck, a lawyer for the NAACP, will quickly remind anyone that the problem is industry-wide. Although the merger with Norwest placed Wells Fargo ahead of all other lenders in the number of residential mortgage loans it originated and serviced, Wells Fargo was responsible for only a portion of the subprime market. By 2006 a number of major banks—including Bank of America, Countrywide, and Citicorp—and smaller banks that specialized in subprime loans were in this lucrative market. Over 25 percent of home purchase loans made in 2006 were subprime loans. And that same year, 31 percent of mortgage refinancing was made on subprime terms.

Kabateck will also be happy to tell you that the organization he represents was one of the first to detect the market practice that would ultimately drain massive amounts of cash from homeowners and would-be homeowners. In early 2007 Kabateck, whose consumer practice goes back to the late 1990s, met with leaders in some of the country's top banks. Surprisingly, according to Kabateck, they were happy to discuss the claims that the NAACP raised about faulty lending practices. General counsels, vice presidents, and diversity representatives from several banks were quick to acknowledge that racial steering and reverse redlining were, in fact, happening. While neither of the banks Kabateck met with acknowledged its own participation in those activities, each was quick to say that other banks definitely engaged in it.[24]

In July 2007, the NAACP announced its own lawsuit against Wells Fargo. Other suits followed. The subprime lending debacle has led to a sea of litigation. In all, the class action suits brought by the NAACP included thirteen more lenders: Ameriquest, Fremont Investment, Option One Mortgage (H&R Block), WMC Mortgage, Countrywide, Long Beach Mortgage, Citigroup, BNC Mortgage, Accredited Home Lenders, Encore Credit (Bear Stearns), First Franklin, HSBC, and Washington Mutual. The cases in Baltimore, Memphis, and Illinois, along with the class action suits filed by the NAACP, attest to the fact that a whole host of lenders may have engaged in destructive practices. On behalf of the NAACP, Kabateck has negotiated settlements with a number of the banks, including Wells Fargo. Wells Fargo's subprime lending was not unique, nor was it limited to a few communities; but by 2007, as the number-one bank in the subprime market, it had become the industry leader, for good or for bad.

GRANNY HUNTING

News in the popular press about the expansion of subprime and predatory lending and the subsequent housing crisis caused me both intellectual and emotional disquiet. As the collapse unfolded, much of the coverage of the devastating effects of the housing debacle focused on its disproportionate impact on minority communities. For example, in October 2007, television cameras followed as the chairman of the House Financial Services Committee, Congressman Barney Frank of Massachusetts, held a public hearing in Roxbury, a predominantly black and Latino neighborhood in Boston. And the *Boston Globe* reported on the findings of housing analyst Jim Campen, who determined that while just 9 percent of white borrowers making more than $152,000 per year received high-interest loans, 71 percent of African Americans and 56 percent of Latinos in the same income bracket were victims of predatory lending.

Yet as the problem grew, the losses attributable to blight in select neighborhoods did not account for the full extent of the mortgage crisis in Boston, let alone nationwide. No major bank could have supported the kind of expansion that Wells Fargo and Countrywide were supporting by lending only to poor minority communities. As I began to look at the problem, I found ample evidence that the problem was a lot more complex than Judge Motz's assessment or even the racial discrimination outlined by the suits in Baltimore, Memphis, and Illinois. Predatory lending may have been launched in minority communities, and Wells Fargo may have been a major player in the market, but the enormity of the crisis suggested a much larger base for the practice than the three suits and the popular press covered. My work in social policy and my interest in women's economic gains suggested that something more was happening. I quickly reached the conclusion that the full breadth of the subprime lending debacle could be explained only through an examination of the gender dimensions of the discriminatory practices.

Why and how did the crisis swell beyond African American and Latino communities? Over time, I pieced together the gender dynamics of subprime lending practices that enabled the spread. I had followed home purchasing trends and knew that a large percentage of recent new home buyers were women on their own. Stories began to appear in both the trade and popular press heralding an increase in the number of women buying homes on their own. As early as 2004, Blanche Evans, writing for the trade publication *Realty Times,* noted what she called a "subtle but seismic shift in the demographics of homebuyers." Simply put, women weren't waiting for marriage to buy houses. Data from Harvard University's Joint Center for Housing Studies backed Evans's observation. Single women were a fast-growing segment in the home-buying market. Moreover, the value of the homes they purchased in a little over a three-year period at the turn of the twenty-first century added up to more than $550 billion. And single women typically entered the market with less money than either unmarried men or married couples.[25]

With so many new female entrants into what had become an aggressive lending market at the height of the home-buying boom, I knew that there was something absent from the telling of the stories of home loss. I suspected that in reporting race bias in the subprime market, gender discrimination was being overlooked. Given that neighborhoods were being targeted, geography helped policy makers, like Frank, and reporters to identify racial disparities. Gender bias was more diffuse, at least geographically, and maybe even harder for interested parties to detect. And masking or ignoring gender issues wasn't new; in 2005 the press had paid little attention to the inordinate impact that Hurricane Katrina had on women and their families, even though the number of households in New Orleans with children under eighteen headed by women alone far outnumbered the households headed by married couples or men alone. Given the history of gender discrimination in the extension of credit and property ownership, it was not difficult for me to imagine its presence in the mortgage crisis.

Even as Marilyn Kennedy Melia, a *Chicago Tribune* finance contributor, was chronicling the rise in single women home buyers, she was cautious. Melia's article advised women to avoid eroding home equity "as lenders aggressively market equity lines of credit and equity loans" and to be wary of adjustable-rate mortgages where "the interest rate could jump later, and they will then struggle to afford payments."[26]

As word of the rise in subprime and high-cost loans spread, the Consumer Federation of America started to expand its research to look at how women in and out of minority neighborhoods were faring in the mortgage market. In December 2006, the fifty-year-old advocacy group reported on a study of over four million mortgage loans in 350 metropolitan areas in 2005. Whether purchasing or refinancing homes, women were overrepresented in the subprime lending market. In some categories, women were almost twice as likely as their male counterparts to get subprime loans.

Elderly women may have been particularly vulnerable. Women, on average, live longer than men and have a greater chance of living alone and being on fixed incomes for longer periods. Rising property taxes and other economic and social realities make elderly women particularly susceptible to abusive home mortgage lending practices that promise ready cash in exchange for second mortgages. Older female homeowners are overrepresented in the subprime refinance market, often losing the equity they have built up in their homes. According to Nina Simon, formerly of the AARP, at least one broker put the pursuit of older women borrowers in blunt terms: "It's time to go granny hunting!"[27]

Ironically, higher-income women received less favorable terms than their white male counterparts on home purchase, refinance, and home improvement loans. The tactics agents employed with high-end borrowers fit the target. According to Brian Kabateck, lenders were eager to advise homeowners to cash in on home equity in order to show their success. A bigger home, a three-car versus two-car garage, new vehicles to fill it, a boat, a second home—all became symbols of the achievement of the American Dream that brokers and lending agents sold.

In 2003, four years into my own mortgage, I responded to the slew of invitations to refinance that lined my mailbox weekly. For thirteen years I had taught contracts and commercial law. I had written about consumer bankruptcy. I was equipped with a vocabulary that would, at the very least, keep me from getting into too much trouble. Nevertheless, I placed the call to my current mortgage holder with trepidation. In my mind, familiarity made my current lender somehow less risky than the hosts of other banks that offered me the chance to "lower my monthly payments" by taking advantage of "historically low rates of interest." Of course, like most borrowers who refinance, I really wanted to pay less than I was currently paying in interest each month.

Over three hours later, I ended the telephone conversation nursing a colossal headache. Nevertheless, I had negotiated a much lower monthly payment, albeit one that could escalate seven years later. Perhaps it was my tenacity, but the agent never suggested a subprime loan. That he offered me only conventional terms may also have been due to my unwillingness to accept the rates he originally offered and to my demand for a cap on the rate adjustments. There was no need for me to add "extra funds" onto the existing loan. I didn't need a new car, furnace, or roof; didn't want a boat or second house; and didn't have children set to go to college. Yet even when the attorney from the bank's signing service showed up at my home with the forty-five legal-size pages of documents for me to sign, I wasn't altogether confident I had gotten the arrangements that I had agreed to over the telephone. Fortunately, the promised lower payments proved to be accurate.

A few years later, when the housing market began its downward spiral and the date on which my interest rates might adjust approached, I was at least thankful that my neighborhood had weathered the worst of the foreclosure crisis. Yet throughout the Boston area, many others fared far worse than I did. In October 2007, according to Attorney General Martha Coakley, weak or subprime credit had led to twenty-five thousand foreclosure actions in Massachusetts over the prior twelve months.

WHO TAKES OUT A SUBPRIME LOAN?

Since the practices of subprime and predatory lending were not limited to neighborhoods in distress, as had been initially suspected, it was clear that neither would the devastation from the meltdown. The pundits who assumed that the problem could be contained were sorely mistaken. But what the stories of blacks, Latinos, and all women had in common was that old-fashioned bias was a contributing factor to who got fleeced. Recall the statement made under oath by the former loan officer at CitiFinancial, the largest consumer financial company in the United States: "If someone appeared uneducated, inarticulate, was a minority, or was particularly old or young, I would try to include all the [extras at additional expense that] CitiFinancial offered." And women's expanded entry into the market just as new, high-cost, and extremely risky mortgage products were booming was a recipe for widespread disaster and, as a writer for *Women's eNews* put it, "crushed dreams." And Debbie Bocian of the Center for Responsible Lending helped to dispel some of the myths about subprime and high-cost lending—myths that many are tempted to believe—by directing me to information she gleaned from 2005 and 2006 Home Mortgage Disclosure Act (HMDA) data:

Myth #1: Subprime borrowers were mainly investors and speculators.
Fact: 90 percent of subprime and high-cost loans to women were for owner-occupied properties (88 percent for all borrowers).

Myth #2: Subprime borrowers got into trouble because they "bought too much house."
Fact: Only 44 percent of 2005–2006 subprime and high-cost loans for owner-occupied properties were for purchase—the rest were for refinance or home improvement loans.

In addition, for those who did purchase homes with subprime and high-cost loans, the loan amounts were modest. For women, median purchase loan = $140K, average = $181K.

For all subprime and high-cost loans, median purchase price = $145K, average = $186K—hardly the "McMansions" that have been highlighted in the media.[28]

Early on in the revelation of the crisis, many of us may have blamed the problem on greedy or irresponsible home buyers who were gaming the system to gain access to places they could not afford. But as we learned more about the enormity of the problem, a different picture emerged. Eventually the mainstream press revealed how female heads of households, whether living in communities of color or primarily white communities, were hit hardest by the burst in the housing bubble. The stability that home ownership promised to these women and their children had vanished. The combined impact of escalating payments and women's typically lower incomes is devastating, even as the housing market recovers. As a 2010 report by the Harvard Joint Center for Housing Studies suggests, "[T]he share of households spending more than half of their incomes on housing," which has always been a concern of single women, will likely escalate.[29] And in 2011, the press is reporting that even those who rent in devastated neighborhoods are at risk of having their belongings put out on the streets as landlords fail to meet mortgage payments.

The legal issue in the court cases is whether lenders targeted African Americans for toxic loans, and there is ample evidence that this is so. There is also evidence that women were targeted, though so far no major suit has been filed against lenders for gender discrimination. That this catastrophe came at a time when many Americans who had been left behind in their quest for the American Dream were starting to catch up makes it even more a crisis of the idea of home.

The issues facing women and people of color are not limited to those groups alone. Yet black women have a history of searching for a place to call home. In so many ways, they had been there before. In the past, black women watched as homes and farms were lost; they and their children were on the front lines of battles against discrimination. Even today they have stood up to keep their families and communities safe and have kept businesses open when patrons' dollars dwindled. African American women know from these experiences that the impact of today's disaster stretches beyond the immediate crisis for them and their extended families, reaching well into the future—that it is likely to set back generations to come by eating up savings for retirement and college.

Sandra Hines, a fifty-five-year-old black woman from Detroit, shared her story with the Applied Research Center for its 2009 report *Race and Recession*. The report's account of how Hines lost her home—which she, her parents, and her two sisters had moved into when Sandra was eighteen—sums up the crisis of home:

> "Our foreclosure was very brutal," she said. "They busted up my mother's antique furniture, our belongings that we had accumulated for 40 years." The sheriff padlocked the door, and the Hines family was evicted. "We lost the home our parents bought," she said. "Now we've lost all of it."
>
> When Hines's middle sister lost her job at General Motors last year, "the family fell on hard times, and we refinanced the house," said Hines. "But we had one of those [adjustable-rate mortgages], and the payment almost doubled. My sister wasn't able to keep it up." They received a notice informing them of their pending foreclosure.
>
> After their eviction, Hines's two sisters and her teenage niece moved into a rental. But shortly after, their landlord defaulted on his mortgage, and that house went into foreclosure, too. "We are facing double foreclosure," she said.[30]

In a video, Sandra Hines stands in front of the home she lost and speaks of her feelings of "uprootedness." This was supposed to be the home passed on to children and grandchildren. This was the place she imagined when she thought of "home." Her words have a familiar ring, reminding me of families a hundred years earlier in a place hundreds of miles away. I think of my grandparents, Henry and Ida Elliott, and their departure from Arkansas and the farm that they must have thought would one day pass to children and grandchildren. I think of the thousands of others like Hines and like the Elliotts, and I ponder whether African Americans have once again been called upon to reimagine their homes and reassess their gains toward equality. The fact that they are being joined by millions of other Americans of all races makes the prospect no less disquieting.

AN AWFULLY BIG MESS

A projected one million homes will be foreclosed on in 2011. What started in poor neighborhoods in Baltimore has spread to glitzy Las Vegas, to rust-belt Detroit, to coastline Florida, and to Katrina-ravaged New

Orleans. A virus first unleashed on poor, minority communities has become an all-embracing pandemic, infecting without regard for race, class, or geography. Whether foreclosures result from the default of subprime or prime loans, the crisis goes back to the "subprime lending spree" that Mayor Dixon complained about in 2008. Ultimately, "those people," "granny," and even women in all income brackets were not enough to feed the growth that bankers like Richard Kovacevich found "exciting." Condemning statements about people who "didn't pay their bills" became self-fulfilling prophesies for a whole host of folks. And the resulting problems are both legal and social, as enormous amounts of wealth have been drained from households throughout the country; no one can escape the consequences. The situation is, in the words of one Securities and Exchange Commission official, "an awfully big mess."[31] In its report *The State of Working America,* the Economic Policy Institute concluded:

> With the bursting of the housing bubble, the decline in the stock market, and the weakness of the labor market, household wealth has taken a substantial hit in the Great Recession. The median net worth of whites fell by around a third from 2004 to 2007, dropping from around $150,000 to around $100,000. The median wealth of blacks, historically much lower than that of whites, took an even bigger hit, dropping by over three-quarters, from around $10,000 to around $2,000.[32]

For many, J. T. Adams's definition of the American Dream, the "dream of a social order in which each man and each woman shall . . . be recognized by others for what they are, regardless of the fortuitous circumstances of birth or position," was eviscerated by the recent lending debacle and subsequent recession. Perhaps the hardest hit is the generation of children whose unfortunate circumstance is to be left homeless or in neighborhoods that are on the brink of complete dissolution. As a result of the housing crisis, everyone's belief in the promises of our democracy is shaken. To be effective, to restore that lost sense of both a place to call home and the state of being at home in our nation, our response must take into account persistent and pernicious biases that have destroyed the American Dream for so many and thereby weakened our democracy. At this point in our history, our collective reimagining of the American Dream should be led by the country's foremost symbol of racial progress and equality, Barack Obama. And he should begin this daunting task by responding not just to the foreclosure crisis but to the crisis of home, by facing squarely the thorny question of what it takes for *every* American to be at home in our great country.

CHAPTER EIGHT

Home at Last

Toward an Inclusive Democracy

Home: 1. A lens through which one can safely view the world.
2. A place where one's ideas, experiences, and work are seen as valuable
and one's body (physical being) and identity are welcome. 3. An ideal state
of being, as much as a place, which is reimagined for each generation.
A.H.

As distressing and seemingly endless as the current crisis of home is, we
can learn from it. But the critical lessons are the ones that will prevent
a similar crisis from happening again, not the ones that will offer short-
term solutions. As difficult as it may seem in the midst of crisis, we must
be willing to face some unattractive truths and ask some difficult questions. Through home ownership, we put a market value on the American
Dream and gave little thought to the larger meaning of home in America.
When the financial industry collapsed, many found themselves priced
out of a sense of safety, security, and being a part of American life. Others
not only lost those aspects of home, but also saw their pathway to equality vanish. In moving forward, we must address the bias and community
detachment at the heart of what Nobel Prize winner Joseph Stiglitz called
the "epicenter of the crisis": subprime mortgages.[1] At this juncture we
must ask ourselves and our leaders: Can we ever restore the place of the
home in the dream in our democracy? How can we make the American
Dream of having a place to which we belong a dream that is inclusive and
sustainable, both socially and economically? What vision of home will
replace our prevailing notions?

A NEW NARRATIVE

As we enter the second full decade of the twenty-first century, it is time for a new narrative, one whose central ideas are place and belonging. An ideology of mobility has prevailed throughout America's history. Women like Abigail Adams abandoned their loyalties to the places of their forebears and helped establish the United States, only to be left out of the U.S. Constitution. From the seventeenth century and the beginning of what historian Ira Berlin calls a "massive relocation" of Africans to the shores of the Virginia Colony, movement has characterized the black American experience.[2] Early in the twentieth century, as African Americans journeyed from the rural South to cities in the Midwest, in the Northeast, and on the West Coast, Booker T. Washington urged blacks to find equality in those new locations by establishing homes and becoming model neighbors. As the century advanced, women ventured outside the home to the public spheres of the workplace and political arenas in search of gender equality and economic freedom. Nannie Helen Burroughs demanded that women be allowed to earn a living and take their place alongside men in the world. In 1964, when President Johnson signed comprehensive legislation outlawing discrimination, both women and blacks found new power in a system governed by civil rights. Yet in many ways, equality eludes us still. We still search for it.

As a self-identified African American man, whose fervent search for home brought him to the presidency, Barack Obama must be the architect of a twenty-first-century vision of equality—not only as a story of movement, but also one of place—embracing belonging, not mere tolerance—a narrative of community as well as rights. This is the narrative that for decades, pioneers in the struggle for equality have attempted to pen. The story of place is the account of our democratic society that Abigail Adams urged upon her husband, John, and that Nannie Helen Burroughs and Booker T. Washington advocated to and for their followers— female and male, black and white. Adams, Washington, and Burroughs found equality in the ability to stay, not in the right to escape. In sum, we must begin to reimagine equality as Abigail Adams did, with all women as equals, having full authority within the home and full citizenship under the law; as Booker T. Washington did, with people of color as welcome neighbors, not as community outcasts; as Nannie Helen Burroughs did, with women's work inside and outside the home deemed both socially and economically valuable.

DREAMS FROM HIS CHILDHOOD

In a now-familiar black-and-white photograph taken in 1996 by Mariana Cook, Barack and Michelle Obama sit on a spare but comfortable-looking sofa in the Hyde Park apartment where they made their home. Behind them are what appear to be Indonesian prints. A lone statue on an end table looks to be from Africa, possibly Kenya, and the thin, rustic rug under their feet could have originated in any number of locations along the Silk Road. All suggest Barack Obama's journey to the place that he would call home and where he would meet his wife-to-be, Michelle Robinson, a Windy City native and fellow Harvard Law School graduate.

Cook, an Ansel Adams protégé, photographed and interviewed the Obamas among a group of intellectuals she planned to feature in *Couples: Speaking from the Heart*, a book exploring marriage. Their portraits didn't make it into the book, but were found on the eve of Barack Obama's inauguration. It's unlikely that at the time, Cook had any idea that she was talking to a future president and First Lady of the United States. He speaks about stitching together his family through "stories . . . memories . . . ideas." Michelle, he notes, represents a different "strand of family life." His own is "traveling" and "mobile." Hers is "very stable, two-parent . . . mother at home . . . living in the same house all their lives." He lapses nostalgic, "imagining what it would be like to have a stable, solid, secure family life." In the end, he relishes the "tension between familiarity and mystery that makes for something strong."[3] Ultimately, one supposes, it was his comfort with the mystery and the willingness to take audacious chances that led to his becoming the leader of the free world just twelve years later. But one could just as easily conclude that it was Michelle Obama's stability that enabled his meteoric ascent.

As the leader of a country struggling to restore its full faith in the American Dream, President Obama can do no less than focus his energy on our larger aspirations and what it takes for all of us to be at home in America. But we must all face a reality: the story of our future will not be the narrative of "mother at home" and may not be one of buying a home and staying in it all our lives, but can and must be one of security, trust, and mutual support. In her journal article "What is the Point of Equality?" philosopher Elizabeth S. Anderson frames the president's challenge well. President Obama, she writes, must help us all to imagine equality as life in a nation where individuals receive "fair value for [their] labor, and recognition by others of [their] productive contribution," where everyone has effective means of accessing and sustaining shelter, and whose members enjoy "the social condition of being accepted by others . . . not being ascribed outcast status."[4] This unique moment in time, and his own personal history, position Barack Obama to address this challenge in a way that perhaps no other president in recent history could.

THE ROAD HOME

Barack Obama's life story is a tale of race, gender, and finding home. In reading his memoir, *Dreams from My Father,* I am reminded of my colleague Tara Brown and how she defined home: "For me, home is identity."

Tara was born in 1966. Her Irish-English-American mother and African American father married in the early days of the 1960s social revolutions that called into question a host of perceived wisdoms. In particular, Tara's parents believed that they were entering an age in which race would cease to be an issue. At the very least—like Barack Obama's parents, who had been married a few years earlier in Hawaii—the couple believed that their love for each other would help them overcome any stigma that might be attached to an interracial family. Consequently, they never discussed race with Tara and their two other children.

In the winter of 1976, when the Browns moved to West Medford, a Boston suburb, the family lived for the first time in a predominantly black neighborhood. What's more, they arrived during the area's heated battles over school integration. White classmates and local residents whispered, snickered, and hurled racial slurs at Tara. The ten-year-old was forced to reckon with race, a concept that she hadn't known existed. Moreover, her race was assigned to her. "I'd been labeled, tied, and bound to an identity," one Tara hadn't chosen. For her African American friends and their parents, there was no such thing as biracial. Just as convinced as their white neighbors of Tara's identity, but more patient and welcoming, they were content to wait for her "to come to terms with and accept [her] African heritage."

In the absence of her parents' guidance, Tara was left on her own to figure out what being a black female meant. So during the summer of 1978, the twelve-year-old, who would one day become an academic, checked books out of the library, hoping to find answers in literary and historical works. For weeks Tara holed up in her bedroom reading Richard Wright's *Native Son* and *Black Boy,* Toni Morrison's *Sula,* and Eugene Genovese's *Roll, Jordan, Roll: The World the Slaves Made.* She emerged as a person with a proud history, "profoundly and irreversibly connected to the black community."

Tara's brother, just eleven months older, evolved differently. "I'm just American," he tells her now. The place and time demanded that Tara embrace her identity as a black woman, even with its burdens. But she allows that in the heat of the era's racial battles, and even in their wake, it might have been too hard for her brother to take on the weight of being a black man.

In his remarkably revealing memoir, Barack Obama brings the reader along with him as he journeys to the place where he would come to terms with what it means to be a black man in America. He chronicles his life as the son of a largely absent black Kenyan father and a white American mother with whom he traveled the world and whose parents took Barack in for much of his childhood. In each location of his early life, his racial identity was always a source of tension that he had to negotiate, often on his own. The future president reveals a longing for a black male role model in his early life.

In 1985 Obama found a job as a community organizer, and, through his work and the people and communities he worked with, he fit into a location in a way he had not previously experienced. The place was Chicago. In *Dreams*, Obama credits the stories that he and the residents of Chicago's South Side exchanged with giving him "the sense of place and purpose [he'd] been looking for."[5] The feelings engendered there brought him "out of the larger sense of isolation" surrounding much of his life to a state of belonging and shared interests. The Chicago experience also helped Obama situate himself in the struggle for racial equality in America.

Dreams from My Father ends with Barack Obama's marriage to Michelle, whose family history includes enslavement in South Carolina and Georgia. Michelle's is the quintessential African American migration story. Generations of her family traveled from Africa to various rural settings in the southern United States, then to northern cities, landing finally in Chicago. Yet one of Michelle Obama's relatives has lived her entire life on the land where their ancestors were enslaved.

In 1964 Michelle LaVaughn Robinson was born into a community much like the one that Lorraine Hansberry's family attempted to integrate and where Robinson's great-grandparents had come as part of the Great Migration. But by the time the future First Lady reached her tenth birthday, the working-class neighborhood that had once been primarily white was predominantly black, since all the whites had fled. The Robinsons owned their home, a three-story bungalow, having previously occupied its top-floor apartment as tenants of one of Michelle's aunts. Barack Obama was drawn to Michelle's stable family, including the aunts, uncles, and cousins from throughout the city who surrounded the couple at family gatherings. With Barack and Michelle's marriage and the birth of daughters Sasha and Malia, the Robinson family's slavery-to-success saga became part of Obama's family story; their sense of place became his.

He had years before declared himself black, but during the early part of his presidential campaign, America was poised to see just how African American Barack Obama was. Pundits speculated about whether he was "black enough" or "too black." The question was much more complicated than it might first appear, as Obama was called on to establish himself in the story of blacks in America. As a candidate, he approached the question of racial identity with delicacy, neither confirming nor denying it as a compelling factor—at least not entirely. Mrs. Obama was much more forthcoming, which might have lent weight to the criticism that she was "militantly" black and "angry."[6] Campaigning for her husband in the critical South Carolina primary, Michelle Obama reminded black voters of Rosa Parks's courage in order to move them to put away their doubts about Barack Obama's chances of becoming the first African American president.[7]

Ironically, arguably the finest moment of his campaign was the occasion on which Barack Obama was compelled to address race squarely.

On March 8, 2008, he gave one of his most famous speeches to date. In "A More Perfect Union," he defended himself against claims that he was a follower of a race-conscious theology that his former pastor and mentor, Chicago minister Jeremiah Wright, preached. In the address, Obama paid homage to the historic struggle against racial discrimination in America and incorporated it into his own narrative, even as he asked people of all races to try to experience the consciousness of others. Months after this speech, according to journalist David Remnick, Barack Obama went beyond acknowledgment of the civil rights movement; speaking to a group of civil rights elders, he "insisted on his place in" it.[8] Americans' positive reaction to "A More Perfect Union" and Obama's embrace of an African American identity suggest a country primed to come to term with its racial past and to move forward.

Nevertheless, as embedded in the American experience of the search for place as Barack Obama's saga is, *New York Times* columnist David Brooks distrusted it. As the presidential race tightened in August 2008, Brooks described Obama's life story as "a peripatetic journey through Kansas, Indonesia, Hawaii *and beyond*" (emphasis added). Despite the decades during which Obama lived in Chicago, Brooks found him "hard to place" and "hard to plant." The former Chicago police reporter contrasted Obama with his opponent. John McCain firmly positioned himself in the American narrative as he "discover[ed] his place in a long line of warriors that produced him," according to Brooks. He disparaged the voyage of a "man who took the disparate parts of his past and constructed an identity."[9] I applaud Obama's effort to find the place where he belonged. But in his criticism, Brooks underscores the social and political significance of place in our imagination of who belongs, and especially of who should lead our country.

With what journalist Gwen Ifill calls Barack Obama's "breakthrough" entry into politics, many were ready to put race aside and elect a junior Democratic senator from Illinois. Nearly two generations earlier, President Lyndon Johnson's support for civil rights prompted states throughout the South to abandon the Democratic Party. Border states and states in the Midwest followed suit, ending histories of straight party-line representation and starting a trend toward straight Republican ticket voting. Economic concerns played a part as well. But from 1964 well into the 1990s, according to Sam Gibbons, a Democrat from Florida, "Republicans [were] able to capitalize on [race], creating what is, in effect, an all-white party."[10] In 2008, over fifty years after that initial shift in voting patterns, some racial memories were either fading or being altered. In a CNN poll prior to the election, seven out of ten said that race was not a factor in their decision in the presidential election.[11]

I have never felt the significance of an election as I did on that brisk morning in November 2008. I woke up early and relished waiting in line to cast my ballot for Obama and talk about the election and its significance with fellow voters. In Massachusetts, I was sure to find like-minded Obama supporters. As it turned out, 61 percent of the Bay State's electorate cast ballots for him. In my native state of Oklahoma, John McCain received 65 percent of the votes. A fellow expatriate, Jan, wrote me:

> I was on the Internet all night looking at the map and the county breakout (yes, I can be a political junkie). I informed my daughter that her county, Madison, in Alabama went for Obama along with about 6 other Alabama counties. East Baton Rouge Parish, Orleans Parish, Caddo (Shreveport) were the bigger parishes in Louisiana that were Obama by up to 15 points. Surprisingly, in Oklahoma, no counties were blue.[12]

Nevertheless, I was encouraged—over half a million people in Oklahoma voted for Barack Obama, a Democrat. And my sister reported that in the Tulsa public elementary school where she is principal, a racially diverse student body elected Obama by a landslide in their mock election. "They don't know we live in a red state," she told me.

On November 4, 2008, as word spread that Barack Obama was the president-elect, people became audaciously and conspicuously hopeful. From Washington, DC, to Los Angeles, people danced in the streets. In Berkeley, California, crowds marched from the university to the People's Park—site of passionate antiwar and antigovernment demonstrations in the 1970s—where they hoisted an American flag and sang the national anthem. An event in Chicago's Grant Park, which had once been considered a dangerous place, brought together people of all races, men and women and children, old, young, and in-between. With Oprah Winfrey in the throng, it's fair to say that the megawealthy and not-so-wealthy were represented, as were assorted religions, sexual orientations, and political backgrounds.

Obama changed America's electoral map by being the first Democratic nominee in decades to win in Virginia, Iowa, and Indiana. Hispanic voters, who helped President George W. Bush capture Colorado and New Mexico, favored Obama over McCain. To be sure, the shifting of political concern that CNN tapped did not mean that race was dead. Twenty-nine percent of those polled said that race was a factor in their choice for president.[13] Out-and-out bias still existed. In an ABC poll, 12 percent of voters said they were "uncomfortable" with an African American president, and the CNN pollsters found 5 out of 100 people who said that race was the single most important factor in their choice.[14] Nevertheless, for the time being, the election of Barack Obama changed racial politics in all corners of the country. In getting moderates to cross party and racial lines, he made the Democratic Party seem all the more inclusive.

On Inauguration Day, January 20, 2009, even as the country was on the brink of a financial crisis that some analysts claimed might match the Great Depression, Americans were generally hopeful. According to a Pew Research Center poll, although they weren't optimistic about much, Americans took pride in an election that showed the country was making racial progress.[15] As history was made, the link between national identity and our president's race was affirmed. While a black couple occupies the nation's most symbolic home—to those within and outside its borders, America is a more inclusive nation.

THE WHITE HOUSE: A HOME FOR THE OBAMAS

The First Family's move into their new space was a media event. Barack Obama woke up to his new home in the White House with a 70 percent approval rating, proving beyond a doubt that the majority of America was ready for a black president. After the election, observers declared that once President and Mrs. Obama, Sasha, and Malia took up residence in the nation's capital, equality was realized. When Mrs. Obama's mother, Marian Robinson, moved in with the family to help with her granddaughters, and when the First Lady independently planted an organic vegetable garden on the South Lawn that would serve as a source of family food and for teaching local children, Michelle Obama's concept for what she called "the people's house" became clearer. Even the selection of their children's new pet, Bo, signaled that the Obamas were shaping a home to suit the needs and style of a young and active "all-American" family. According to press reports, not even the president is exempt from dog duty. Mrs. Obama walks Bo in the morning and "I'm the guy with the nightshift," Mr. Obama told a reporter.[16]

A month into the new president's term, Michelle Obama's approval rating of 49 percent surpassed that of four former First Ladies. (Forty-four percent of those polled had no opinion.) Some had been offended by her comment during the primaries that she was "proud of America" for the first time in her life, but many of us who share the desire to embrace America as our home, as well as to be embraced by America as full citizens, understood what she meant. The efforts of Barack Obama's critics to cast Michelle as angry and militantly unpatriotic didn't stick; only 5 percent of those polled viewed her negatively. A year after moving into the White House, the self-described "mom in chief" enjoyed soaring approval ratings, even as the president's dipped.[17] Even so, her high approval rating leaves open the question of whether America would embrace a woman commander in chief, as opposed to the mom-in-chief role Michelle assigned herself. More specifically, Barack Obama's election provided very limited context for extrapolating how the public would respond to the candidacy of a black woman.

Despite the goodwill engendered by the presidential election, issues of gender, race, and place linger. Questions about Obama's "place," like the ones raised during the campaign by David Brooks, have resurfaced. Months into his presidency, members of the so-called "birther movement" clamored for the public's attention with calls for proof of Obama's citizenship. They and others cited Barack Obama's childhood experiences in Indonesia as evidence that, as a "non-native," he did not belong in the White House. The calls for proof of President Obama's place of origin, Hawaii birth certificate notwithstanding, indicate that a vocal minority of Americans are still not "at home" with Barack Obama as president. President Obama's detractors have characterized his few acknowledgments of race as reverse discrimination. Radio talk-show hosts assign a racial preference label to race-neutral policy. One dimwitted and callous pundit characterized humanitarian aid extended in 2010 to earthquake-ravaged Haiti as "racial pandering"; health care reform has been dubbed "racial reparations."[18]

Barack Obama's presidency is another milestone in the full citizenship of African Americans and others who have felt left out politically or marginalized. For all Americans, it shows that the country can accept a black man as its best representative. African Americans enjoy the right to be represented by the government and to represent the people of the United States. But the first black president's achievements must mean more.

As Gwen Ifill noted in her 2009 book *The Breakthrough: Politics and Race in the Age of Obama,* "There is evidence that Barack Obama has not transcended race," but there is also "proof that he has redefined what racial politics is." Others, like political scientist Andra Gillespie, assert that Barack Obama won by adopting a posture that was "race neutral." But Gillespie admits that "deracializing" is not a simple concept, whether it's applied to a political identity or a specific political agenda.[19] No political contest can be entirely devoid of race, nor can it be gender neutral. Whether by supporters or foes, the categories that we like to think don't matter continue to be raised. What's more, race and gender neutrality can come back to haunt a candidate who wins with this approach. They can even amount to "golden handcuffs," inhibiting the elected official from ever addressing race- or gender-specific issues. With so many left adrift by the recession, I ponder whether racial progress should be measured by one black family's occupation of the White House, as those responding to the Pew poll asserted.

One of the defining features of *The America Play* by Suzan-Lori Parks is a huge hole dug by her character Foundling Father, a black grave digger who finds purpose in his life through impersonating Abraham Lincoln, reenacting Lincoln's assassination for a penny. The hole is a replica of "the Great Hole of History," an amusement park attraction where visitors view renditions of past events. Each performance seems to generate a new understanding of what America is and wants to be. Barack Obama's election and his presidency add to an understanding of America and what it means to be black in America. Yet he also reminds me of Parks's character Brazil, Foundling Father's son, who at the play's end asserts the need to climb out of the "Great Hole of [American] History."

A MORE INCLUSIVE DEMOCRACY

Notwithstanding the strident opposition to his presidency, and even the setback the Democrats suffered in the 2010 midterm election, I have no doubt that Barack Obama's election bridged a political divide. As president, he has an opportunity to bring us even closer to the inclusive democracy that his election portended.

In times of turmoil, by confronting prejudice, past U.S. presidents have shaped who is at home in America and with whom America is at home. Like no other document in our country's history, Abraham Lincoln's Emancipation Proclamation expanded our thinking about who belonged. Lincoln's legacy to African Americans was the opportunity he gave them to become citizens, something that had been denied them by the Supreme Court in the Dred Scott case. Early in the Civil War, President Lincoln signed the Homestead Act of 1862 into law, giving people who had no chance of inheriting property an opportunity to own acreages, considered a critical condition for prosperity in mid-nineteenth-century America. For a majority of the newly freed slaves, land was essential, as farm work and rural culture were all that they knew. The Homestead Act, despite its flawed origins in manifest destiny, combined with the Emancipation Proclamation to give people like my grandfather Henry Elliott chances well beyond what they were born into. The legislation gave blacks, and others who had been locked out of the American Dream because they lacked the resources to buy land, opportunities to belong, to enjoy the benefits of citizenship, and to be represented by their government. Through these acts, Lincoln expanded our democracy.

As the country descended into the Great Depression, Franklin Delano Roosevelt's New Deal suggested a type of egalitarianism that attracted throngs who were dispossessed and others who saw their fates linked to the destitute. Despite some New Deal policies' accommodation of racism and President Roosevelt's failure to secure rights for blacks, the democratic appeal of his proposals was so strong that it prompted African Americans to reinvest in the country's political system and defect from the party of Lincoln to the Democratic Party. In this respect, Roosevelt succeeded, in large part, because of his wife Eleanor's overtures to the black community. But without a doubt, Franklin Roosevelt's efforts to provide a safety net were not limited to blacks and other racial minorities.

To this day, people of all backgrounds enjoy New Deal programs, and the country is better off because the government insures safe working conditions, a minimum wage, and financial security for the elderly. Moreover, Roosevelt's efforts to stem the Depression-era housing crisis by promoting home ownership opportunities opened the door for Harry Truman's post–World War II building projects, which put fifteen million returning GIs in homes and helped give rise to a middle-class ownership rank.

Progress toward bridging America's racial gap stagnated following World War II. As the country grappled with racial disenfranchisement at the protests of the civil rights movement, President Lyndon Johnson utilized his political might to move the passage of landmark civil rights legislation. By including prohibitions against housing discrimination and protections against gender discrimination in work and in the granting of credit, the law set the stage for residential integration in urban and suburban settings. Johnson's highly criticized War on Poverty brought attention to the limited opportunity for homes available to the poor. It was under President Johnson's watch that the concept of rights truly became inclusive and progressive. But Johnson's approach to inclusion came at a political cost. White voters' support of the Democratic Party dwindled in the decades that followed. Many went straight to the party of Lincoln, which would be rebranded as the party of Ronald Reagan.

Glaring inconsistencies and violent contests over home were apparent in each president's agenda. Various populations, often identifiable by race or gender, were simply left out in the cold. Lincoln's definition of citizenship never seemed to include women or Native Americans. Indeed, well after his death, even with the enactment of laws granting protections to newly freed male slaves, neither women nor indigenous people were invited to become full members of the country's political community. Tribes were still suffering from being uprooted from their homelands, and there was no attempt to address that loss.

Through Executive Order 9066, Franklin Roosevelt authorized the forcible removal of over one hundred thousand people of Japanese ancestry from their homes, confining them to government internment camps for years. Initially, even Roosevelt's benevolent pension plans were flawed. Household workers—a large majority of whom were women, and many of whom were racial minorities—were excluded from benefits, as were agricultural workers. And Lyndon Johnson and fellow Democrats, as well as the Supreme Court itself in *Milliken v. Bradley,* refused to see how local, state, and federal policy encouraged, according to Justice Thurgood Marshall in his dissent, "our great metropolitan areas to be divided up each into two cities—one white, the other black."[20] Democratic leadership seemingly accepted the 1960s and 1970s "white flight" from the Democratic Party, and from the homes that became accessible to blacks, as a fait accompli. Very little leadership effort seemed to be put into stemming the tide on either front. Southern white Democrats were seemingly content to go with the political flow by becoming Republicans.

Yet despite the shortcomings and inconsistencies in each president's plan, each moved the country toward a stronger democracy for all. If President Obama is to do the same, he must be mindful of the deficiencies in earlier plans. He must call upon all of us, this time, to dig deeper to make sure no one is left out, or even sacrificed for what is conveniently seen as the "greater good."

A vision of a more inclusive America, an enlarged concept of home, must guide us as we address the problems of those displaced by the housing crisis and those still awaiting their chance for the American Dream. The Obama administration's plans to help homeowners of all stripes retain their houses included a $75 billion loan modification program. Yet this amount barely covered the millions of borrowers at risk of foreclosure. The federal foreclosure mediation program to help train counselors and pro bono attorneys who can counsel and support homeowners is lofty, but administrative efforts must go beyond policies that help home buyers pay their mortgages.

Residents feeling the pain of the foreclosure crisis vary, and so do their needs. Three categories are worth pointing out. Buyers who have been in homes that they struggled to purchase and to keep for decades may now find themselves or their neighbors on the verge of foreclosure. At the very least, many of these long-termers have seen their property values drop and their nest eggs dwindle. In abandoned or dubious areas, security issues are particularly acute for them. Their prospects for retirement and passing on family wealth are greatly diminished. In fact, they may be passing on debt to their children and grandchildren. Demographics and life expectancy being what they are, many of these homeowners are women.

People who before the meltdown were ten, fifteen, or even twenty years into their home mortgage face a different predicament. These midlifers are confronted with the prospect of foreclosure and additional years in the workplace to rebuild pensions and depleted college funds for their children. Moreover, their ability to borrow money to make sure their children get a university degree is jeopardized by their foreclosure status. Even if they keep their homes, the value has declined, and there will be no borrowing against it to make sure their offspring's education matches or surpasses their own. Many midlifers are couples; many are single, and those one-parent households are most likely headed by women. They are what we once thought of as the solid middle class, the bedrock of the country's economic and social structure. Ironically, the foundation we thought was sound badly needs shoring up.

Finally, there are the new entrants to the housing market. Not only are many of them facing foreclosure, but they are the ones who find themselves under the burden of the greatest debt because they bought high and, if they can sell at all, will have to sell low. This category is filled with buyers whose loans are being repaid from one income. The potential fallout from the loss of that income is tremendous but, given the slow jobs recovery, not unimaginable. The new entrants' category is filled with single women, women of color, and young couples, many of whom are in lower-paying jobs and perhaps bought into neighborhoods in transition because that's all they could afford. Given the downturn in the entire economy, it's likely that the upward transition they anticipated has halted. New entrants may walk away from mortgages and turn (or return) to renting, but that market too suffers the same capriciousness as the home-buying market. The combination of compromised credit records and the poor quality of renting opportunities may result in marginalization of these would-be owners. The future for them and their children is in limbo.

In short, one or more government policies won't fit all. Renegotiating loans is a start, but is not a make-whole solution.

The Obama Justice Department supports cities like Memphis and Baltimore in their lawsuits against Wells Fargo. But punishing a handful of lenders in isolated lawsuits throughout the country is not a national strategy for addressing the displacement of millions, a problem that is now spreading to rural areas. Administrative policies like Making Home

Affordable, which helps buyers restructure loans, and the Neighborhood Stabilization Act, which provides grants to cities for purchasing and rehabilitating foreclosed properties, have the potential to help stem the dislocation of families, but can cover only a fraction of the households suffering from the collapse of the market. Yes, more must be done to rebuild our cities—especially the pockets that are public and private service wastelands—and those efforts will have to involve the banking industry.

Of special concern to the problem of home is the lack of financial services available in many inner-city neighborhoods, where people rely on check cashing services that charge fees as high 20 percent and payday loan outlets and rent-to-own stores that command appallingly high interest rates. These precursors to subprime lending continue to flourish in many communities. I have no doubt that the acceptance of these credit options as the norm contributed to the culture inside the banking industry that declared that certain neighborhoods deserved no more than toxic credit products, like the subprime and high-cost devices that even the country's largest banks peddled. Indeed, researchers Jacob Rugh and Douglas Massey have concluded that years of racial segregation and isolation in America's cities created a natural market for subprime loans, resulting in high rates of foreclosure and leaving "minority group members uniquely vulnerable to the housing bust."[21] If communities remain racially isolated and devoid of employment opportunities, retail clothing and food outlets, and options for viable credit, our entire society will continue to be susceptible to additional catastrophes.

Just as not all residents are the same, neither are all cities in the same predicament. Places like Baltimore, Detroit, New Orleans, and Los Angeles have their own unique genealogy. Where they are today is shaped by their past. Within each city's history is the special place it held as the ground where the hopes and aspirations of migrants would be met, where they would find a more hospitable home. Those stories are part of a larger American story of promise that must be taken into account as we revitalize our cities.

As middle-income people of color begin the reverse migration to the South, cities lose social capital and a portion of their economic base. Farming in rural areas by people of color is not a workable option. Urban policy must give people a place and a reason to stay. Yes, critics will choose to deny this part of our national narrative and even claim that efforts directed at inner-city neighborhoods amount to racial reparations. So be it. If we've learned nothing over the past two years, we've surely learned that the fate of urban areas and those who live in them is linked to the health of the entire nation. As they suffer, so suffers the American Dream. Refusal to address problems in distressed communities is tantamount to cutting off the country's nose.

CAN WE TALK?

Sadly, experience tells us that President Obama will have a difficult time addressing race publicly. Since his election, the president's one attempt to broach the topic proved problematic and ultimately unfruitful. In what Harvard law professor Charles Ogletree calls a teaching moment on the lingering issues of racial inequality, President Barack Obama called for a "beer summit" on the White House lawn.[22] Joining him were Vice President Joe Biden, Harvard professor Henry Louis Gates, and Cambridge police officer James Crowley.

Chance brought the cast of characters together on that summer night in July 2009. Weeks earlier, Officer Crowley had responded to a call from a passerby who saw Gates trying to enter his Cambridge home and suspected that he might be a burglar. Even after Gates produced identification showing that he belonged in the neighborhood, and indeed in that home, Crowley arrested him for disorderly conduct. What ensued was a series of comments by the president about the imprudent arrest and a public ruckus—never really a full-fledged debate—over racial profiling.

After a forty-minute chat on the Rose Garden patio, the president declared his hope that we would all draw a positive lesson from the episode. But in fact, the "beer summit," intended to serve as a moment of reconciliation and illumination, fell flat. The topic, context, and even players failed to offer America a lasting engagement in a conversation on race.

Gender won't be easy for President Obama to speak to either, especially given his contentious primary battles with Hillary Clinton in which gender and race collided. Even though he has not made speeches about gender equality, he has signed important legislation designed to protect women against workplace discrimination. On January 29, 2009, the Lily Ledbetter Fair Pay Act was one of the first bills President

Obama signed into law. His order establishing the White House Council on Women and Girls was hailed as a landmark as well. But that council has been relatively quiet. If we are to achieve the more inclusive America his presidency promises, the Obama administration cannot shy away from talking about either gender or race bias in the country.

My experience in the years since the 1991 Clarence Thomas confirmation hearing convinces me of the power of public discourse. Following my testimony about Supreme Court nominee Thomas's egregious conduct toward me, the nation began an earnest, though often contentious and painful, conversation on the issue of sexual harassment. Talking publicly and privately about the problem changed our collective understanding of the nature of a behavior that had been the bane of women's and girls' workplace experience for centuries, notwithstanding laws that prohibited it. Changing the way we talked and thought about sexual harassment encouraged individuals and the legal system to combat it. Employers instituted zero-tolerance workplace policies. Women and men filed complaints in record numbers. Many succeeded. The Supreme Court, which had decided only one sexual harassment case in its history, in one year (1998) heard three claims. In one claim against automobile manufacturer Mitsubishi Motors, the Equal Employment Opportunity Commission, the federal government's office for enforcing anti–sexual harassment laws, negotiated a record $34 million settlement. Though the problem of sexual harassment still exists, in the years since the hearing, we as a country have learned a lot about the pernicious nature of gender inequality. We are better off for having started a long-overdue conversation about sexual harassment.

The foreclosure crisis and the loss of homes should serve as the impetus for another public conversation that would include national, state, local, community, and business leaders, as well as regular people. The times call for a "Home Summit," not at the White House but in communities around the country. President Obama has two offices at his disposal to help orchestrate such a discussion. Together, the Council on Women and Girls (CWG) and the White House Domestic Policy Council (DPC) are made up of representatives from Cabinet-level federal agencies. The DPC coordinates the domestic policy-making process in the White House, offers advice to the president, and supervises the execution of domestic policy.[23] Given the housing crisis and the effort it is taking for us to recover from it, it's hard to imagine a more critical domestic concern than the search for home in America.

The CWG, chaired by Obama's adviser and friend Valerie Jarrett, is the only White House agency with equality written into its mission. When Obama established the council, he noted that the issues facing women today "are not just women's issues." In particular, he observed that "when women make less than men for the same work, it hurts families who find themselves with less income."[24] Likewise, in the housing crisis, women and their families often find themselves shut out of the American Dream. As an issue impacting the entire country, home is a fitting topic for the council to tackle.

One may question whether an agency whose mission is to address gender inequality is up to responding to racial inequities. It can, but only if the leadership is truly multiracial. If they know anything about social bias, women of color know that their equality can be achieved only through the elimination of both race and gender inequality. When the CWG was established, its mandate was quite broad. Obama cited "the true purpose of our government" in signing the presidential order commissioning the group "to ensure that in America, all things are still possible for all people." Moreover, the council must make sure that federal agencies consider "the needs of women and girls in the policies they draft, the programs they create, the legislation they support."[25] In working with Congress to make sure that the administration's policies are implemented, the DPC's role is complementary to that of the CWG.

The DPC's and CWG's first order of business would be to convene discussions of the concerns of those set adrift by the home crisis. Together these two agencies have the authority to bring together the myriad of buyers, government agencies, and private financial institutions implicated in the collapse of the housing market. The dialogue model could be adapted from President Bill Clinton's Conversation on Race. Clinton himself took the lead in that 1997 initiative calling for a "great and unprecedented conversation."[26] With the guidance of an advisory board headed by John Hope Franklin, the late historian, town hall talks aimed at engaging the

American public took place in Little Rock, Arkansas; San Francisco, California; Washington, DC; and points in between. Clinton's initiative was a critical start in a long-overdue racial discourse.

Like Clinton's Conversation on Race, the conversation about home must take place not just in Washington, but throughout the country, especially in cities like Baltimore, Memphis, and Chicago—those ravaged by the housing crisis. But even with the illustrious John Hope Franklin behind it, Clinton's Conversation on Race did not do its subject justice. As law professor Lani Guinier noted in commenting on the Clinton talks, the country deserved a "dialogue with depth" with a "problem solving format" that was "neither conducted in campaign mode nor politician-centered."[27] Instead, we got a discussion that avoided worrisome and controversial issues, like affirmative action. Today, a focused conversation, one that engages longstanding and even painful issues related to gender and race and the struggles of diverse individuals to find a place they can call home, is needed.

In earlier chapters I began the discussion of questions we must address to restore our faith in America as the place of great promise. As we move beyond the immediate housing crisis, there are important questions we must ask ourselves:

- How do we stop further social and economic isolation of communities of color?
- How do we incorporate gender equality into our vision for racial equality and residential integration?
- What steps will we take to avoid visiting the impact of foreclosures on the children of those whose homes and neighborhoods have been lost?
- Within our cities, what are our plans to build community and put an end to the notion that individualism and neighborhood isolation will protect us from violence and crime in economically distressed areas?
- Will we challenge the undemocratic exclusivity of an American Dream that can be achieved only by families with two incomes buying large suburban homes?

- Can we imagine an American Dream founded on the idea that one's gender or race will not predestine where one finds home—both the place and the state of being?

Structuring a conversation about these and many other issues won't be easy. It is perhaps unprecedented, but others have contemplated just this kind of public discourse. In his work on poverty alleviation among inner-city youth, William Julius Wilson, a sociologist and adviser to President Obama, offers guidance for resolving entrenched and often complicated racial problems. In his book *More Than Just Race*, Wilson advises that consideration of cultural and institutional forces are key to frank, hopeful, and fruitful discussion and problem solving. Indeed, Wilson advises that in order to "make people feel at home in this country," cultural and institutional factors *must* be considered.[28]

In the Home Summit, the apparent cultural and behavioral factors that disadvantage women and people of color in their efforts to find home, both as a place and as a state of being, have to be dealt with. In the subprime meltdown, borrowers and lenders both engaged in ill-advised, and often potentially illegal, behavior. Yet discussing individual behavior alone, or even group behavior, too easily lends itself to "victim blaming" and will not move the conversation forward. The meltdown was made possible by institutional failures to halt what John Kenneth Galbraith called a global game of "pass the bad penny to the greater fool."[29] Women's lower wages have also been built into our employment and credit institutions. The confluence of structural forces cannot be divorced from the racial isolation and gender bias that have existed for decades in the home purchasing market. All must be taken into account if America is to dig out of the "awfully big mess" of the housing crisis and move toward a better future. According to Wilson, only after "policymakers, philanthropists, educators, community leaders, and others" have addressed these structural impediments that contributed to the crisis and interfered with peoples' ability to "realize their values in calling a place home" should they focus on "problematic cultural behavior" that impeded home building.[30]

Consideration of these factors alone makes a Home Summit a tall order. Yet as worthy a beginning as such a summit would be, the American public will expect more than a brainstorming session from the DPC's and CWG's effort. Vetting of issues and ideas should ultimately lead the council to make policy recommendations.

To make sure the needs of women and girls are taken into account when developing policies, programs, and legislation, government agencies should adopt some sort of analytic procedure that lets them evaluate the impact of their actions on people who we know are at risk of being shut out of the housing market. Ultimately, that means a number of government agencies that influence home buying, housing, and transportation should put into operation a process that assesses every aspect of their work for its ability to protect the interests of all women, regardless of color. Since a myriad of national, state, and local agencies have made decisions that influenced housing patterns and neighborhood demographics in the past, it stands to reason that their participation is needed to stop further racial, gender (family makeup), and income isolation.

Recall that before the crisis, single women—many with children—were an emerging market for home ownership. Given the income disparities that exist, they are unlikely to be able to purchase homes in higher-income areas. Therefore, the cost and types of homes built will shape who becomes part of the communities that are developed. How much affordable housing to build and where to locate it have to be part of the discussion of the Home Summit. The analysis of rules and regulations governing new developments must tell us who is being shut out when building permits are granted and streets are being paved.

The ultimate purpose of a population impact analysis (PIA) would be to make certain that government resources are spent more effectively, particularly with respect to the buyers who were hardest hit as the housing and financial markets collapsed. Clearly, many of the buyers and communities that fared worst during this crisis were the ones who were most vulnerable even before the advent of subprime markets. While one can reasonably argue that the best antidote to the problem of loss of home ownership is the growth of jobs, that approach ignores the fact that the buildup to the housing crisis occurred when unemployment was low. Earnings did not keep up with upwardly spiraling housing costs, and those who were employed in chronically low-paying jobs—women and black and brown men—were always at a disadvantage for home ownership, even in a job-rich economy. Consequently, the ultimate goal of any policy analysis would be to address those vulnerabilities, not to get the new entrants, midlifers, or long-termers back to exactly where they were before the collapse.

Currently gender, racial, and ethnic demographic and economic information, the kind needed for such an analysis, is collected by the Census Bureau, but not all government agencies utilize it in decision making. And some, sensitive to the potential for discrimination, will be suspicious of its use. Again, the Domestic Policy Council would be an excellent home base for this project. In its pivotal role as a central point for coordination of, and cooperation with, the overall goals of the administration and for full implementation of administrative policy, it could standardize the PIA procedures, as well as determine how federal agencies collaborate with state and local agencies and private entities. The DPC could establish rules for when a PIA is required, how it is to be used, and how to disseminate the information gathered from the PIA, as well as the consequences for failing to do such analysis.

A number of policies related to the home and home ownership will need to be evaluated for their impact on individuals and communities. Policy advisers have already suggested some candidates for scrutiny. For example, an eighteen-member bipartisan White House commission hinted that eliminating the federal tax write-off for mortgage interest payments might be an option for addressing the deficit. This suggestion started a debate about the benefit of what has become an expectation for some taxpayers. Arguably, the mortgage interest write-off and other federal policies have encouraged the growth of the suburbs whose histories are steeped in white homeowners' efforts to avoid residential integration. And while federal policy should not punish or abandon those neighborhoods, a balance between suburbs, cities, and rural areas must be struck. As it is, economists note that only one-third of those eligible deduct their mortgage interest payments from the amounts they owe on taxes. Low-income taxpayers are often better off taking the standard deduction rather than itemizing their deductions. Those most likely to itemize, and thus take the interest deduction, are upper-income taxpayers, often those residing in suburbs. According to one *Wall Street Journal* blog, "Around 70% of the benefits from mortgage-interest and property-tax deductions go to the top 20% of taxpayers in terms of income." A taxpayer can write off interest on as much as one million dollars of debt, arguably encouraging individuals to overleverage and take on more debt than they otherwise would, which can inflate the cost of housing. Today the mortgage interest deduction is, according to the same blog, "the largest single subsidy for housing and one of the largest deductions in the U.S. tax code . . . projected to reduce tax revenue by \$131 billion in 2012."[31] As such, it amounts to tax subsidization for a few. At the very least, we must begin to debate whether the policy is in the best interest of all neighborhoods or whether some tailored approach to mortgage deduction is in order.

Policies already in place will be up for consideration as we move into a new period of projected record foreclosures. Under the Home Affordable Modification Program, the Obama administration set aside \$30 billion to help homeowners renegotiate troubled loans. The billion-dollar Emergency Homeowners' Loan Program was designed to help unemployed homeowners who have fallen behind on their mortgage payments. Buyers who owe more on their homes than they are worth might be helped by the FHA Short Refinance Option to refinance mortgages. And the Neighborhood Stabilization Program promises to assist states, cities, and nonprofits to purchase and refurbish abandoned properties. All are programs that might alleviate some of the problems caused by the crisis of home, but all should be evaluated under a PIA to measure their ability to address the long-term concerns of those whose chance at the American Dream has been the most diminished, through no fault of their own.

No matter whether people rent or own their homes, the area in which they live often determines education and employment opportunities and chances to engage in civic activities. Even after years of civil rights gains, where and how one lives in America often correlates to race and gender disparities. In order to move the country forward, President Obama will have to do as his predecessors did and confront lingering inequality. Among other ideas, Obama could make our democracy more inclusive by tying financial support for home buyers to purchases that promote community sustainability and stability. He could urge the Justice Department to systemically combat discrimination in public and private housing markets. He could fund community development that draws on women's community-building leadership capacities and the social networks that they develop through their workplaces, places of worship, children's schools, and even beauty shops. But whatever Obama's policies, they must all follow a vision for equality, one that embraces a community of equals. As we climb out of this crisis, we must ask ourselves whether the housing market is a safe repository for our vision of equality, much less the American Dream. Will President Obama continue to follow the path of moderate efforts to help individual homeowners renegotiate bad loans? Or will he work with other leaders to broaden our vision of equality and help us reimagine a democracy in which we are all at home?

The discussion of how to strengthen our democracy and reimagine the home and its relationship to equality should not be left to one person, not even one as powerful as President Obama. We—educators, community and business leaders, local politicians, philanthropists, media, and individuals—are all responsible for moving the country forward on these critical issues. And our responsibility is independent of what the White House or Congress does. Education, work, civic engagement, ready availability of goods and services—all correlate to where and how one lives. Thus teachers, employers, city officials, and any others with something to offer the public have a stake in this conversation.

In sorting out topics of concern, let's begin with education. Take, for example, an elementary school teacher with a passion for her students' learning, Ms. Young. Given that our schools are funded through property taxes, where and how Ms. Young's students live will determine what she can do in the classroom. The number of students assigned in her classes and the kinds of basic materials Ms. Young has at her disposal are often beyond her control. A frank conversation between Ms. Young, local school board members, a store owner or manufacturer near her school, and a charity devoted to the health and well-being of children about the local housing market and property values in her school's neighborhood will shed light on the structural challenges Ms. Young and her students face and should lead to some practical solutions for addressing those challenges. This conversation about the role the home plays in school funding may help Ms. Young and the others understand why every one of her pupils doesn't have a textbook or access to a computer and what needs to be done structurally to change that situation.

A COMMUNITY OF EQUALS

Author John Edgar Wideman reminds us that home is more than a place; it is a "way of seeing and being seen."[32] What I have learned from my experiences at multiple addresses throughout the country began with my childhood on a farm in Oklahoma. For most of us, home is a structure (a house or apartment) and a household of family members or kin, as defined not only by blood but by close relationships, love, or marriage. Home is physical when defined by shared space—a domicile—and emotional when defined by the connections between the people who live in that space. Sharing a home assumes shared intimacy, emotions, good and bad times. The home where I grew up is the same place where my mother and father raised their thirteen children. Though we never all lived there together, we all call it home, having had common experiences there. Home signifies belonging. Belonging to a house set back from a dirt road and surrounded by fields shaped how our family saw a world where the majority of people of our race lived in cities. And no doubt, the fact that we were farm people shaped what others expected us to say and believe in, and even how we were supposed to look. Years later, when I went to law school in New Haven, Connecticut, with people from around the country, I was one of two Oklahomans. Many of my classmates seemed surprised by the mere presence of someone from a state that few of them had visited, and even more surprised that natives of rural Oklahoma who were black actually existed.

Home can also refer to a community or neighborhood. For me, the Lone Tree community where I grew up was also a place that felt like home. I knew its residents, not in the same way that I knew my family, but they were indeed familiar. Work, church and school, birthdays and funerals were community affairs. Having crafted a sense of security over the objections of the area's prejudices, black members of the community felt connected to each other and, oddly and with reservations, to our white neighbors. We were not all equals, but we all felt rooted in the place.

It's worth noting that this sphere, the community, was as far as my mother, Erma Hill, ventured in her concept of where she belonged. She felt at home on our farm and with her black friends, but that was it. She never looked beyond that limited landscape for her own sense of home, but she expected more for her children.

My mother's experience tells me that in order to find a nation-home, we must do more than inhabit a space within a national boundary. We must find a connection with a country. That connection is expressed through our civic participation and identification with national representatives. It's reinforced when those leaders make policies that show they understand what we care about. Home, even a nation-home, not only offers us privileges, but also demands responsibility. We don't often think of what having a nation-home means. Even black artists' ability to connect us with a nation-home is anxiety ridden. Langston Hughes wrote, "I, too, am America," even as he situated the "darker brother" in our nation's "kitchen."[33] Today thousands, maybe even millions, feel relegated to the America's back rooms, waiting to be let into the parlor in full view of company.

Most often those of us, regardless of race, who are born citizens take being an American for granted and rarely think about what it means to have a nation-home, let alone that the meaning might be influenced by race or gender. Yet when tragedy strikes, we rummage around for ways to symbolize our belonging to America. We rely on recognized emblems, and sometimes we find symbols in peculiar places. We even reprioritize our desire for a haven. After the attacks on the World Trade Center and Pentagon, we began to fly flags and wear lapel pins to let our neighbors know of our shared sentiments. During seventh-inning stretches at professional baseball games, we stopped asking to be taken to the ball game and asked God to bless America, our "home sweet home." National security became our primary political, as well as personal, issue—underscoring that of utmost importance is the sense that home, in any of these forms, should make those who are within its boundaries feel secure and valued, even during recreational activities.

More important, to see yourself and be seen as having a home in America, you must feel valued and secure in your place in the nation. When I look back on my mother's life and consider her and Iola Young, the two women who sent me out to find my home in America, I realize how they struggled to find their place in a nation that never heard their stories and thus never began to fully value their contributions. If not outcasts, they were seen as peripheral to the story of America. They are joined today by many Americans, some of whom look like them, others of whom do not. I cannot help but think that if they are just seen and included in the universe of American discourse, to adapt a phrase coined by anthropologist Clifford Geertz, the country will be better off.[34]

As the story goes, President Barack Obama spends the last few minutes of each day in the Oval Office reading ten letters from the public. On occasion, he responds to one or two. I have no doubt that Obama's correspondence is compelling and much more massive than my own. But with respect to mail, I do have one thing over the president. The now more than twenty-five thousand letters I have received from the public span nearly two decades, extending beyond the specific issues of the day. The writers live in every state—red, blue, and purple—in this country. Women and men, writing on all manners of topics, share their stories with me. Consequently, my letters offer long-view lessons about living together in a community. And through them I have found home—not simply the place, but perhaps more important, the state of being. I believe that these letters could benefit President Obama, or anyone who is privileged to read them, as much as they have benefited me.

Among the many messages of these letters is that at its best, the American Dream is an application of our shared values. Today I am privileged to witness the coming of age of a generation that seeks to move beyond historic race and gender divisions. For them, the American Dream means nothing if it is not inclusive. Because of the financial crisis, and because of their having grown up in an era of less strident racial discrimination and in homes where women are breadwinners, they will be less willing and able to pay a premium to live in a racially isolated (predominantly white) community.

I also know that this new generation will never love rights the way that I do. And why should they? Individuals born after the passage of civil rights laws have never lived without legal protections against race and gender discrimination. For them, the rights discussion is abstraction. If we are to engage them in a struggle for progress, we must find a new way to talk about equality. Indeed—because the aspects of our lives that cannot be adjudicated in a courtroom will ultimately help define equality—as important as rights are, we do the next generation a disservice by limiting our talk about progress and equality to a discussion of rights. For them, rights are a starting point, Equality 1.0. They are ready for the 4G version of equality. Before long they will no doubt be clamoring for the 10G version.

But one thing that a generation that has grown up in an era of social networking understands is community. Even as abstract as the concept may seem to some, the burgeoning industry of technology that keeps us linked shows that young people understand and crave connectedness in ways that many in my generation never imagined and cannot fully appreciate. The perennial question my generation asks people whom we meet is "Where are you from?" I would encourage a generation of Facebook users to forego that query and ask instead, "Where is your home?" In answering that question, give some thought to how you found your own place—what role your race played in the choices you had and the choices you made before settling into a home. When you look out your window, what are the races of the people you expect to see? Are they the same as those you see on your Facebook page, on YouTube, at your job, or on the streets as you make your way to work? For men, I'd ask you to also think about whether your choices for a place that gives you a sense of belonging and security are different from your sisters' or those of other women in your life. I'd like young women and men to think about whether your possibilities are the same as your parents'. Will your children's options be the same? Finally, I'd ask you to imagine how any of your answers might be different in a world of true equality.

Urban geographer Elvin Wyly wisely tempers my optimism about a younger generation's ability to get beyond gender and racial limitations. Even though today's twenty-year-olds may have good intentions to change their behavior, Wyly reminds me that "for those who follow the path of marriage, parenthood, and home ownership, there is a built-in suburban bias, and this will trigger all of the structural biases of property markets, municipal fiscal disparities, and, especially, school-district inequalities."[35] In short, the institutional incentives that encourage separation are firmly in place and will trump the best intentions for more inclusive racial and gender. Again, our conversation must include frank talk about how personal choices can only be realized through changes in a host of local and national policies.

Barack Obama, whose fervent search for home brought him to the presidency, must seize the moment of crisis to enlarge our concept of home for all Americans, but especially the next generation. I would call on all of the nation's leaders—political and social—to take up this cause. Americans are in need of a twenty-first century vision of our country— not a vision of movement, but one of place; not one of tolerance, but one of belonging; not just of rights, but also of community—a community of equals. This new vision will lead to an inclusive American democracy that stays alive and remains real for everyone.

On October 16, 2011, I will celebrate the one hundredth birthday of my mother, Erma Hill. The place where I live, with its long, snowy winters, is not likely what she contemplated thirty-five years ago when she sent me off with two sets of luggage. But it is my home, and each day I honor her by working to live up to her dream that I will find a more just America than the one she lived in and that, as she did, I will leave it better than I found it.

ACKNOWLEDGMENTS

Thanking everyone who has contributed to this book is a daunting task, but there is one logical place to start—home. Charles Malone's insight, patience, good humor, and unflinching commitment to me and my work sustained me daily through years of research and writing. My cousin Willie Faye Parker was the link between me and the grandparents we shared. Her stories of their lives in Arkansas gave vitality and new meaning to our family's written oral history and the information generously provided me by historian Richard Buckelew and researchers at the Little River County (Arkansas) Genealogical Society and the National Archives and Records Administration. Siblings Elreatha, Albert, Billy, Doris, Allen, Joyce, Carlene, John, Ray, and JoAnn each shared stories about our farm and community in Oklahoma that enriched the book and my appreciation of our upbringing. My brothers Alfred and Winston, who passed during this project, deserve special thanks for their poignant remembrances and their gentle but insistent encouragement. Eric, my nephew, who read, researched, and advised from the start, was especially helpful to my understanding of popular culture and the meaning of home for young African American men today. My family's support and love serve as the base from which I dared reenvision equality in America.

During the twelve years that Brandeis University has been my intellectual home, many colleagues at the Heller School for Social Policy and Management and the Women's and Gender Studies Program have given generously of their time and talents to help me understand the complexity of equality in a way that made this project possible. Yet the book may not have happened had Robert Reich, then a colleague at Brandeis, not coaxed me to write about my mother as I was grieving her death and pondering her life. Lisa Lynch, dean of the Heller School, offered enormous support and just the right amount of prodding to "finish the manuscript." Andreas Teuben, Robin Feuer Miller, Mari Fitzduff, Theodore Johnson, James Mardrell, and Dennis Nealon, whose thoughtful contributions to early drafts and enthusiasm for the book's ideas energized my efforts, were kind and supportive beyond anything in their job descriptions. Donna Einhorn, who eagerly assisted me in structuring the work on this book and all my projects, makes my time at Brandeis all the more productive and enjoyable. Together with Lindsay Markel's research and editorial assistance, these colleagues, along with many on the staff and a host of students, helped me conceptualize and develop the design for the project.

With their vast knowledge of books and the publishing world, Larry Kirshbaum, my agent, and Joy Johannessen, my friend and an exceptional editor, took what were ideas for *Reimagining* and shaped it into a solid proposal for a manuscript. Friends and colleagues Susan Hoerchner, Shirley Wiegand, William Rhoden, William J. Wilson, Sydney Goldstein, Kathleen Peratis, Emma Coleman Jordan, Susan Faludi, Russ Rhymer, Stacy Blake-Beard, Lillian Rubin, and Lani Guinier raised important questions that both broadened and refined my thinking as I wrote each chapter.

NOTES

INTRODUCTION

1. Throughout the book I use the term "race." Though I talk mostly about African Americans and European Americans, I realize the value in the stories of people of different races as they search for home. Indeed, in writing this book I hope to open exploration into the ways each of us searches for belonging and, ultimately, how we can all feel at home in America.

2. T. S. Eliot, "East Coker," in *The Complete Poems and Plays: 1909–1950* (New York: Harcourt, 1980), 129.

3. On March 31, 1776, Abigail Adams wrote to her husband, John Adams, who was attending the Continental Congress: "[I]n the new Code of Laws which I suppose it will be necessary for you to make I desire you would Remember the Ladies, and be more generous and favourable to them than your ancestors. Do not put such unlimited power into the hands of the Husbands." Available at "Selected Manuscripts: Remember the Ladies," Massachusetts Historical Society, accessed April 27, 2011, www.masshist.org/adams/manuscripts_1.cfm.

4. "A Speech at the Memorial Service for Samuel Chapman Armstrong," in *The Booker T. Washington Papers*, ed. Louis R. Harlan, vol. 3, *1889–95*, eds. Stuart B. Kaufman and Raymond W. Smock (Urbana: University of Illinois Press, 1974), 317.

5. See, for example, Traki L. Taylor, "'Womanhood Glorified': Nannie Helen Burroughs and the National Training School for Women and Girls, Inc., 1909–1961," in "New Perspectives on African American Educational History," special issue, *Journal of African American History* 87, no. 4 (Fall 2002): 390–402; Audrey Thomas McCluskey, "'We Specialize in the Wholly Impossible': Black Women School Founders and Their Mission," *Signs* 22, no. 2 (Winter 1997): 403–26.

6. Hansberry v. Lee, 311 U.S. 32 (1940). See also Allen R. Kamp, "The History Behind *Hansberry v. Lee*," *UC Davis Law Review* 20, no. 3 (1986–87): 481–99.

7. Daniel Patrick Moynihan, *The Negro Family: The Case for National Action* (Washington, DC: U.S. Department of Labor, 1965).

8. See, for example, Sharon Epperson and Peter Chin, "You Can Buy a Home," *Essence*, June 2006, 170, describing how three black women fulfilled their dream of owning a home.

9. Allen J. Fishbein and Patrick Woodall, *Women Are Prime Targets for Subprime Lending: Women Are Disproportionately Represented in High-Cost Mortgage Market* (Washington, DC: Consumer Federation of America, 2006), www.consumerfed.org/elements/www.consumerfed.org/file/housing/Women PrimeTargetsStudy120606.pdf.

10. Mayor of Baltimore v. Wells Fargo Bank, N.A., 324 Fed. Appx. 251, 2009 U.S. App. LEXIS 9127 (4th Cir. Md. 2009); John Fritze, "Lawsuit by City Targets Lender," *Baltimore Sun*, January 8, 2008. See also Kenneth C. Johnston et al., "The Subprime Morass: Past, Present, and Future," *North Carolina Banking Institute Journal* 12 (2008): 127, www.law.unc.edu/documents/journals/articles/99.pdf.

11. Mayor of Baltimore v. Wells Fargo Bank, N.A., 677 F. Supp. 2d 847, 2010 U.S. Dist. LEXIS 834 (D. Md. 2010). The January 6, 2010, order dismissing the City of Baltimore's complaint is available at www.mdd.uscourts.gov/Opinions/Opinions/WellsFargo06jan10.pdf.

12. Mayor of Baltimore v. Wells Fargo Bank, N.A., 677 F. Supp. 2d 847, 2010 U.S. Dist. LEXIS 44731 (D. Md. 2010). Amended complaint, filed April 7, 2010; in author's possession.

13. Christopher Clausen, "Moving On," *Wilson Quarterly* 32, no. 1 (2008): 22.

14. *The White House: Inside America's Most Famous Home*, Adobe Flash video and transcript, C-SPAN Video Library, December 6, 2008, www.c-spanvideo.org/program/282748-8.

CHAPTER ONE—HOME: SURVIVAL AND THE LAND

1. Henry Louis Gates Jr., quoted in WNET.ORG, *"African American Lives*, Acclaimed PBS Series by Harvard Scholar Henry Louis Gates, Jr., Becomes a Summer Course in Spain," news release, July 9, 2009, www.thirteen.org/pressroom/pdf/company/WNETAALSummerCourseRelease.pdf.

2. F. Heinemann, "The Federal Occupation of Camden as Set Forth in the Diary of a Union Officer," *Arkansas Historical Quarterly* 9, no. 3 (Autumn 1950): 215.

3. Laura F. Edwards, "'The Marriage Covenant Is at the Foundation of All Our Rights': The Politics of Slave Marriages in North Carolina after Emancipation," *Law and History Review* 14, no. 1 (Spring 1996): 101.

4. Randy Finley, "In War's Wake: Health Care and Arkansas Freedmen, 1863–1868," *Arkansas Historical Quarterly* 51, no. 2 (Summer 1992): 144.

5. William Rogers, quoted in Kenneth C. Barnes, *Journey of Hope: The Back-to-Africa Movement in Arkansas in the Late 1800s* (Chapel Hill: University of North Carolina Press, 2004), 174.

6. Rogers, quoted in Barnes, *Journey*, 173.

7. *Christian Recorder* (Philadelphia), March 24, 1892, reprinted in Herbert Aptheker, ed., *A Documentary History of the Negro People in the United States,* vol. 2 (Citadel: New York, 1970), 793.

8. "Race War Is On: Whites of Arkansas Killing Off the Colored Men," *Nebraska State Journal,* March 24, 1899, accessed May 12, 2011, http://yesteryears news.wordpress.com/2009/01/19/; and P. Butler Thomkins, letter to the editor, *New York Times,* August 5, 1899, http://query.nytimes.com/mem/archive-free/ pdf?res=F40E11FC3C5911738DDDAC0894D0405B8985F0D3.

9. "Mob at Ashdown Lynches a Negro," *Arkansas Gazette,* May 15, 1910, in the author's possession.

10. Little River County Mortgage Record No. 4, 1896–7, 254, obtained from Little River County Genealogical Society, e-mail message to author, August 8, 2008.

CHAPTER TWO—BELONGING TO THE NEW LAND

1. For a general discussion, see Michael J. Shapiro, *Methods and Nations: Cultural Governance and the Indigenous Subject* (New York: Routledge Press, 2004), 74. See also Andrea Most, "'We Know We Belong to the Land': The Theatricality of Assimilation in Rodgers and Hammerstein's *Oklahoma!*," *PMLA* 113, no. 1 (January 1998): 77–89, for a discussion of Jud Fry's racialization and the assimilation theme of the musical; and Bruce Kirle, "Reconciliation, Resolution, and the Political Role of *Oklahoma!* in American Consciousness," *Theatre Journal* 55, no. 2 (May 2003): 252–74.

2. Shapiro, *Methods*, 74.

3. Sandra Baringer et al., letter to the editor, *PMLA* 113, no. 3 (May 1998): 452–55.

4. Dianna Everett, "Lynching," *Encyclopedia of Oklahoma History and Culture,* Oklahoma Historical Society, accessed April 27, 2011, http://digital.library .okstate.edu/encyclopedia/entries/L/LY001.html. See also Daniel F. Littlefield Jr. and Lonnie E. Underhill, "The 'Crazy Snake Uprising' of 1909: A Red, Black, or White Affair?," *Arizona and the West* 20, no. 4 (Winter 1978): 322–23.

5. Daniel F. Littlefield Jr. and Lonnie E. Underhill, "Black Dreams and 'Free' Homes: The Oklahoma Territory," *Phylon* 34, no. 4 (4th Quar. 1973): 342–57; M. Jeff Hardwick, "Homesteads and Bungalows: African-American Architecture in Langston, Oklahoma," *Shaping Communities: Perspectives in Vernacular Architecture* 6 (1997): 21–32; James M. Smallwood, "Segregation," *Encyclopedia of Oklahoma History and Culture*, Oklahoma Historical Society, accessed March 19, 2011, http://digital.library.okstate.edu/encyclopedia/entries/S/SE006 .html.

6. "In all things that are purely social we can be as separate as the fingers, yet one as the hand in all things essential to mutual progress," was Booker T. Washington's proposal for model interaction between blacks and whites, as presented in his September 18, 1895, "Atlanta Compromise" speech to a mostly white audience. *Booker T. Washington Papers*, 583–87.

7. Ben Brantley, "Wilson's Wanderers, Searching for Home," *New York Times,* April 17, 2009, http://theater.nytimes.com/2009/04/17/theater/reviews/17turn.html.

8. Kevin Boyle, "Promised Land," *New York Times,* March 19, 2010, www.nytimes.com/2010/03/21/books/review/Boyle-t.html.

9. Ira Berlin, *The Making of African America: The Four Great Migrations* (New York: Viking, 2010), 18.

CHAPTER THREE—GENDER AND RACE AT HOME IN AMERICA

1. Abigail Adams, "Remember the Ladies" (see introduction, n. 3).

2. Gail Collins, *America's Women: 400 Years of Dolls, Drudges, Helpmates, and Heroines* (New York: Perennial, 2003), 80, 83.

3. Ibid., 80.

4. John Edgar Wideman, *The Homewood Books* (Pittsburgh, PA: University of Pittsburgh Press, 1992), 155. See also Wilfred D. Samuels, "Going Home: A Conversation with John Edgar Wideman," *Callaloo* 6, no. 1 (Feb. 1983): 41–42.

5. Dolores Hayden, "Biddy Mason's Los Angeles, 1856–1891," *California History* 68, no. 3 (Fall 1989): 86–99.

6. Karen A. Johnson, "Undaunted Courage and Faith: The Lives of Three Black Women in the West and Hawaii in the Early 19th Century," in "The African American Experience in the Western States," special issue, *Journal of African American History* 91, no. 1 (Winter 2006): 4–22.

7. Brantley, "Wilson's Wanderers."

8. Berlin, *Making,* 290.

9. Barbara Burlison Mooney, "The Comfortable Tasty Framed Cottage: An African American Architectural Iconography," *Journal of the Society of Architectural Historians* 61, no. 1 (March 2002): 48–67. See also *American Victorian Cottage Homes* (Bridgeport, CT: Palliser, Palliser & Co., 1878; repr., New York: Dover, 1990), 15–16, plate 19, "Design 29—Shows plan, elevations and perspective view of a tasty little Cottage of six rooms, with necessary conveniences for making a comfortable and attractive home."

10. *The Booker T. Washington Papers*, ed. Louis R. Harlan, vol. 3, *1889–95,* eds. Stuart B. Kaufman and Raymond W. Smock (Urbana: University of Illinois Press, 1974), 503–4.

11. *Booker T. Washington Papers*, 317.

12. Booker T. Washington, "Educational Engineers," *Outlook* 95 (June 4, 1910): 266.

13. Booker T. Washington, "Signs of Progress among the Negroes," *Century Magazine* 59 (1900): 472–78, http://xroads.virginia.edu/~hyper/washington/signs.html.

14. *Booker T. Washington Papers*, 498–501.

15. Justice Joseph P. Bradley, concurring opinion, Bradwell v. Illinois, 83 U.S. 130 (1873), 141–42.

16. Jessica Sewell, "Sidewalks and Store Windows as Political Landscapes," *Constructing Image, Identity, and Place: Perspectives in Vernacular Architecture* 9 (2003): 85–98.

17. Tera W. Hunter, "African-American Women Workers' Protest in the New South," *OAH Magazine of History* 13, no. 4 (Summer 1999): 52–55.

18. Dorothy Sterling, *Black Foremothers: Three Lives* (New York: The Feminist Press at CUNY, 1988), 133.

19. Nannie Helen Burroughs, quoted in Evelyn Brooks Higginbotham, *Righteous Discontent: The Women's Movement in the Black Baptist Church, 1880–1920* (Cambridge, MA: Harvard University Press, 1993), 229.

CHAPTER FOUR—LORRAINE'S VISION: A BETTER PLACE TO LIVE

1. Herbert Hoover, "Address to the White House Conference on Home Building and Home Ownership," December 2, 1931, http://www.presidency.ucsb.edu/ws/index.php?pid=22927#axzz1LbRl5lpJ.

2. See, generally, Janet Hutchison, "Building for Babbitt: The State and the Suburban Home Ideal," *Journal of Policy History* 9, no. 2 (1997): 184–210. See also Jeffrey M. Hornstein, *A Nation of Realtors: A Cultural History of the Twentieth-Century American Middle Class* (Durham, NC: Duke University Press, 2005), 128–32.

3. Paul C. Luken and Suzanne Vaughan, " 'Be a Genuine Homemaker in Your Own Home': Gender and Familial Relations in State Housing Practices, 1917–1922," *Social Forces* 83, no. 4 (June 2005): 1614.

4. Ibid., 1611.

5. Andrew Wiese, *Places of Their Own: African American Suburbanization in the Twentieth Century* (Chicago: University of Chicago Press, 2004).

6. Isabel Wilkerson, *The Warmth of Other Suns: The Epic Story of America's Great Migration* (New York: Random House, 2010), 269.

7. Allen R. Kamp, "The History Behind *Hansberry v. Lee*" (see intro., n. 6).

8. Enoch P. Waters Jr., "Hansberry Decree Opens 500 New Homes to Race," *Chicago Defender*, November 23, 1940, 1.

9. *To Be Young, Gifted and Black: Lorraine Hansberry in Her Own Words*, adapted by Robert Nemiroff (Englewood Cliffs, NJ: Prentice-Hall, 1969), 20.

10. Sidney Fields, "Housewife's Play Is a Hit," *New York Daily Mirror,* March 16, 1959, cited in Margaret B. Wilkerson, "'A Raisin in the Sun': Anniversary of an American Classic," *Theatre Journal* 38, no. 4 (December 1986): 442.

11. Langston Hughes, "Harlem," in *The Norton Anthology of African American Literature*, eds. Henry Louis Gates Jr. and Nellie Y. McKay (New York: W. W. Norton, 1999), 1267.

12. Collins, *America's Women*, 422.

13. Jane Riblett Wilkie, "Changes in U.S. Men's Attitudes toward the Family Provider Role, 1972–1989," *Gender and Society* 7, no. 2 (June 1993): 268.

14. Lyndon B. Johnson, "Remarks at the University of Michigan," May 22, 1964, www.lbjlib.utexas.edu/johnson/archives.hom/speeches.hom/640522.asp.

15. For a discussion of the trend, see Martin Gilens, *Why Americans Hate Welfare: Race, Media, and the Politics of Antipoverty Policy* (Chicago: University of Chicago Press, 1999), 111–30. See also Joe Soss and Sanford F. Schram, "A Public Transformed? Welfare Reform as Policy Feedback," *American Political Science Review* 101, no. 1 (February 2007): 112.

16. Martin Gilens, "Race and Poverty in America: Public Misperceptions and the American News Media," *Public Opinion Quarterly* 60, no. 4 (Winter 1996): 514–15, 521.

17. U.S. Department of Labor, Office of Policy Planning and Research, "The Tangle of Pathology," chap. 4 in *The Negro Family: The Case for National Action* (Washington, DC: U.S. Department of Labor, 1965), www.dol.gov/oasam/programs/history/moynchapter4.htm.

18. Dorothy Height, in President's Commission on the Status of Women, *Report of Consultation on Problems of Negro Women*, April 19, 1963, 35, quoted in U.S. Department of Labor, "Tangle."

19. Thomas Pettigrew, *A Profile of the Negro American* (Princeton, NJ: Van Nostrand, 1964), 16, quoted in U.S. Department of Labor, "Tangle."

20. Pauli Murray, "The Right to Equal Opportunity in Employment," *California Law Review* 33, no. 3 (September 1945): 388–433.

21. Justice Thurgood Marshall, dissenting opinion, Milliken v. Bradley, 418 U.S. 717 (1974).

22. Frank Rich, "Theater: 'Raisin in Sun,' Anniversary in Chicago," *New York Times*, October 5, 1983, www.nytimes.com/1983/10/05/theater/theater-raisin-in-sun-anniversary-in-chicago.html.

23. Margaret B. Wilkerson, "'A Raisin in the Sun': Anniversary of an American Classic," Theatre of Color Issue, *Theatre Journal* 38, no. 4 (December 1986): 447.

24. Kristin L. Matthews, "The Politics of 'Home' in Lorraine Hansberry's *A Raisin in the Sun*," *Modern Drama* 51, no. 4 (Winter 2008): 578.

CHAPTER FIVE—BLAME IT ON THE SUN

1. Luken and Vaughan, "Be a Genuine Homemaker," 1603–25.

2. Adam Gordon, "The Creation of Homeownership: How New Deal Changes in Banking Regulation Simultaneously Made Homeownership Accessible to Whites and Out of Reach for Blacks," *Yale Law Journal* 115, no. 1 (October 2005): 189.

3. Wiese, *Places*, 161 (see ch. 4, n. 5).

4. Ibid., 131.

5. Ibid, 43.

6. Tayari Jones, quoted in Christian Boone, "30 Years Ago, Atlanta Battled Most Infamous Killing Spree in City's History," *Atlanta Journal-Constitution*, August 7, 2009, www.ajc.com/news/atlanta/30-years-ago-atlanta-110448.html.

7. Tricia Rose, quoted in Gilbert Cruz, "Q&A: Tricia Rose, Author of *The Hip Hop Wars*," *Time*, December 11, 2008, www.time.com/time/arts/article/0,8599,1866048,00.html.

8. William Oliver, "'The Streets': An Alternative Black Male Socialization Institution," *Journal of Black Studies* 36, no. 6 (July 2006): 918–37.

9. William Julius Wilson, *When Work Disappears: The World of the New Urban Poor* (New York: Knopf, 1996), 64.

CHAPTER SIX—LESSONS FROM A SURVIVOR: ANJANETTE'S STORY

1. John Leland, "Baltimore Finds Subprime Crisis Snags Women," *New York Times,* January 15, 2008, www.nytimes.com/2008/01/15/us/15mortgage.html.

2. Fishbein and Woodall, *Women*.

3. Vikas Bajaj and Ford Fessenden, "What's Behind the Race Gap?," *New York Times*, November 4, 2007, www.nytimes.com/2007/11/04/weekinreview/04bajaj.html.

4. Alan Zibel, "Latino, Black Homeownership Rates Falling," *SFGate.com*, January 25, 2009, http://articles.sfgate.com/2009-01-25/real-estate/17197108_1_homeownership-hispanic-white-households.

5. Jeff Crump, sample quotes from interviews with African American women with subprime loans, e-mail message to author, July 24, 2008.

6. "Declaration of Gail Kubiniec Pursuant to 28 U.S.C. § 1746," July 20, 2001, 7, www.ftc.gov/foia/citigroup.pdf.

7. Mean Sartin, "Blame the Borrowers for the Housing Crisis," *Parkerized Ohioan* (blog), May 13, 2008, http://parkerizedohioan.blogspot.com/2008/05/blame-borrowers-for-housing-crisis.html.

8. Eric Lipton and Steve Labaton, "The Reckoning: Deregulators Look Back, Unswayed," *New York Times,* November 16, 2008, www.nytimes.com/2008/11/17/business/economy/17gramm.html.

9. John W. Dienhart, "Who Are Our Hairdressers? A Plea for Institutions and Action," *Business Ethics Quarterly* 13, no. 3 (July 2003): 391–401.

10. Judge J. Frederick Motz, opinion, Mayor and City Council of Baltimore v. Wells Fargo Bank and Wells Fargo Financial Leasing, Inc., 1, www.mdd.uscourts.gov/Opinions/Opinions/WellsFargo06jan10.pdf.

CHAPTER SEVEN—HOME IN CRISIS: AMERICANS ON THE OUTSIDE OF THE DREAM

1. James Truslow Adams, *The Epic of America* (New York: Little, Brown, 1931), 404. Adams is credited with popularizing the term "the American dream."

2. Financial Crisis Inquiry Commission, *The Financial Crisis Inquiry Report: Final Report of the National Commission on the Causes of the Financial and Economic Crisis in the United States* (Washington, DC: U.S. Government Printing Office, 2011), xxiv, http://fcic-static.law.stanford.edu/cdn_media/fcic-reports/fcic_final_report_full.pdf.

3. Motz, *Baltimore v. Wells Fargo,* 4–5.

4. "The gist of Motz's opinion is that the Maryland law—which was enacted despite a veto from Gov. Robert Ehrlich—runs afoul of the Employee Retirement Income Security Act (ERISA), a complex federal law that is intended to ensure that multistate employers have only one set of rules to follow in the area of health benefits—federal rules.

"The Maryland bill, the judge said, would have required one Maryland employer, Wal-Mart, to run a special benefit system for Maryland employees only. '[A]s a consequence of the [Maryland] law,' Motz wrote, 'a nationwide employer like Wal-Mart must segregate a separate pool of expenditures for its Maryland employees and structure its contributions—and employees' deductibles and co-pays—with an eye to' that law." Diane Cadrain, "'Wal-Mart' Health Care Law Overturned," *HR Magazine,* September 2006, http://findarticles.com/p/articles/mi_m3495/is_9_51/ai_n26993566.

5. Mayor of Baltimore v. Wells Fargo Bank, amended complaint, 3, filed April 27, 2010; in author's possession.

6. Elizabeth Jacobson, quoted in Michael Powell, "Bank Accused of Pushing Mortgage Deals on Blacks," *New York Times,* June 6, 2009, www.nytimes.com/2009/06/07/us/07baltimore.html.

7. Ibid., 23.

8. Ibid.

9. Martha Neil, "Judge Dismisses Baltimore Blight Suit Against Wells Fargo,

Will Allow Refiling," *ABA Journal*, September 14, 2010, http://www.abajournal .com/news/article/judge_dismisses_baltimore_blight_suit_against_wells_ fargo_with_leave_to_ref/.

10. "Illinois Attorney General Madigan Issues New Subpoenas to Country-wide and Wells Fargo," news release, Illinois Attorney General's Office, March 6, 2008, www.illinoisattorneygeneral.gov/pressroom/2008_03/20080306.html.

11. "Madigan Sues Wells Fargo for Discriminatory and Deceptive Mortgage Lending Practices," news release, Illinois Attorney General's Office, July 31, 2009, http://www.illinoisattorneygeneral.gov/pressroom/2009_07/20090731.html.

12. Complaint for injunctive and other relief, People of the State of Illinois v. Wells Fargo and Company, Wells Fargo Bank, and Wells Fargo Financial, Illinois, Inc., 8; in author's possession.

13. Ibid.

14. "Single Black Female, in Her Own House," *Economist,* November 18, 2004, www.economist.com/node/3403447.

15. Glenn Townes, "Booker Promotes Homeownership for Newark Residents," *New York Amsterdam News*, October 5, 2006, 4.

16. U.S. Department of Housing and Urban Development, "Bush Signs American Dream Downpayment Act," news release, December 16, 2003, http:// archives.hud.gov/news/2003/pr03-140.cfm.

17. U.S. Department of Housing and Urban Development, Office of Policy Development and Research, "Unequal Burden in Baltimore: Income and Racial Disparities in Subprime Lending," May 2000, 4, accessed May 12, 2011, http:// www.huduser.org/publications/pdf/baltimore.pdf.

18. Andy Meek, "House of Cards: How Risky Loans Spurred the Local Foreclosure Crisis—and a Suit against Wells Fargo," *Memphis Daily News,* February 1, 2010, http://www.memphisdailynews.com/editorial/Article.aspx?id=47557.

19. Richard Kovacevich, "Leadership in a Time of Financial Crisis" (speech at Commonwealth Club of California, October 21, 2008), Adobe Flash video and transcript, C-SPAN Video Library, www.c-spanvideo.org/program/281905-1.

20. Nils Pratley, "The Day the Ticking Time Bombs Went Off," *Guardian* (UK), September 16, 2008, www.guardian.co.uk/business/2008/sep/16/market turmoil.lehmanbrothers1.

21. Kristopher Gerardi et al., "Making Sense of the Subprime Crisis," *Brookings Papers on Economic Activity* 2 (Fall 2008): 69–160.

22. "Wells Fargo, Wachovia Agree to Merge" (news release), Wells Fargo website, October 3, 2008, https://www.wellsfargo.com/press/2008/20081003 _Wachovia; "Wells Fargo and Wachovia Merger Completed" (news release), Wells Fargo website, January 1, 2009, https://www.wellsfargo.com/press/2009/ 20090101_Wachovia_Merger.

23. Kovacevich, "Leadership."

24. Brian Kabateck, telephone conversation with author, January 29, 2011.

25. Blanche Evans, "The Rising Minority—Single Female Homebuyers," *Reality Times*, March 24, 2004, http://realtytimes.com/rtpages/20040324 _minority.htm; Rachel Bogardus Drew, *Buying for Themselves: An Analysis of Unmarried Female Home Buyers* (Cambridge, MA: Joint Center for Housing Studies, Harvard University, 2006), 1, www.jchs.harvard.edu/publications/mar kets/n06-3_drew.pdf.

26. Marilyn Kennedy Melia, "Women Propel Housing Market," *Chicago Tribune,* August 22, 2004, http://articles.chicagotribune.com/2004-08 -22/business/0408220274_1_allegra-calder-single-women-equity-loans.

27. As quoted in Molly M. Ginty, "In Subprime Fallout, Women Take a Heavy Hit," *Women's ENews*, January 14, 2010, www.womensenews.org/story/ economyeconomic-policy/100113/in-subprime-fallout-women-take-heavy-hit.

28. Debbie Bocian, e-mail message to author, March 21, 2011. "One caveat: there has been evidence that some of the loans listed as 'owner-occupied' in HMDA may actually have been investor properties (since there is a rate premium for investor properties, some investors may have lied and said they planned to live in the property). We have no way of knowing what proportion of owner-occupied properties were, in fact, investor properties, but even if you assume that 10% were, that would still leave 4 out of 5 of subprime loans to women being owner-occupied." See also Debbie Gruenstein Bocian, Wei Li, and Keith S. Ernst, *Foreclosures by Race and Ethnicity: The Demographics of a Crisis* (Durham, NC: Center for Responsible Lending, 2010), www.responsiblelending.org/ mortgage-lending/research-analysis/foreclosures-by-race-and-ethnicity.pdf.

29. *The State of the Nation's Housing 2010* (Cambridge, MA: Joint Center for Housing Studies, Harvard University, 2010), 1, www.jchs.harvard.edu/son/ index.htm.

30. *Race and Recession: How Inequity Rigged the Economy and How to Change the Rules* (Oakland, CA: Applied Research Center, 2009), 32, http:// arc.org/downloads/2009_race_recession_0909.pdf.

31. Financial Crisis Inquiry Commission, *Financial Crisis Inquiry Report*, 153.

32. "Great Recession: Other Fallout," *The State of Working America*, Economic Policy Institute, accessed March 19, 2011, www.stateofworkingamerica .org/articles/view/14.

CHAPTER EIGHT—HOME AT LAST: TOWARD AN INCLUSIVE DEMOCRACY

1. Joseph Stiglitz, *Freefall: America, Free Markets, and the Sinking of the World Economy* (New York: W. W. Norton, 2010), 78.

2. Berlin, *Making of African America,* 14.

3. Mariana Cook, "A Portrait of a Couple in Chicago," *New Yorker,* January 19, 2009, www.newyorker.com/reporting/2009//01/19/09011fa_fact_cook. See also interview of Mariana Cook by Todd Zwillich, *The Takeaway,* streaming audio, January 16, 2009, www.thetakeaway.org/2009/jan/16/nadias-cms -tk/.

4. Elizabeth S. Anderson, "What Is the Point of Equality?," *Ethics* 109, no. 2 (January 1999): 318.

5. Barack Obama, *Dreams from My Father: A Story of Race and Inheritance* (New York: Crown, 2004), 190.

6. See, for example, the July 18, 2008, cover of the *New Yorker,* where Ms. Obama is portrayed as an AK-47-toting black militant. See also "Juan Williams Says Michelle Obama 'Sometimes Uses' a 'Kind of Militant Anger,'" *Media Matters for America* website, August 25, 2008, http://mediamatters.org/research/ 200808250013.

7. Gwen Ifill, *The Breakthrough: Politics and Race in the Age of Obama* (New York: Doubleday, 2009), 67.

8. David Remnick, *The Bridge: The Life and Rise of Barack Obama* (New York: Alfred A. Knopf, 2010), 20.

9. David Brooks, "Where's the Landslide?," *New York Times,* August 5, 2008, www.nytimes.com/2008/08/05/opinion/05brooks.html.

10. Sam Gibbons, quoted in Craig Crawford, "Southern Politics Has GOP Accent," *Orlando Sentinel,* October 2, 1994, http://articles.orlandosentinel.com/ 1994-10-02/news/9410020216_1_democrats-in-congress-republicans-could -win-north-carolina.

11. Paul Steinhauser, "Poll: Age May Play Bigger Role Than Race on Election Day," *Political Ticker* (blog), CNN Politics, October 24, 2008, http://political ticker.blogs.cnn.com/2008/10/24/poll-age-may-play-bigger-role-than-race-on -election-day/.

12. Jan Jackson, e-mail message to author, November 5, 2008.

13. Steinhauser, "Poll."

14. ABC News/*Washington Post* poll, "No Rush for Clinton to Go, But It's Still Advantage Obama," news release, May 12, 2008, http://abcnews.go.com/ images/PollingUnit/1064a208Election.pdf; Steinhauser, "Poll."

15. "Gains Seen on Minority Discrimination—But Little Else: Americans Assess Progress on National Problems," Pew Research Center, January 7, 2009, http://people-press.org/report/480/progress-on-national-problems.

16. Associated Press, "The Poop on Bo's First Month in White House," *Today* website, September 1, 2009, http://today.msnbc.msn.com/id/32633503/ns/ today-today_people/.

17. Ed Henry, "The Sweep: 'Reluctant Warrior' Michelle Obama Dives into

Midterms," CNN.com, October 13, 2010, www.cnn.com/2010/POLITICS/10/13/sweep.michelle.obama/index.html.

18. Rush Limbaugh, *The Rush Limbaugh Show*, streaming audio and transcript, January 13, 2010, www.rushlimbaugh.com/home/daily/site_011310/content/01125106.guest.html.

19. Andra Gillespie, ed., *Whose Black Politics? Cases in Post-Racial Black Leadership* (New York: Routledge, 2010), 311–12.

20. Justice Thurgood Marshall, dissenting opinion, Milliken v. Bradley, 418 U.S. 717 (1974).

21. Jacob S. Rugh and Douglas S. Massey, "Racial Segregation and the American Foreclosure Crisis," *American Sociological Review* 75, no. 5 (October 2010): 634.

22. Elizabeth Williamson and John Hechinger, "'Teachable Moment' Observed with Beer," *Wall Street Journal*, July 31, 2009, http://online.wsj.com/article/SB124899365578295227.html.

23. Domestic Policy Council website (main page), accessed March 27, 2011, www.whitehouse.gov/administration/eop/dpc/.

24. Barack Obama, "Remarks by the President at Signing of Executive Order Creating the White House Council on Women and Girls" (speech, East Room of the White House, Washington, DC, March 11, 2009), www.whitehouse.gov/the-press-office/remarks-president-signing-executive-order-creating-white-house-council-women-and-gi.

25. Obama, "Remarks."

26. "A Dialogue on Race with President Clinton," *NewsHour*, PBS, July 9, 1998, http://www.pbs.org/newshour/bb/race_relations/OneAmerica/transcript.html (accessed March 15, 2011).

27. Lani Guinier, "Dialogue without Depth," *New York Times*, December 16, 1997, www.nytimes.com/1997/12/16/opinion/dialogue-without-depth.html.

28. William Julius Wilson, *More Than Just Race: Being Black and Poor in the Inner City* (New York: W. W. Norton, 2009).

29. James K. Galbraith, statement before the Subcommittee on Crime, Senate Judiciary Committee, May 4, 2010, http://utip.gov.utexas.edu/Flyers/GalbraithMay4SubCommCrimeRV.pdf.

30. William J. Wilson, e-mail message to author, March 21, 2011.

31. Nick Timiraos, "Is It Time to Roll Back the Mortgage-Interest Deduction?," *Developments* (blog), *Wall Street Journal* online, November 12, 2010, http://blogs.wsj.com/developments/2010/11/12/is-it-time-to-roll-back-the-mortgage-interest-deduction/.

32. John Edgar Wideman, *The Homewood Books* (Pittsburgh: University of Pittsburgh Press, 1992), vii.

33. Langston Hughes, "I, Too," in *The Norton Anthology of African American Literature*, eds. Henry Louis Gates Jr. and Nellie Y. McKay (New York: W. W. Norton, 1999), 1259.

34. As cited in Michael R. Dove, "Dreams From His Mother," *New York Times*, August 10, 2009, www.nytimes.com/2009/08/11/opinion/11dove.html.

35. Elvin Wyly, e-mail message to author, February 27, 2011.

INDEX

Adams, Abigail, xiv, 40–41, 53, 141–42
Adams, John, xiv, 40, 41
Adams, J. T., 138
An American Dilemma (Myrdal), 62
American Dream: democracy and, 138–39, 140; equality and, xix, xxiv, 116–18, 164; gender and, 95–96, 112, 124–26, 167; home and, xiv, xix–xxii, 54, 55–57, 116–18, 138–39, 140, 142–43, 153; home ownership and, xviii, 95–96, 112, 124–26, 133, 159, 164; housing crisis and, xi, xviii–xxii, 112, 116–18, 124–26, 133, 138–39, 140, 153, 163; migration and, xxi; mortgage lending and, xviii–xxii, 95–96, 124–26, 133, 138–39, 140; Obama and, 142–43; race and, 95–96, 112, 124–26, 167
The America Play (Parks), 150
Anderson, Elizabeth S., 143
Arkansas, 3–8, 12–13, 20–23

Baker, Dean, 116
Baltimore, xix, 96, 113–15, 118–21, 126–27
beauty salons, 107–13
Berlin, Ira, xxi, 39, 44, 141
Better Homes movement, 55–56
Biden, Joe, 156
Birth of a Nation (Griffith), 45

Bocian, Debbie, 135
Booker, Anjanette, xix, 96–99, 107–8, 109–10, 111–13
Booker, Corey, 125
Born, Brooksley, 129
Bradwell v. Illinois, 48
Brantley, Ben, 36
Brooks, David, 146, 149
Brown, Lizzie McClain, 15, 17
Brown, Tara, 143–44
Brown, Willie, 17
Brown v. Board of Education, 31, 66, 71
Buffett, Warren, 128
Burroughs, Nannie Helen, xiv, 9, 47, 50–54, 107–8, 141–42
Bush, George W., 117, 125–26, 129, 148

Campen, Jim, 131
Carter, Jimmy, 71–72
citizenship: civil rights movement and, 45–46; education and, 45–47; equality and, xiv, 40, 44–54; gender and, 47–54; home and, xiv, 40, 44–54, 114–15, 165–69; home ownership and, xviii, 82, 114–15, 117; Obama and, 149–50; race and, 44–54, 149–50
civil rights movement: citizenship and, 45–46; equality and, xiii–xiv, xvi–xvii, 68–69; family

and, xvi–xvii, 67–69; gender
and, xvi–xvii, 67–69; Hill
family and, xiii–xiv, 33; home
and, xv–xvii, 45–46; home
ownership and, 57–61, 70–71,
83; housing crisis and, xix; law
in, 66–67, 83, 141, 152, 167;
limitations of, xii, xix; migration
and, xv–xvi, 70–71; Obama's
place in, 146; poverty and, 66–
67; states' rights and, 71, 72;
suburbanization and, 70–71;
violence and, xvi, 69–70; work
and, 68–69. *See also* women's
rights movement
Civil War, 4–5
Clausen, Christopher, xxi
Clinton, Bill, 38, 117, 125, 158–59
Clinton, Hillary, 156
Coakley, Martha, 134
Cole, Nat King, 81–82
The Color Purple (Walker), 73–74
Combs, Sean "P. Diddy," 76
Consumer Federation of America,
133
consumer lending, 101–5, 155
Cook, Mariana, 142
Council on Women and Girls
(CWG), 157–64
Countrywide, 123
Crooks, Danny, 8, 13, 20
Crowley, James, 156

democracy: American Dream and,
138–39, 140; discrimination
and, 62; emancipation and, 151;
equality and, 62, 151–56; gender
and, 152; home and, xi, xiv, 138–
39, 140, 151–56; home ownership
and, 140, 152, 163–64; housing
crisis and, 138–39, 140; presiden-

cies and, 151–56; race and, 62,
151–56
Dienhart, John, 111
discrimination: democracy and, 62;
education and, 30–31, 71, 103;
equality and, 62; home ownership and, xv–xvi, 57–61, 63–64,
70–71, 80–84, 163–64; legal-
ization of, 13, 25, 26–27, 57, 64,
81, 83; migration and, xv–xvi,
34–35; mortgage lending and,
57, 81, 120–27, 131–37; suburbanization and, 63–64; women's
rights movement and, 48–49;
work and, 64, 156–57
Dixon, Sheila, 96, 113, 119, 138
Domestic Policy Council (DPC),
157–64
Douglass, Charles R., 51–52
Dreams from My Father (Obama),
143, 144–45
drug use, 97
Du Bois, W. E. B., 52–53
Duke University, 37–38

Eagleson, William L., 26
education: citizenship and, 45–47;
discrimination and, 30–31, 71,
103; equality and, xxiv, 32–33,
45–47, 50, 52; gender and, 50, 52;
of Anita Hill, 1, 31, 32–33; home
and, 45–47; home ownership
and, 164; race and, 103; women's
rights movement and, 50, 52;
work and, 50, 52
Elliott, George, 21, 22–23, 33, 34
Elliott, Ida Crooks: family and,
8–9, 10–11; home of, 12–13,
27–28, 29; migration by, xiii,
20–23, 24, 44; research on,
34, 36

Elliott, Sam, 4, 6
Elliott, William Henry: childhood
    of, 5, 7; family and, 11; home of,
    8–9, 12–13, 27–28, 29, 41–42;
    migration by, xiii, 20–23, 24,
    44; research on, 34, 36
Elliott Taylor, Mollie (née Mary),
    xiii, 3–8, 36, 41–42
Emancipation, xxii–xxiii, 5–9, 151
equality: American Dream and,
    xix, xxiv, 116–18, 164; citizen-
    ship and, xiv, 40, 44–54; civil
    rights movement and, xiii–xiv,
    xvi–xvii, 68–69; democracy
    and, 62, 151–56; discrimination
    and, 62; education and, xxiv,
    32–33, 45–47, 50, 52; family and,
    xvi–xvii; gender and, xi–xii,
    xiv–xv, xvi–xvii, xxiv, 40–41,
    47–54, 62–63, 68–69, 141–42,
    158; for Anita Hill, xiii–xiv,
    36–37; home and, xi–xii, xiv–xv,
    xvi–xvii, xviii, xix, xxiii–xxiv,
    40–41, 44–54, 73–77, 114–15,
    116–18, 141–43, 164–69; home
    ownership and, xv–xvi, 57–61,
    114–15, 163–64; housing crisis
    and, xix, 116–18; migration and,
    xxi, 39; Obama and, xxiii–xxiv,
    141–43, 148, 168–69; Oklahoma
    and, 38; race and, xi–xii, xiv–xv,
    xxiv, 40, 44–54, 57–61, 62, 158;
    work and, 46–47, 49, 50–54,
    68–69, 141
Evans, Blanche, 132
Evers, Medgar, xvi, 70

family: civil rights movement and,
    xvi–xvii, 67–69; emancipation
    and, 5–6, 7–8, 10–11; equal-
    ity and, xvi–xvii; gender and,

xvi–xvii, 63, 64–66, 67–69;
    home and, xvi–xvii, 8–9, 64–66,
    78–81, 84–94, 97–99; home
    ownership and, 55, 56, 63, 79–80,
    84–86, 98; race and, 67–69; slav-
    ery and, 4; street culture and,
    90–94; suburbanization and,
    63; violence and, 10, 11, 13–20,
    86–88, 90–94
farming, 7, 13, 22, 24
Faye (Anita Hill's cousin), 19, 21
feminism, 78
Ferroll, 92
Financial Crisis Inquiry Commis-
    sion (FCIC), 117–18, 129
Ford, Gerald, 71
Frank, Barney, 131
Franklin, John Hope, 37–38, 158–59

Galbraith, John Kenneth, 160
Gates, Henry Louis, Jr., 3, 156
gender: American Dream and,
    95–96, 112, 124–26, 167; citizen-
    ship and, 47–54; civil rights
    movement and, xvi–xvii, 67–69;
    consumer lending and, 101–5;
    democracy and, 152; educa-
    tion and, 50, 52; equality and,
    xi–xii, xiv–xv, xvi–xvii, xxiv,
    40–41, 47–54, 62–63, 68–69,
    141–42, 158; family and, xvi–
    xvii, 63, 64–66, 67–69; home
    and, xi–xii, xiv–xv, xvi–xvii,
    40–43, 46, 47–54, 64–66,
    73–77, 78–79, 136–37, 158–64,
    167–69; home ownership and,
    56, 65–66, 79–81, 95–96, 99–101,
    106–8, 124–26, 132–34, 158–64;
    housing crisis and, xix, 105–15,
    124–26, 131–37, 158–64; identity
    and, 149–50; migration and,

xxi, 42–43; mortgage lending
and, xix, 95–96, 99–101, 105–15,
124–26, 131–37; Obama and,
156–57, 158; public discourse
on, 156–57, 158–64; race and,
47–54, 158; work and, 50–54, 63,
64, 68–69, 78, 80, 107–13, 141,
156–57, 160, 161
Gibbons, Sam, 147
Gillespie, Andra, 150
Goody, 18, 19, 20, 35
Gramm, Phil, 106
Great Migration, xv–xvi, 44, 47
Greener, Richard T., 51
Greenspan, Alan, 125, 129
Griffith, D. W., 45
Grimké, Angelina Weld, 9–10
Guinier, Lani, 159

hairstyling, 107–13
Hale, Archie, 19
Hale, Ernest, 13–20, 35–36
Hale, Lillian, 18–19, 20
Hammerstein, Oscar, II, 24–25
Hansberry, Carl, xv–xvi, 58–61
Hansberry, Lorraine, xv–xvi, 59–
62, 64, 65–66, 69–70, 74–77,
93
Hansberry v. Lee, xv–xvi, 58–61
Height, Dorothy, 68
Hernandez, Aileen, 68
Hill, Albert, xiii, 29–30
Hill, Anita: childhood of, xiii, 1–2,
30; education of, 1, 31, 32–33;
family research by, 34–36; home
and, xiii–xiv, xviii, 1–3, 30,
36–37, 164–69; mortgage lend-
ing and, 134; Thomas hearing
and, xxii, 157
Hill, Bill, 2

Hill, Erma: birth of, 169; childhood
of, 27; equality and, 37; home of,
xiii, 29–34, 165, 166; research on,
34–35, 36
Hines, Sandra, 136–37
home: American Dream and, xiv,
xix–xxii, 54, 116–18, 138–39, 140,
142–43, 153; in Arkansas, 3–8,
12–13, 20–23; citizenship and,
xiv, 40, 44–54, 114–15, 165–69;
civil rights movement and, xv–
xvii, 45–46; democracy and, xi,
xiv, 138–39, 140, 151–56; education and, 45–47; of Henry and
Ida Elliott, 8–9, 12–13, 20–23,
24–29, 41–42; Emancipation
and, 41–43; equality and, xi–xii,
xiv–xv, xvi–xvii, xviii, xix, xxiii–
xxiv, 40–41, 44–54, 73–77,
114–15, 116–18, 141–43, 164–
69; family and, xvi–xvii, 8–9,
64–66, 78–81, 84–94, 97–99;
gender and, xi–xii, xiv–xv, xvi–
xvii, 40–43, 46, 47–54, 64–66,
73–77, 78–79, 136–37, 158–64,
167–69; for Anita Hill, xiii–xiv,
xviii, 1–3, 29–34, 36–37, 164–69;
home ownership and, xxi–xxii,
114–15, 140; housing crisis and,
xi, xviii–xxii, 116–18, 136–39,
140, 153; identity and, 143–48;
of Jane James, 43; of Marla,
xvii–xviii; of Biddy Mason,
42–43; migration and, xv–xvi,
96, 141, 142, 144–45; mortgage lending and, 136–39, 140;
Obama and, xxii, xxiii–xxiv,
139, 141–43, 144–50, 168–69;
in Oklahoma, 1–3, 24–30; public discourse on, 157–64; race

and, xi–xii, xiv–xv, 40, 41–43,
44–47, 73–77, 136–37, 143–47,
158–64, 167–69; religion and,
43; slavery and, 41–42, 141, 145;
street culture and, 90–94; of
Mollie (née Mary) Elliott Taylor, xiii, 4, 6–8, 41–42; violence
and, 78–79, 86–88, 90–94;
women's rights movement and,
xiv, 40–41, 47–54; work and,
xiv, 46–47, 50–54, 107–13, 141.
See also home ownership
home ownership: American Dream
and, xviii, 55–57, 95–96, 112,
124–26, 133, 159, 164; citizenship
and, xviii, 82, 114–15, 117; civil
rights movement and, 57–61,
70–71, 83; democracy and, 140,
152, 163–64; discrimination and,
xv–xvi, 57–61, 63–64, 70–71,
80–84, 163–64; education and,
164; by Henry and Ida Elliott,
12–13, 22; equality and, xv–xvi,
57–61, 114–15, 163–64; family
and, 55, 56, 63, 79–80, 84–86,
98; gender and, 56, 65–66,
79–81, 95–96, 99–101, 106–8,
124–26, 132–34, 158–64; by
Albert and Erma Hill, 30; home
and, xxi–xxii, 114–15, 140;
housing crisis and, xviii–xxii,
xviii, 96, 105–7, 124–26, 132–34,
140; Biddy Mason, and, 42–43;
migration and, xv–xvi, 60–61,
70–71; mortgage lending and,
124–26, 132–34, 140; poverty
and, 125–26; public discourse
on, 157–64; race and, 56, 57–61,
63–64, 65–66, 70–71, 80–84,
95–96, 99–101, 106–8, 124–26,

158–64; suburbanization and,
57, 61, 63–64, 70–71; work and,
80, 86, 107–13, 161–62. *See also*
mortgage lending
Home Owner's Loan Corporation
(HOLC), 56–57
Homestead Act, 151
Home Summit, 157–64
The Honeymooners, 65
Hoover, Herbert, 55–56, 117
Housing and Urban Development
(HUD) Department, 126–27
housing crisis: American Dream
and, xi, xviii–xxii, 112, 116–18,
124–26, 133, 138–39, 140, 153,
163; civil rights movement and,
xix; democracy and, 138–39, 140;
discrimination and, 120–27,
131–37; equality and, xix, 116–18;
gender and, xix, 105–15, 124–26,
131–37, 158–64; home and, xi,
xviii–xxii, 116–18, 136–39, 140,
153; home ownership and, xviii,
xviii–xxii, 96, 105–7, 124–26,
132–34, 140; lawsuits over, xix,
xx, 96, 113–15, 118–27, 130–31;
Obama and, 153–56; onset of,
96–97, 127–30; poverty and,
125–26; public discourse on,
157–64; race and, xix, 105–15,
120–27, 131–37, 155, 158–64;
solutions for, 157–64; work
and, 107–13. *See also* mortgage
lending
Hughes, Langston, 62, 166
Hutton, Ralph, 30

identity, 143–48, 149–50, 164–69
Ifill, Gwen, 146, 150
Illinois, xx, 123–24, 126–27

Jackson, Michael, 88
Jacobson, Elizabeth, 120, 127
James, Jane, 43
Jarrett, Valerie, 158
Joe Turner's Come and Gone
    (Wilson), 36
Johnson, Lyndon, xxiii, 66–67, 141,
    146, 152, 153
Jones, Tayari, 87

Kabateck, Brian, 130–31, 133
Kelly, Barbara M., 61
King, Martin Luther, Jr., 66, 70
Kovacevich, Richard M., 127–31, 138

law, xviii, 66–67, 83, 141, 152, 167. *See
    also* civil rights movement
lawsuits, xix, xx, 96, 113–15, 118–27,
    130–31. *See also* Supreme Court
Levitt, William J., 61
Liberia, 11–12
Lincoln, Abraham, xxii–xxiii, 5, 150,
    151, 152
Loved Ones Victims Services, 92
Luken, Paul, 56
lynching. *See* violence

Madigan, Lisa, 123–24
The Making of African America
    (Berlin), xxi, 39
Marla, xvii–xviii
marriage. *See* family
Marshall, Thurgood, 70–71, 153
Mason, Biddy, 42–43
Massey, Douglas, 155
Matthews, Kristin, 76
McCabe, Edward P., 26
McCain, John, 146
McClain, Dock, 13, 14–20, 35
McClain, Ezekiel, 15, 17, 35

McClain, Lizzie, 15, 17, 35
McClain, Mary, 13, 14–20, 35
McDonald, Audra, 76
Melia, Marilyn Kennedy, 133
Memphis, xx, 124, 126–27
migration: American Dream and,
    xxi; civil rights movement and,
    xv–xvi, 70–71; discrimination
    and, xv–xvi, 34–35; by Henry
    and Ida Elliott, xiii; Emancipa-
    tion and, 42–43; equality and,
    xxi, 39; Gates on, 3; gender and,
    xxi, 42–43; Great Migration,
    xv–xvi, 44, 47; home and, xv–
    xvi, 96, 141, 142, 144–45; home
    ownership and, xv–xvi, 60–61,
    70–71; to Liberia, 11–12; Obama
    and, 142, 144; to Oklahoma, 12,
    21, 22–23, 24–29; race and, xxi,
    144–45; slavery and, 141, 145;
    violence and, 13, 20–23, 25–26,
    34–35, 36, 44
Milliken v. Bradley, 70–71, 153
Morrison, Toni, 28–29
mortgage-backed securities, 117–18,
    124, 127–30
mortgage interest, 162–63
mortgage lending: American Dream
    and, xviii–xxii, 95–96, 124–26,
    133, 138–39, 140; in Baltimore,
    xix, 96; democracy and, 138–39,
    140; discrimination and, 57, 81,
    120–27, 131–37; gender and, xix,
    95–96, 99–101, 105–15, 124–26,
    131–37; home and, 136–39, 140;
    home ownership and, 124–26,
    132–34, 140; Home Owner's
    Loan Corporation (HOLC)
    and, 56–57; lawsuits over, xix,
    xx, 96, 113–15, 118–27, 130–31;

mortgage-backed securities and, 117–18, 124, 127–30; Obama and, 153–56; poverty and, 125–26; race and, xix, xx, 57, 81, 95–96, 99–101, 105–15, 120–27, 131–37, 155; solutions for, 157–64; work and, 107–13

Motz, J. Frederick, 113, 118–19, 119–20, 122, 131–32

Moynihan, Daniel Patrick, xvii, 67–68, 69

Murray, Pauli, 68–69

music, 88–90

Myrdal, Gunnar, 62–63

National Association for the Advancement of Colored People (NAACP), 10, 15, 130–31

National Baptist Convention, 51, 52, 53

National Council of Negro Women, 68

National Organization for Women (NOW), 68

New Kids in the Neighborhood (Rockwell), 70

Newsome, Arthur, 9, 20, 23

Nickles, Don, 72, 73

Obama, Barack: American Dream and, 142–43; citizenship and, 149–50; democracy and, 153–56; *Dreams from My Father*, 143, 144–45; election of, xxii, 145–48; equality and, xxiii–xxiv, 141–43, 148, 168–69; gender and, 156–57, 158; home and, xxii, xxiii–xxiv, 139, 141–43, 144–50, 168–69; housing crisis and, 153–56, 157–64; life story of, 143,

144; presidency of, xxiii–xxiv, 148–51, 166–67; race and, 143, 144–50, 156

Obama, Michelle, xxii, xxiii, 3, 142, 145, 148–49

O'Connor, Sandra Day, 72–73

Ogletree, Charles, 156

Oklahoma, 1–3, 12, 21, 22–23, 24–30, 38

Oklahoma! (Rodgers and Hammerstein), 24–25

Oklahoma State University, 1

Oliver, William, 90–91

Owens, Sybela, 42

Own Your Own Home (OYOH) campaign, 55–56, 79, 84–85

Paradise (Morrison), 28–29

Parker, A. W., 46–47

Parks, Rosa, 145

Parks, Suzan-Lori, 150

Paschal, Tony, 121, 127

Plessy v. Ferguson, 13, 26–27

poverty, 66–67, 71, 72, 101–5, 106, 125–26

public discourse, 156–64

race: American Dream and, 95–96, 112, 124–26, 167; citizenship and, 44–54, 149–50; consumer lending and, 101–5; democracy and, 62, 151–56; education and, 103; equality and, xi–xii, xiv–xv, xxiv, 40, 44–54, 57–61, 62, 158; family and, 67–69; gender and, 47–54, 158; home and, xi–xii, xiv–xv, 40, 41–43, 44–47, 73–77, 136–37, 143–47, 158–64, 167–69; home ownership and, 56, 57–61, 63–64, 65–66, 70–71,

80–84, 95–96, 99–101, 106–8,
124–26, 158–64; housing crisis
and, xix, 105–15, 120–27, 131–37,
155, 158–64; identity and, 143–
48; migration and, xxi, 144–45;
mortgage lending and, xix, xx,
57, 81, 95–96, 99–101, 105–15,
120–27, 131–37, 155; music and,
88; Obama and, 143, 144–50,
156; poverty and, 66–67; public
discourse on, 156, 158–64; suburbanization and, 63–64, 70–71;
work and, 46–47, 49, 50–54,
107–13
Rachel (Grimké), 9–10
A Raisin in the Sun (Hansberry),
xv–xvi, 59–60, 61–62, 65–66,
69–70, 74–77, 93
Rashad, Phylicia, 76
Rawlings-Blake, Stephanie, 119
Reagan, Ronald, 71–73, 118
Reitman v. Mulkey, 83
religion, 43
Remnick, David, 146
Robinson, Marian, 148
Rockwell, Norman, 70
Rodgers, Richard, 24–25
Roosevelt, Eleanor, 151
Roosevelt, Franklin Delano, xxiii,
56–57, 151–52, 152–53
Roosevelt, Theodore, 9, 26
Rubin, Robert, 129
Rugh, Jacob, 155

Sadler, Georgia, 110–11
segregation. *See* discrimination
sexual harassment, 157
Shelley v. Kraemer, 59, 64, 82
Sheryl, 91–92
Simon, David, 113

Simon, Nina, 133
slavery, xiii–xiv, 3–5, 41–42, 141, 145.
See also Emancipation
Smith, Robert, 42
Spielberg, Stephen, 74
states' rights, 71, 72
Stiglitz, Joseph, 140
street culture, 90–94
Stumpf, John G., 128
suburbanization, xvii, 57, 61, 63–64,
70–71
suffrage movement, 48–50
Summers, Lawrence, 129
Supreme Court: *Bradwell v. Illinois*,
48; *Brown v. Board of Education*,
31, 66, 71; *Hansberry v. Lee*, xv–
xvi, 58–61; *Milliken v. Bradley*,
70–71, 153; *Plessy v. Ferguson*,
13, 26–27; *Reitman v. Mulkey*,
83; sexual harassment cases in,
157; *Shelley v. Kraemer*, 59, 64,
82

tax policy, 162–63
Taylor, Charley, 7–8
Taylor, Juanita, 108–9
Terrell, Mary Church, 51–52
Thomas, Clarence, xxii, 157
Truman, Harry, 63
Tuskegee Institute, 45–46

Vaughan, Suzanne, 56
violence: civil rights movement and,
xvi, 69–70; after Emancipation,
7, 8; family and, 10, 11, 13–20,
86–88, 90–94; home and, 78–
79, 86–88, 90–94; migration
and, 13, 20–23, 25–26, 34–35, 36,
44; National Association for the
Advancement of Colored People

(NAACP) and, 15; street culture and, 90–94; suburbanization and, xvii

Walker, Alice, 73–74
Walker, C. J., 108
Walker-Thomas Furniture Company, 101–5
Walsh, Adam, 87
Warren, Elizabeth, 101
Washington, Booker T., xiv, 44–47, 50, 53, 60, 141–42
welfare programs, 71, 72
Wells, Ida B., 49, 52
Wells Fargo Bank, xix, xx, 96, 113–15, 118–24, 126, 127–32
White House, xxii, xxiii–xxiv, 148–49
Wideman, John Edgar, 42, 164–65
Williams, Ora Lee, 101–5, 107, 111
Williams v. Walker-Thomas Furniture Company, 101–5
Willis, Hiram F., 7
Wilson, August, 36
Wilson, Margaret, 75
Wilson, William Julius, 90, 160
The Wire, 113

women's rights movement, xiv, 40–41, 47–54, 141–42. *See also* civil rights movement
work: civil rights movement and, 68–69; discrimination and, 64, 156–57; education and, 50, 52; equality and, 46–47, 49, 50–54, 68–69, 141; gender and, 50–54, 63, 64, 68–69, 78, 80, 107–13, 141, 156–57, 160, 161; home and, xiv, 46–47, 50–54, 107–13, 141; home ownership and, 80, 86, 107–13, 161–62; housing crisis and, 107–13; mortgage lending and, 107–13; race and, 46–47, 49, 50–54, 107–13; women's rights movement and, 49, 50–54
Wright, Jeremiah, 146
Wyatt, Leonard, 79–81, 84–85
Wyatt, Marla, 78–81, 84–94
Wyatt, Sam, 78–79, 86–87, 88–94
Wyly, Elvin, 100, 168

Young, Iola B., 2, 30–33, 164, 166
Young, Joseph, 15, 21
Young Women's Christian Association (YWCA), 49